Scotland
and the Crusades

For Hazel

Scotland and the Crusades
1095-1560

ALAN MACQUARRIE

Department of Scottish History
University of Glasgow

JOHN DONALD PUBLISHERS LTD.
EDINBURGH

ISBN 0 85976 115 0

Exclusive distribution in the United States of
America and Canada by Humanities Press Inc.,
Atlantic Highlands, NJ 07716, USA.

The publishers acknowledge the financial assistance
of the Scottish Arts Council in the publication of this
volume.

Filmset by Wright Printers, Dundee
and printed in Great Britain by Bell & Bain Ltd., Glasgow

Preface

What was the impact of the crusading movement on medieval Scotland? This was the question which I set myself in my Edinburgh Ph.D. thesis, 'The Impact of the Crusading Movement in Scotland, 1095-1560' (1982), on which the present work is based. It must be said that my thesis has undergone very considerable changes of structure and organisation in the course of its transformation into a book: parts of my thesis which have been published elsewhere and which are not central to the theme have been omitted, and in the remainder the chapters have been made shorter and their number increased, while large parts have been totally rewritten. Short sections have been drawn from articles already published, and my thanks are due to the publishers for permission to draw upon the following articles: 'The Crusades and the Scottish *Gaidhealtachd* in Fact and Legend', *The Middle Ages in the Highlands*, ed. L. Maclean (Inverness Field Club, 1981), 130-41; 'The Ideal of the Holy War in Scotland, 1296-1330', *Innes Review*, xxxii (1981), 83-92; 'Anselm Adornes of Bruges: Traveller in the East and Friend of James III', *Innes Review*, xxxiii (1982), 15-22; 'A Problem of Conflicting Loyalties? The Knights Hospitallers in Scotland in the Later Middle Ages', *Records of the Scottish Church History Society*, xxi (1983), 223-32; and my contribution to the introduction to *The Knights of St John of Jerusalem in Scotland* (Scottish History Society, 1983), edited jointly by myself and by Dr. I. B. Cowan and Dr. P. H. R. Mackay.

It is a pleasant duty to acknowledge those who have helped me with advice and criticism. In particular I must thank my supervisors, Professors G. Donaldson and G. W. S. Barrow, who have pointed me in many directions in which I would not otherwise have looked, and have striven hard to keep inaccuracies and omissions to a minimum. Whatever merit this work contains is due largely to their efforts.

Others who have helped me are too numerous to mention all by name, so I must be content to single out a few. At Edinburgh I must acknowledge the advice of Mr E. J. Cowan and Dr. J. W. M. Bannerman; and since moving to Glasgow, that of Dr. John Durkan and Professor I. B. Cowan. Mention must also be made of Sir Steven Runciman, Professor Jonathan Riley-Smith, Dr. A. T. Luttrell, Dr. G. G. Simpson, the late Mgr. David McRoberts, Mr R. W. Munro, Dr. S. D. Lloyd and Mr Geoffrey Stell, who have all given generously of their time and expertise on various points.

I have been ably assisted by the staffs of various institutions in Scotland and abroad: Edinburgh, Glasgow and Aberdeen University Libraries; the National Library of Scotland; the Scottish Record Office; in England,

Cambridge University Library and the British Library; in France, the Archives Nationales and Bibliothèque Nationale in Paris, the Archives Départementales de l'Aube in Troyes and the Bibliothèque Municipale and Bibliothèque des Facultés Catholiques in Lille; in Belgium, the Stadsarchief in Bruges; and in Malta, the National Library in Valletta.

The Ross Fund of the University of Glasgow provided me with a grant to visit Malta in the winter of 1981. My mother-in-law, Mrs Joan Sutton, has kindly helped with the typing of a long and often difficult manuscript, both at thesis and book stage, and has remained cheerful throughout. My parents have provided generous financial and incalculable moral support while this work has been in progress.

No-one over the years has deserved my thanks more than my wife Hazel. She has read my typescript in its entirety and made many helpful comments on style and phrasing, without which this would be a poorer piece of work. For that, but more for her cheerfulness and patience, she deserves my deepest thanks, and the dedication of this book.

Alan Macquarrie

Glasgow, July 1984

Contents

Abbreviations

Note: Except in the case of journals and society publications, place of publication is London unless stated otherwise.

AANHSC	*Ayrshire Archaeological and Natural History Society Collections*
Aberdeen Registrum	*Registrum Episcopatus Aberdonensis* (Spalding and Maitland Clubs, 1845)
Aberdeen St Nicholas Cartularium	*Cartularium Ecclesie S. Nicolai Aberdonensis* (Spalding Club, 1888-92)
Acta Sanctorum, AASS	*Acta Sanctorum*, ed. Bollandists (Antwerp and elsewhere, 1643-)
Anderson, *ES*	*Early Sources of Scottish History, 500-1286*, ed. A. O. Anderson (Edinburgh, 1922)
Anderson, *SAEC*	*Scottish Annals from English Chroniclers, 500-1286*, ed. A. O. Anderson (1908)
Ann. Monast.	*Annales Monastici*, ed. H. R. Luard (RS, 1866)
APS	*Acts of the Parliaments of Scotland*, ed. T. Thomson and C. Innes (Edinburgh, 1814-75)
Arbroath Liber	*Liber S. Thome de Aberbrothoc* (Bannatyne Club, 1848-56)
ASC	*Anglo-Saxon Chronicle*, ed. G. N. Garmonsway (Everyman, 1953)
AU	*Annals of Ulster*, ed. W. M. Hennessy and B. MacCarthy (Dublin, 1887-1901)
Boece, *Chronicles*, trans. Bellenden	Hector Boece, *The Chronicles of Scotland*, trans. John Bellenden (STS, 1938-41)
BIHR	*Bulletin of the Institute of Historical Research*
Cal. Close Rolls	*Calendar of Close Rolls preserved in the Public Record Office* (1902-62)
Cal. Fine Rolls	*Calendar of the Fine Rolls preserved in the Public Record Office* (1911-61)
Cal. Pat. Rolls	*Calendar of the Patent Rolls preserved in the Public Record Office* (1901-)
Cal. Scot. Papers	*Calendar of State Papers relating to Scotland and to Mary Queen of Scots* (1898-1965)
CDS	*Calendar of Documents relating to Scotland*, ed. J. Bain (Edinburgh, 1881-8)

Chron. Benedict	*Gesta Regis Henrici Secundi Benedicti Abbatis*, ed. W. Stubbs (RS, 1867)
Chron. Bower	*Joannis de Fordun Scotichronicon cum Supplementis et Continuatione Walteri Boweri*, ed. W. Goodall (Edinburgh, 1759)
Chron. Extracta	*Extracta e variis Cronicis Scocie* (Abbotsford Club, 1842)
Chron. Fordun	*Johannis de Fordun Chronica Gentis Scottorum*, ed. W. F. Skene (Historians of Scotland, Edinburgh, 1871-2)
Chron. Froissart	*Les Chroniques de Sire Jean Froissart*, ed. J. A. C. Buchon (Paris, Société du Panthéon littéraire, 1837-8)
Chron. Holyrood	*A Scottish Chronicle known as the Chronicle of Holyrood*, ed. M. O. Anderson (SHS, 1938)
Chron. Lanercost	*Chronicon de Lanercost*, ed. J. Stevenson (Maitland Club, 1839)
Chron. le Baker	*Chronicon Galfridi le Baker de Swynebroke*, ed. E. M. Thomson (Oxford, 1889)
Chron. le Bel	*Les Vrayes Chroniques de Jehan le Bel*, ed. L. Polain (Brussels, 1863)
Chron. Man	*Chronica Regum Manniae et Insularum*, ed. P. A. Munch (Manx Society, Douglas, 1874)
Chron. Melrose	*The Chronicle of Melrose* (facsimile edn.), ed. A. O. and M. O. Anderson and W. C. Dickinson (1936)
Chron. Richard I	*Chronicles and Memorials of the Reign of Richard I*, ed. W. Stubbs (RS, 1864-5)
Chron. Rishanger	*Chronica et Annales regnantibus Henrico Tertio et Edwardo Primo Willelmi Rishanger*, ed. H. T. Riley (RS, 1865)
Chron. Wyntoun (Laing)	Androw of Wyntoun, *The Orygynale Cronykil of Scotland*, ed. D. Laing (Historians of Scotland, Edinburgh, 1872-9)
Clement VII Letters	*Papal Letters to Scotland of Clement VII of Avignon*, ed. C. Burns (SHS, 1976)
CLP Henry VIII	*Calendar of Letters and Papers, foreign and domestic, of the Reign of Henry VIII*, ed. J. S. Brewer and others (1864-1932)
Coupar Angus Charters	*Charters of the Abbey of Coupar Angus*, ed. D. E. Easson (SHS, 1947)

CPL	*Calendar of Entries in the Papal Registers relating to Great Britain and Ireland: Papal Letters,* ed. W. H. Bliss and others (1893-)
CSP Rome	*Calendar of State Papers preserved in Rome* (1895-1965)
CSP Venice	*Calendar of State Papers preserved in Venice* (1864-1947)
CSSR	*Calendar of Scottish Supplications to Rome,* ed. A. I. Dunlop and others (SHS, 1934-70, Glasgow, 1983-)
DNB	*Dictionary of National Biography* (1921-)
Dowden, *Bishops*	J. Dowden, *The Bishops of Scotland* (Glasgow, 1912)
Dryburgh Liber	*Liber S. Marie de Dryburgh* (Bannatyne Club, 1847)
Dunfermline Registrum	*Registrum de Dunfermelyn* (Bannatyne Club, 1842)
Dunkeld Rentale	*Rentale Dunkeldense, 1505-17,* ed. R. K. Hannay (SHS, 1915)
Edinburgh Sciennes Liber	*Liber Conventus S. Katherine Senensis* (Abbotsford Club, 1841)
Edinburgh St Giles Registrum	*Registrum Cartarum Ecclesie S. Egidii de Edinburgh* (Bannatyne Club, 1859)
EHR	*English Historical Review*
ER	*Exchequer Rolls of Scotland,* ed. J. Stuart and others (Edinburgh, 1878-)
Glasgow Registrum	*Registrum Episcopatus Glasguensis* (Bannatyne and Maitland Clubs, 1843)
Glasgow Rental	*Rental Book of the Diocese of Glasgow* (Grampian Club, 1875)
Hardwicke Papers	Philip Yorke, earl of Hardwicke, *Miscellaneous State Papers, 1501-1726* (1778)
HMC Reports	*Reports of the Royal Commission on Historical Manuscripts* (1870-)
Iona Inventory	*Argyll, an Inventory of the Monuments:* vol. iv, *Iona* (Royal Commission on the Ancient and Historical Monuments of Scotland, 1982)
IR	*Innes Review*
James IV Letters	*The Letters of King James IV, 1505-13,* ed. R. K. Hannay, R. L. Mackie and A. Spilman (SHS, 1953)
James V Letters	*The Letters of James V,* ed. R. K. Hannay and D. Hay (Edinburgh, 1954)

Kelso Liber	*Liber S. Marie de Calchou* (Bannatyne Club, 1846)
Lindores Chartulary	*Chartulary of the Abbey of Lindores,* ed. J. Dowden (SHS, 1903)
Malta Cod.	Codex in the Archives of the Knights of St John of Jerusalem, National Library of Malta, Valletta, Malta
Matthew Paris, *Chron. Maiora*	Matthew Paris, *Chronica Maiora,* ed. H. R. Luard (RS, 1872-3)
Matthew Paris, *Historia Minor*	Matthew Paris, *Historia Anglorum sive Historia Minor,* ed. F. T. Madden (RS, 1866-9)
Melrose Liber	*Liber S. Marie de Melros* (Bannatyne Club, 1837)
MGH Script	*Monumenta Germaniae Historica: Scriptores,* ed. G. H. Pertz and others (Hanover, 1826-)
Midlothian Charters	*Charters of the Hospital of Soltre, of Trinity College Edinburgh, and of other Collegiate Churches in Midlothian* (Bannatyne Club, 1861)
Migne, *PL*	*Patrologiae Cursus Completus, Series Latina,* ed. J.-P. Migne (Paris, 1844-65)
Newbattle Registrum	*Registrum S. Marie de Neubotle* (Bannatyne Club, 1849)
Paisley Registrum	*Registrum Monasterii de Passalet* (Maitland Club, 1832)
Palgrave, *Documents*	*Documents and Records illustrating the History of Scotland,* ed. F. Palgrave (1837)
Pipe Rolls, 1191-92	*The Great Rolls of the Pipe for the third and fourth years of the Reign of King Richard I, 1191 and 1192,* ed. D. M. Stenton (Pipe Roll Society, 1926)
Pontefract Cartulary	*Cartulary of St John of Pontefract,* ed. R. Holmes (Leeds, 1899-1902)
PPTS	Palestine Pilgrims Text Society
PSAS	*Proceedings of the Society of Antiquaries of Scotland*
Report of Philip de Thame	*The Knights Hospitallers in England: the Report of Prior Philip de Thame, 1338* (Camden Society, 1837)
RHC Occ	*Recueil des Historiens des Croisades: Historiens occidentaux* (Académie des Inscriptions et Belles-Lettres, Paris, 1844-1906)
RMS	*Registrum Magni Sigilli Regum Scottorum,* ed. J. M. Thomson and others (Edinburgh, 1882-1912)

Rot. Scot., Rotuli Scotiae	Rotuli Scotiae in Turri Londinensi et in Domo Capitulari Westmonasteriensi asservati, ed. D. Macpherson and others (1814-19)
RRS	Regesta Regum Scottorum, ed. G. W. S. Barrow and others (Edinburgh, 1960-)
RS	'Rolls Series': Rerum Britannicarum medii aevi Scriptores, or Chronicles and Memorials of Great Britain and Ireland during the Middle Ages, published under the direction of the Master of the Rolls, 1858-1911
RSCHS	Records of the Scottish Church History Society
RSS	Registrum Secreti Sigilli Regum Scottorum, ed. M. Livingstone and others (Edinburgh, 1908-)
Rymer, Foedera	Foedera, Conventiones, Literae, et cuiuscunque generis Acta publica, ed. T. Rymer (1816-69)
SHR	Scottish Historical Review
SHS	Scottish History Society
SHS Misc., SHS Miscellany	The Miscellany of the Scottish History Society (SHS, 1893-)
SP, Scots Peerage	The Scots Peerage, ed. J. Balfour Paul (Edinburgh, 1904-14)
Spalding Misc.	Miscellany of the Spalding Club (Spalding Club, 1841-52)
SRO	Scottish Record Office
St Andrews Liber	Liber Cartarum Prioratus S. Andree in Scotia (Bannatyne Club, 1841)
Stones, Anglo-Scottish Relations	Anglo-Scottish Relations, 1174-1328: some selected Documents, ed. E. L. G. Stones (2nd edn., Oxford, 1970)
STS	Scottish Text Society
SWHIHR	Society of West Highland and Island Historical Research
TA	Accounts of the Lord Treasurer of Scotland (Edinburgh, 1877-)
Taymouth Bk	The Black Book of Taymouth (Bannatyne Club, 1855)
TDGNHAS	Transactions of the Dumfriesshire and Galloway Natural History and Antiquarian Society
TELAFNS	Transactions of the East Lothian Antiquarian and Field Naturalists' Society

TGSI	*Transactions of the Gaelic Society of Inverness*
Theiner, *VM*	*Vetera Monumenta Hibernorum et Scottorum Historiae Inlustrantia,* ed. A. Theiner (Rome, 1864)
TRHS	*Transactions of the Royal Historical Society*
West Lothian Inventory	*Report of the Royal Commission on the Ancient and Historical Monuments of Scotland: Midlothian and West Lothian* (Edinburgh, 1929)
Yester Writs	*Calendar of Writs preserved at Yester House, 1166-1503,* ed. C. C. H. Harvey and J. Macleod (Scottish Record Society, 1930)

Wars and Rumours of Wars

More than thirty years have passed since Professor A. A. M. Duncan drew attention to a passage from the Picard chronicler Guibert de Nogent, in which he described the outlandish clothing of the Scottish participants on the first Crusade.[1] In his article, Professor (then Mr) Duncan commented that to assess the rôle played by the Scots in the first Crusade would require a close analysis of the sources. If that were so for one Crusade, it follows that the same is true for the whole of the Crusading movement. It might appear at first sight that the subject is an unpromising one, owing to the relative sparseness of medieval Scottish source material and the lack of any previous treatment of the subject. However, the fact that a subject has not been tackled before does not *ipso facto* mean that it is not worth tackling; and it is hoped that the present study will be judged to have been worthwhile.

Scottish historians in the past have tended to regard the level of Scottish participation in the Crusades as negligible. A. O. Anderson, for instance, found it impossible to believe that Scots could have joined the first Crusade, and concluded that the *Scoti* who did so must have been Irish.[2] P. Hume Brown was so ignorant of the history of the Crusading movement that in his three-volume *History of Scotland* he associated St Bernard of Clairvaux with the third Crusade.[3] His work has now been superseded, but the standard textbook for the high middle ages, Professor Duncan's *Scotland: the Making of the Kingdom*, devotes only some two pages to the subject of Scottish involvement in the Crusades. Professor Duncan speaks of a 'marked lack of enthusiasm for the recovery of Jerusalem after its fall in 1187', and comments that 'the number of known participants in the crusades is not large. ... Their fewness suggests an isolation of Scotsmen from the cosmopolitan junketings of later thirteenth-century Europe'.[4] But Professor Duncan does take the subject sufficiently seriously to concede that the apparent lack of enthusiasm 'was modified as the thirteenth century progressed and the spiritual benefits of the crusade were preached assiduously by the church'.[5]

If received opinion is that Scottish participation in the Crusades was slight, there have been few attempts to contradict this view. Some historians, with an anachronistic view based on concepts of modern nationalism (which have limited relevance for medieval kingdoms), have regarded crusades unfavourably as 'unpatriotic'; Herkless and Hannay, in their *Archbishops of St Andrews*, comment of one archbishop that 'though an obedient servant of the pope, he was an unpatriotic Scot when he agreed, as

Apostolic nuncio, to levy taxes for a crusade'.[6] Logically, one should then regard Robert Bruce as unpatriotic for expressing a longing to go on crusade in 1329, and Sir James Douglas as unpatriotic for actually doing so. Douglas has been criticised for affording himself the luxury of getting killed on crusade in 1330 at a time when his country needed him;[7] but such an attitude ignores the value of Douglas's crusade, in restoring Scotland to international respectability, and winning for himself and King Robert international prestige and renown. Modern historians have perhaps tended to view the past in quantitative terms, while medieval people were concerned, as often as not, with the salvation of their souls and with performing what they believed to be the will of God. Crusading in itself does not convey any quantifiable benefits, such as wealth or national security; and so some historians, especially those concerned with the development of nations, have found it difficult to understand.

Some modern historians have striven for a more balanced view based on a genuine attempt to understand the workings of the medieval mind. Professor Ranald Nicholson, for instance, wrote some years ago that 'nineteenth-century historians, and some of the present century as well, were all too prone to see evidence of nationalism in the Scotland of Robert Bruce. Ignoring the climate of thought in the medieval world, they paid little heed to such concepts as cosmopolitan chivalry, which sometimes vied with nascent nationalism in fourteenth-century Europe'.[8]

Such a balanced view of medieval Scottish attitudes must take in a European perspective. Few historians have done more to set Scotland within its European context than the late Mgr. David McRoberts, whose pioneering essay, 'Scottish Pilgrims to the Holy Land', opened up to historians new and hitherto unimagined vistas.[9] Mgr. McRoberts asserted that 'Life in medieval Scotland cannot be fully understood or appreciated without some assessment of its foreign contacts. . . . Curiously, no-one has attempted to gather together the records of pilgrim traffic. . . . Our sources show clearly that Scotsmen were as much addicted to pilgrimage as any other nation in Christendom'.[10] In his concern to break new ground, Mgr. McRoberts was necessarily summary in his treatment of some aspects of his subject, and was able only to survey the evidence rather than to examine it thoroughly; but his pathfinding work is nonetheless a great achievement, for which researchers who come after must be grateful.

If Scottish historians have had little to say about members of their nation taking part in the Crusades, historians of the Crusading movement have equally little to say about Scottish participation. In Sir Steven Runciman's great *History of the Crusades,* Scotland is mentioned seven times in over 1,400 pages.[11] In the equally vast *History of the Crusades* edited by K. M. Setton, references to Scotland and the Scots are equally infrequent.[12] The

Crusades were in origin a Frankish venture, and most of the participants and beneficiaries in the Crusades were French. On only a few occasions can Scotland's political position be seen to have had an effect on the Crusades, as for instance when Henry II and later Richard I had to delay their departure for the Holy Land because they required a settlement with the Scots before the third Crusade.[13] Edward I claimed that he was planning a new Crusade in the 1290s which had to be abandoned because of the Scottish 'rebellion', and he blamed the Scots for hindering the recovery of the Holy Land; but in the 'Declaration of Arbroath' (1320) the Scots replied that they themselves wished to fight for the Holy Land, but were prevented by English aggression; the English, they claimed, preferred to make war on their smaller neighbours and reap the material benefits rather than to gain the spiritual reward of fighting in the Holy Land.[14] One should not be too surprised at Scotland's relative lack of resources and influence in cosmopolitan Europe as a whole, which meant that the number of Scottish crusaders was always smaller than the number of French, and even of English and Germans. But the contingents of Scottish crusaders were often respectable, or even substantial, by Scottish standards; and there can be no doubt that the Crusading movement with its many facets – preaching, finance, institutions, participation – did make its impact in Scotland as in every other part of western Christendom. It is that impact which is the subject of the present study.

Although historians of the Crusades have little to say about Scotland, and until recently most historians of Scotland have had little to say about their compatriots' participation in the Crusades, this has not always been the case. The realm of folklore is one which the historian enters with reluctance and extreme caution, but it remains the case that traditions about the Crusades abound in many parts of Scotland. Perhaps the most famous such tradition concerns the *bratach shithe* or fairy banner of Dunvegan: 'The legend of its origin is that a MacLeod who had gone on a Crusade to the Holy Land when returning in the garb of a pilgrim was benighted on the borders of Palestine in a wild and dangerous mountain pass, where by chance he met a hermit who gave him food and shelter. The hermit told him that an evil spirit guarded the pass and never failed to destroy the true believer; but by the aid of a piece of the true cross and certain other directions given by the hermit, this MacLeod vanquished and slew the "she-devil" ... around whose loins this banner had been tied; and in reward for conveying certain secrets which she wished some earthly friends to know, she revealed to her conqueror the future destinies of his clan ... and desired that her girdle be converted into this banner, which was to be attached to her spear, which became the staff which is now lost'.[15]

It would be wasted labour to try to recover the true facts behind this supposed crusader's relic. The same is probably true of another mysterious object in the possession of the MacPhersons of Cluny. In 1883 James Mitchell was shown round the hall of Cluny Castle by the chief: 'In the hall there are various relics of the olden time. . . . There is . . . a very curious belt of thick red morrocco leather, with clasps and devices in silver of a religious and oriental character. This had been in the family since the time of the Crusades, one of the Cluny race having gone to Palestine to fight against the Turks. The country people believe there is a charm in the belt, particularly for the safe delivery of women in childbirth'.[16]

There are other examples from the Highlands of charm-stones and mysterious objects which have been connected with the Crusades. The Stewarts of Ardvorlich were proud possessors of the *clach dearg* of Ardvorlich, a small red charm-stone which had properties to cure sick cattle when they drank water in which it had been dipped. Its owners were reckoned the chiefs of the Stewarts of Balquhidder, and family tradition is that it was brought back from a Crusade.[17] In 1890 the National Museum of Antiquities received 'a charm-stone used in Argyll, a polished slice of silicious fossil wood, set in silver, and said to have been brought from the Holy Land'.[18] Sir Colin Campbell of Glenorchy (d. 1480) had an amulet which he 'woir when he fought in battell at the Rhodes agaynst the Turks', and which was still at Taymouth Castle long after his time, being used for 'more homely purposes'.[19]

It is not only the *Gaidhealtachd* which has produced folklore and tradition about the Crusades. The 'Lee Penny' is a famous lowland example of a crusader's talisman, said to have been brought back from the Holy Land by Sir Simon Lockhart of Lee in the fourteenth century; he had used it 'as a medical amulet, for the arrestment of haemorrhage, fever, etc. . . .'[20] An alternative version of the tradition states that 'It is said to have been given, along with ransom money, to Sir Simon Lockhart of Lee by the wife of a Saracen chief whom he had taken prisoner in Palestine'.[21] Its magical properties to cure human and animal diseases are no longer respected, but it has become more famous as the centre round which Sir Walter Scott wove his romantic novel *The Talisman*.

At Bonshaw Tower (Annan) there is a stone built into a ceiling of the tower known as the Crusader Stone: 'The tradition of the Irvings is that an Irving on the First Crusade brought a stone back from the walls of the Old Temple at Jerusalem, had it blessed by the pope at Rome, and fixed it where it now rests in the tower at Bonshaw'.[22] A more sober modern judgement is that the stone is of local origin, that the carving on it is of the same sixteenth-century date as the rest of the tower, and that 'of course it has nothing whatever to do with the Crusades'.[23] This contemptuous dismissal is perhaps a little unfair to a family who were only trying to add a little lustre to their pedigree. Others had done it before: John Barbour had written a genealogy of the Stewarts in the course of which he sent Alan son of Walter Stewart off to the siege of Antioch with Godfrey de Bouillon. Walter Bower pointed out that Antioch fell to the Christians in 1098, while Alan son of Walter died more than a hundred years later.[24] However, the possibility that Alan son of Walter joined the third Crusade (1190-92) does require serious consideration.[25] It is also worth noting that a Breton ancestor of the Stewarts *had* been present on the first Crusade (1096-1099), and that in the sixteenth century an Irving joined the Knights of St John of Malta.[26]

Other relics of the Holy Land are known to have existed. An inventory of the relics of Aberdeen cathedral drawn up in 1498 mentions relics of St Catherine of Alexandria, St Helen mother of Constantine, St Margaret of Antioch, and the patriarch Isaac.[27] In 1533 King James V was much impressed by the relics and miracles of Thomas Doughty, who claimed to have fought against the Turks and established a hermitage of Loretto at Musselburgh; but contemporaries influenced by reforming ideas from the continent were more sceptical.[28] Another sixteenth-century hermit, John Scott of Jedburgh, was under suspicion from men of reforming opinions for his doubtful relics of the Holy Land.[29] Probably the Reformation has been largely responsible for the disappearance of many relics of the Holy Land, so that the only ones that survive are in the hands of private families.

Traditions of crusading or pilgrimage do not always relate necessarily to a mysterious object or talisman. In Gaelic-speaking areas the voice of bard or *seanchaidh* has preserved unwritten lore and history over many generations, and one of the most striking examples of this phenomenon is found in a quatrain collected in Argyllshire in the nineteenth century, attributed to the thirteenth-century bard Muiredhach Albanach; said to have been spoken 'at the head of Lochlong in Argyllshire when he sat down to rest himself when he returned thither from Rome' and from the fifth Crusade, it ends with the line: *Is fada Roimh o Lochlong*, 'Far is Rome from Lochlong'.[30] The survival of other poems by Muiredhach Albanach and his companions on crusade seem to confirm the authenticity of this scrap of oral tradition relating to his Mediterranean adventures.

In other cases, it is less easy to be certain. Hector Boece in his *Scotorum Historia* has a long, circumstantial, and very largely fabulous account of Earl David's presence on the third Crusade; in this David is instrumental in the capture of Acre by the Crusaders, and on his return journey he is subjected to such a series of shipwrecks and disasters, including enslavement, that it is a wonder that he got back to Scotland alive.[31] The whole could be easily dismissed were it not for the fact that a hazy tradition of Earl David's having been on crusade was in existence in the early fifteenth century, when Andrew de Wyntoun wrote his *Orygynale Cronykil:*

> As sum men saide, in Sarzenes
> He trawylit, quhen Wilyham crownyt wes.[32]

William the Lion became king in 1165, but it is highly unlikely that his brother David was on crusade at that time. The story of David's absence on crusade resurfaces in a late-fifteenth-century manuscript of Fordun's *Chronica Gentis Scottorum* before blossoming into Boece's fantasy;[33] but it is unlikely that the truth behind these stories will ever be known.

Some post-reformation catholic apologists wrote with the same pride as Boece of their forefathers' crusading zeal before their hearts were corrupted by reforming ideas. In 1594, Father George Thomson wrote in his *De Antiquitate Christianae Religionis apud Scotos:*

> The Catholic religion . . . counted among its adherents men of a physical courage which brought them fame at home and abroad for their military glory . . . Of the splendid proof of this valour that they gave in Germany when they fought on the side of Charlemagne . . . and afterwards many times in Gaul and Italy . . . and also in Palestine itself, we learn from the annals of many nations.[34]

There is a picturesque tall story in an early seventeeth-century French book concerning the Scottish contingent on the Crusade of 1248. It relates how, after the capture of Damietta and the surrounding area, King Louis IX drove out *le roy des Arsacides* (i.e., the Assassins), *Prince Payen appellé le Vieil de la Montagne.* The latter, bent on revenge, chose certain Assassins to go disguised to the crusaders' camp; but as they plotted near the camp, they were spotted by a group of Scottish crusaders whose suspicions were aroused, and who reported what they had seen to King Louis. He told the Scots to remain with him when the Assassins came into his tent; and so the Scots were able to identify them and they were seized and made to confess before the plot could be carried out.[35] Louis was so impressed by the Scots' conduct that he formed them into his personal bodyguard of Scots Archers.

Although this story is a romantic concoction of the seventeenth century by a man anxious to remind Scots what good catholics they had once been, it may be inspired by Joinville's account of the Assassin embassy sent to Louis IX at Acre in 1250; during this a dagger was shown to the king as a token of defiance, and a winding-sheet as a symbol of death.[36] In fact, Louis was not greatly impressed by the Scots whom he met on crusade; at some time between 1254 and 1260 he told his son Louis, 'I would prefer that a Scot should come from Scotland and govern the people of the kingdom well and faithfully, than that you were seen to govern it badly'.[37]

The Scottish crusader as hero resurfaces in the romantic historical novels of Sir Walter Scott in the early nineteenth century. The best example is surely *The Talisman,* which skilfully weaves together the heroic tradition of Richard the Lionheart, Boece's stories of Earl David's crusading activity, and the tradition of the origins of the 'Lee Penny', with little regard for historical realism. In this novel Scott makes Earl David assert that the Scots and English together 'can furnish forth such a body of men-at-arms as may go far to shake the unholy hold which [Saladin] hath laid upon the cities of Sion'.[38] Although *The Talisman* is the most famous example, Scott hearkens back to romantic crusading traditions in others of his novels as well. In *Guy Mannering* he makes a Galloway laird tell an English visitor: 'I wish ye could have heard my father's stories about the auld fights of the Mac-Dingawaies . . . wi' the Irish, and wi' the Highlanders, that came here in their berlings from Islay and Cantire – and how they sailed to the Holy Land – that is, to Jerusalem and Jericho, wi' a' their clan at their heels . . . and how they brought hame relics, like those the Catholics have, and a flag that's up yonder in the garret'.[39] Scott thus neatly transfers the *Bratach Shithe* from Dunvegan to Caerlaverock to add a touch of romantic realism to his story.

Scott's death in 1832 is not the end of the romantic crusader tradition in Scotland. In modern times the 'Scottish Priory of the Venerable Order of St John of Jerusalem' exists as a reminder of the time when Scottish members of crusading orders travelled frequently to Jerusalem, Acre, Rhodes and Malta to serve their grand masters.

The writing of history nowadays requires greater discipline than did the production of folk-traditions or romantic novels. But it also should avoid the excessive scepticism of narrow nationalism, and the negative attitudes of modern protestantism towards what was, after all, an institution closely connected with the papacy. An examination of the facts, such as they can be discovered, seems to show that the truth lies somewhere in between.

NOTES

1. *SHR,* xxix (1950), 210-12.
2. Anderson, *ES,* ii, 98.
3. P. Hume Brown, *History of Scotland* (Cambridge, 1911-29), i, 74.
4. A. A. M. Duncan, *Scotland: the Making of the Kingdom* (Edinburgh, 1975), 446-7.
5. Ibid., 446.
6. J. Herkless and R. K. Hannay, *The Archbishops of St Andrews* (Edinburgh, 1907), i, 66-7.
7. I. M. Davis, *The Black Douglas* (London, 1974), 164.
8. R. Nicholson, 'Magna Carta and the Declaration of Arbroath', *University of Edinburgh Journal* xxii (1965-6), 140-44, at 142.
9. *IR,* xx (1969), 80-106.
10. Ibid., 80.
11. S. Runciman, *A History of the Crusades* (Cambridge, 1951-4).

12. K. M. Setton and others, *A History of the Crusades* (Madison, Wisconsin, 1969-in progress).

13. See below, pp. 27-8.

14. See below, pp. 72-3.

15. F. T. MacLeod, 'Notes on the Relics preserved in Dunvegan Castle', *PSAS,* xlvii (1913), 99-129, at 111.

16. J. Mitchell, *Reminiscences of my Life in the Highlands* (1883, reprinted London, 1971), i, 192.

17. I. Moncreiffe, *The Highland Clans* (London, 1967), 21.

18. *PSAS,* xxiv (1890), 411.

19. *Taymouth Bk,* pp. ii, 10, 15.

20. *PSAS,* iv (1860-62), 222-4.

21. F. M. McNeill, *The Silver Bough* (Glasgow, 1957), i, 94.

22. A. M. T. Maxwell-Irving, 'The Crusader Stone at Bonshaw', *TDGNHAS,* xxxix (1960-61), 124-6.

23. R. C. Reid, 'Bonshaw', *TDGNHAS,* xx (1935-6), 147-56, at 149.

24. R. L. G. Ritchie, *The Normans in Scotland* (Edinburgh, 1954), 288 and n.

25. See below, pp. 29-30

26. Orderic Vitalis, *Ecclesiastical History,* ed. M. Chibnall (Oxford, 1969-81), v, 58; see below, pp. 118-9.

27. *Aberdeen Reg.,* ii, 167.

28. *RMS, 1513-46,* 309-10; *TA,* vi, 200-1, 299; *A Diurnal of Remarkable Occurents* (Maitland Club, 1833), 17; John Knox, *Works,* ed. D. Laing (Wodrow Soc., 1895), i, 72-6.

29. David Calderwood, *History of the Kirk in Scotland* (Wodrow Soc., 1842), 101.

30. D. Mackintosh, *Collection of Gaelic Proverbs* (2nd edn, Edinburgh, 1819), 190-1.

31. Hector Boece, *Chronicles of Scotland,* trans. J. Bellenden (STS, 1941), 11, 209-12.

32. *Chron. Wyntoun* (Laing), ii, 213.

33. *Chron. Fordun,* xxix ff., 257.

34. G. Thomson, 'De Antiquitate Christianae Religionis apud Scotos', *SHS Miscellany,* ii (1904), 115-32, at 130.

35. *Papers relative to the Royal Guard of Scottish Archers in France* (Maitland Club, 1835), 74.

36. J. de Joinville, *Histoire de Saint Louis,* ed. N. de Wailly (Paris, Société de l'histoire de France, 1868), 160-4.

37. Ibid., 7.

38. Walter Scott, *The Talisman* (various editions), cap. i.

39. Walter Scott, *Guy Mannering* (various editions), cap. v.

1

The Land of Promise, 1095-1187

Although historians have looked for precursors of the Crusades,[1] the Crusading movement is generally acknowledged to have had its origin on 27th November, 1095, when Pope Urban II exhorted the chivalry of western Europe to go to the aid of the Holy Places of Christendom.[2] The Council of Clermont, to whom his appeal was addressed, was composed mainly of French and Italian clergy; the only participant from the British Isles was a disciple of St Anselm called Boso, who reported to the archbishop what had passed at the council.[3]

It is uncertain whether Pope Urban had expected the tremendous outburst of enthusiasm which greeted his appeal. But an outburst there certainly was, and it was not confined to those who first heard the call of Clermont, or for whose ears it seems to have been intended. Early chroniclers stress how the pope's appeal travelled far and wide, stirring the hearts of all social classes. The twelfth-century chronicler Sigebert of Gembloux wrote:

> The western peoples, sorrowing that the Holy Places of Jerusalem were profaned by the gentiles, and that the Turks had invaded the borders of Christendom from many sides, moved in great numbers by a single hope and having been shown many signs, inspired one by another – dukes, counts, potentates, noble and ignoble, rich and poor, free men and slaves, bishops, clerics, monks, old and young, even boys and maidens – they came together from all sides with a single spirit and without animosity, from Spain, Provence, Aquitaine, Brittany, Scotland, England, Normandy, France, Lorraine, Burgundy, Germany, Lombardy, Apulia, and from other lands; and armed with virtue and signed with the holy cross, they set out for the injuries of God against the enemies of the Christians.[4]

About 1115, the chronicler Ekkehard of Aura wrote a similar account of the reaction to Pope Urban's appeal:

> So much were the souls of all aroused . . . that about 100,000 men were presently enrolled in the army of the Lord, from Aquitaine and Normandy, England, Scotland and Ireland, Brittany, Galicia, Gascony, France, Flanders, Lorraine, and from other Christian peoples, whose names are hardly ever heard at this time.[5]

Ekkehard describes how the news travelled across the sea and caused the men of the islands to join the Crusading army, and how the army came to contain both those who subsisted on bread and water, and those who dined entirely from silver utensils.[6]

These lists provided the basis for later historians writing about the first Crusade.[7] In the middle of the twelfth century Otto of Freising added at the end of Ekkehard's list of nationalities:

> . . . and other peoples, not only dwelling on land but also on the islands of the sea and of the furthest ocean.[8]

One contemporary eyewitness, the Picard chronicler Guibert de Nogent, provides a detailed description of some of these exotic strangers encountered by the Frankish Crusaders:

> You might have seen groups of Scots, ferocious among themselves but elsewhere unwarlike, with bare legs, shaggy cloaks, a purse hanging from their shoulders, rolling down from their marshy borders; and those who seemed ridiculous to us bore copious arms, offering us their faith and devotion as aid. God be my witness, I have heard of men from I know not what barbarous nation driven in to our seaport, whose speech was until then unknown, so that, having no voice, they crossed one finger over another in the sign of the cross; thus showing us, since they could not speak, that they had set out for the cause of the faith.[9]

It has been noted that elsewhere Guibert uses the word *Scoti* to indicate Scots rather than Irish,[10] though the word had not yet come to mean Scots exclusively. The interesting reference to 'a purse hanging from their shoulders' may not be an early description of a sporran, but rather of a leather pouch for holding sacred books or relics; these are depicted on Irish crosses and on the figures of evangelists in the Book of Deer, and so were familiar in tenth-century Scotland.[11]

Chroniclers from the British Isles also describe the outburst of enthusiasm which greeted Pope Urban's sermon. The annal for 1096 in the *Anglo-Saxon Chronicle* states:

> At Easter [13 April] there was a very great stir throughout this nation, and in other nations too, because of Urban who was called pope. . . . A countless number of people with their wives and children set out wishing to fight against the heathen.[12]

Writing some twenty-five years after the events he describes, the historian William of Malmesbury gives a rather uncomplimentary description of the reaction among England's neighbours to the summons of Clermont, and the pursuits which they abandoned to go to Jerusalem:

> Then the Welshman abandoned his poaching, the Scot his familiarity with fleas, the Dane his continuous drinking, and the Norwegian gorging himself on fish.[13]

He goes on to describe how the fields were abandoned by their farmers, and houses deserted by their inhabitants, while the populations of whole cities marched away to the East. The details are a little picturesque, but not at variance with the accounts of other historians of the period. All stress that the first Crusade was an international movement, which involved not only France and Italy (from which lands the principal leaders came), but also remote parts of northern Europe, including Scotland.

This should not come as a surprise. Before the Viking raids of the ninth century the Scots had been great travellers; Adomnán's *De Locis Sanctis* displays an interest in the Holy Places as far back as c. 690.[14] Later the Irish annals record frequent pilgrimages to Rome, and Macbeth king of Scotland was in Rome in 1050 'spending money like seed'.[15] English travellers of the eleventh century sometimes went further afield: Swein Godwineson, brother of the later King Harold, went on pilgrimage to Jerusalem in 1052 and died at Constantinople;[16] Archbishop Ealdred of York visited the Holy Sepulchre in 1058.[17] Harold Hardrada, king of Norway, who died at Stamford Bridge in 1066, had taken military service at the imperial court in Constantinople, visited the Holy Land, and been in action against the Saracens in Sicily.[18] After the Norman Conquest, the Varangian Guard at Constantinople came increasingly to include Englishmen as well as Scandinavians; the seal of a Byzantine recruiting officer of c. 1080 has been found at Winchester.[19] It would be surprising not to find Scottish involvement in the eastern Mediterranean in the late eleventh century.

It is less easy to discover what part the Scots did play in the first Crusade. Who were they? When did they set out and by what route? Under what commander did they serve? Did they reach Jerusalem, and did they return home? These are vital questions, and to most of them there is at least a partial answer.

Only one Scottish participant in the first Crusade is known by name. He was Lagmann, king of Man and the Western Isles, who, struck with remorse after blinding and mutilating his rebellious brother,

> freely renounced the kingdom, and signed with the sign of the Lord's cross, took up the journey to Jerusalem, in which also he died.[20]

Probably the king of the Isles was not one of Ekkehard of Aura's 'bread and water' crusaders, though he would certainly have seemed like an outlandish barbarian to Guibert de Nogent. He would have been accompanied by a substantial retinue, perhaps of the kind which Guibert could have described as a *cuneus* (group or phalanx of soldiers), when he wrote of 'groups of Scots' (*Scottorum cuneos*). The names of the leaders of other groups are unknown.

The news of the summons of Clermont reached the British Isles around April 1096.[21] Lagmann and those who went with him probably crossed the channel in the summer of 1096 and joined the assembling forces of Duke Robert of Normandy, whose army included most of the peoples from northern Europe who took part:

> In the month of September [1096] Robert count of the Normans, brother of King William, accompanied by Robert of Flanders and Stephen of Blois, his sister's husband, set out on that wonderful journey. . . . With them went the English and Normans and western Franks, the Flemings and groups (*cunei*) of all the peoples from the British ocean as far as the Mediterranean Alps.[22]

It is interesting to note that William of Malmesbury here uses the same word, *cuneus*, as Guibert de Nogent.

How far did the Scottish contingent get on the first Crusade? They might not have been expected to survive under the rigours of an unfamiliar climate, and were 'unwarlike' away from home; one might wonder whether they even reached Constantinople in the winter of 1096-7. But in the following summer they were noted among the many nations marching across Asia Minor by the French chronicler Fulcher of Chartres:

> But who ever heard such a multitude of tongues in a single army, since it contained Franks, Flemings, Frisians, Gauls, Allobroges, Lotharingians, Germans, Bavarians, Normans, Englishmen, Scots, Aquitanians, Italians, Danes (*Daci*), Apulians, Spaniards, Bretons, Greeks and Armenians? If any of the Bretons or Germans had asked me a question, I would not have known how to reply.[23]

The writer was travelling in the retinue of Stephen of Blois, one of Robert of Normandy's companions, and so would certainly have been rubbing shoulders with Germans and Bretons; and it is known from the writings of Orderic Vitalis that in 1097 the Bretons were still in company with Robert of Normandy.[24] Fulcher's description of the army in 1097 can therefore be taken to be reasonably accurate.

This is the last glimpse that can be caught of the Scottish contingent on the first Crusade. It is not known how they fared at the siege of Antioch (1098), or whether they were present at the capture of Jerusalem in the following year.

There is evidence which suggests that some of these Scots did return home. The Irish *Annals of Innisfallen* contain the following curious entry for the year 1105:

> In the above year a camel (*camall*), an animal of remarkable size, was brought from the king of Scotland (*ríg Alban*) to Muirchertach Ua Briain.[25]

It is difficult to imagine how King Edgar (assuming he is the *ríg Alban* referred to) could have acquired this 'animal of remarkable size' unless its arrival in Scotland is to be connected in some way to the return of the crusaders from the Holy Land in 1100 and the following years. Another Scottish crusader may have brought back a less ambitious souvenir: a North African gold coin bearing the date AH 491 (AD 1097) has been unearthed in Monymusk churchyard.[26] It could be argued that the coin originated in Morocco rather than in Syria, and could have come into Scotland by a more indirect route; but on the other hand, the fact that it was virtually uncirculated at the time of its burial points to a date of arrival in Scotland soon after 1097, and that points in the direction of the first Crusade.

The enormous success of the first Crusade and the establishment of Latin principalities in Syria led others to follow in the footsteps of the Crusaders. Notable among them was Edgar Atheling, brother-in-law of King Malcolm III, who 'after Michaelmas' 1097 had led an English army into Scotland and placed Malcolm's son Edgar on the throne in place of his brother Donald Bàn.[27] Among those who accompanied the Atheling on his Scottish campaign was Robert son of Godwine, an Anglo-Norman knight whom King Edgar rewarded with lands in Lothian on which he began to build a castle.[28] Robert's building work was interrupted in 1099, when he was arbitrarily seized and imprisoned by Ranulf Flambard bishop of Durham.[29] He was released in 1099, and subsequently went with Edgar Atheling to the Holy Land. Orderic Vitalis places Edgar's arrival in the East in the spring of 1098,[30] but this seems too soon after his campaign in Scotland in the last months of 1097, and is certainly impossible for his companion Robert son of Godwine, who was imprisoned in the bishop of Durham's castle at the time. According to Orderic, Edgar was in charge of the Greek emperor's fleet off Antioch in March 1098, and sailed to the capture of Lattakieh soon after. William of Malmesbury has a very different and much more likely account of Edgar's movements. He states that Edgar Atheling and Robert son of Godwine arrived together at the siege of Ramleh in May 1102, where Robert was captured and carried off to 'Babylon' (i.e., Cairo) and martyred by being pierced with arrows when he refused to renounce the name of Christ.[31] The manner of his death may be fanciful, but the chronology of the rest of the story is more credible than Orderic's account. Edgar seems to have returned to the West *via* the imperial court at Constantinople and Germany. He was back in Normandy by 1106, when he fought on Duke Robert's side at the battle of Tinchebrai, was captured by Henry I, and released without ransom.[32]

Robert son of Godwine seems to have been a fairly isolated figure, and to have contrasted with the Scottish crusaders noted by Guibert de Nogent and others.[33] It has been suggested that Thor Longus, an Anglian landowner in Ednam (Merse), had a brother who was captured on the first Crusade, but the evidence of a single charter referring to his 'redemption' is hardly substantial enough to bear any weight.[34] Apart from Lagmann king of the Isles, most Scottish participants in the first Crusade were not men of substance or importance; they were regarded as barbarous and of little use in war outside their own country. The Scottish participants had not the wealth or resources of the Franks and Normans, nor did they share the same land-hunger which existed in northern France in the late eleventh century.[35]

Although they did not benefit from the rich pickings of the first Crusade, powerful men from northern Europe showed an early interest in the Latin states in the Holy Land. One of the earliest visitors to the new kingdom of Jerusalem was Sigurd king of Norway, who had been earl of Orkney before his accession in 1103. He set out from Bergen in 1107, coasting Scotland and England, passing through the English Channel and the Bay of Biscay, past the Straits of Gibraltar into the Mediterranean and on to Acre.[36] King

Baldwin I greeted him and conducted him personally to Jerusalem, and persuaded him to use his fleet to blockade Sidon, which the crusaders were besieging at the time. Sidon fell to the Christians on 4 December 1107. Sigurd's voyage was so famous that he was subsequently known as the *Jorsalafara* ('Jerusalem-farer'), and later Scandinavian pilgrims to the Holy Land sought consciously to emulate his feats. [37]

At the time of Sigurd's pilgrimage to Jerusalem, the king of Scotland was Alexander I (1107-1124), of whom it has been remarked that 'in spirit he was a crusader'. [38] Certainly King Alexander possessed an Arab horse and Turkish armour, which he had proudly displayed during a visit to the church of St Andrews (probably the present St Regulus' church). [39] Whether or not this is convincing evidence that Alexander was imbued with crusading spirit, it shows further links between Scotland and the eastern Mediterranean during the early years of the Latin states.

These links are also apparent in the career of John bishop of Glasgow, tutor and friend of Alexander's brother David, who was prince of Cumbria and Strathclyde before his accession as king in 1124. Bishop John's career is remarkable both for his tenacious resistance to the claims of overlordship of the archbishops of York and for his wide travels. He may have been a Tironensian monk before being appointed bishop c. 1117. In 1122, in response to a letter from Pope Calixtus II enjoining his immediate submission to the archbishop of York, John set out for Rome to state his case in person. His appeal before the pope was unavailing; but instead of returning to Scotland, he set out on a further journey to Jerusalem, where he lodged as the guest of the patriarch Gormond for several months. [40] He may have joined a Venetian fleet which sailed down the Adriatic in August 1122, and arrived at Acre the following spring after besieging Corfu. [41] His visit to the Holy Land may have been made out of a mixture of pilgrim spirit and natural reluctance to return to Scotland to confront David with the news of the failure of his mission to Rome. Calixtus was insistent, however, and in 1123 ordered John to return to his diocese and make his submission to York. [42]

Soon after John's return to Scotland, Alexander I died and was succeeded by his brother David, who throughout his reign displayed an interest in the Holy Land and in the crusading movement, which may have been due in part to the influence of John bishop of Glasgow. David's interest was further stimulated a few years later by the visit to Scotland of brother Hugh de Paiens, first master of the Knights Templars, in 1128. Hugh had been attending the Council of Troyes, at which the rule and habit of the Templars were established under the influence of St Bernard of Clairvaux. The *Anglo-Saxon Chronicle* thus describes Hugh's visit to the British Isles:

In this year [1128] Hugh of the Knights Templars came to the king [Henry I] in Normandy from Jerusalem; and the king received him with great ceremony, and sent him thereafter into England, where he was welcomed by all good men. He was given treasure by all, and in Scotland too; and by him much wealth, entirely in gold and silver, was sent to Jerusalem. He called for people to go out to Jerusalem. As a result more people went, either with him or after him, than ever before since the first Crusade, which was in the days of Pope Urban.[43]

The Holy Land historian William of Tyre confirms that Hugh's recruiting drive had considerable success:

In the following year [1129] Hugh de Paiens, first master of the knights of the Temple, and certain other religious men, who had been sent to the princes of the West by the king [Baldwin II] and other princes of the kingdom to rouse the people to come to our aid, and specifically for powerful men to come to the siege of Damascus, returned; and with them came a great throng of noble men to the kingdom, having faith in their words.[44]

In February 1128 the emir of Damascus had died, and it was hoped that the unrest following his death would provide the crusaders with an opportunity to capture the strongest and wealthiest city in Syria. The undertaking was so ambitious that it required not only the fresh recruits from the West, but also contingents from all the Latin states, including Tripoli, Antioch and Edessa.[45]

The assault on Damascus was a complete failure. The English chronicler Henry of Huntingdon describes how an advance party of Christians was surprised and routed by the Damascenes, after which bad weather made further fighting impossible:

In that year [1129] evil befell those whom Hugh de Paiens had led with him to Jerusalem. . . . On the eve of Saint Nicholas's day [5 December 1129] many Christians were defeated by a few pagans . . . at the siege of Damascus; while a great many Christians had gone forth foraging for victuals, the pagans were amazed at so many and so strong Christians fleeing in such womanly fashion, and killed many while pursuing them. God punished those who sought to save themselves by flight that night by a snowstorm in the mountains, so that they barely escaped.[46]

The storm made the plain of Damascus impassable, and the princes of Outremer decided to abandon the attack. The overseas recruits were disheartened at this failure; the *Anglo-Saxon Chronicle* comments that they were 'pitiably duped to find it was nothing but lies'.[47]

Hugh de Paiens's visit to Scotland in 1128 had a more permanent effect than to send recruits to their death or disillusionment before the walls of Damascus. He also impressed upon King David I the virtues of his new order of knights of the Temple, who at this time became established in Scotland. Ailred of Rievaulx describes the influence exerted by Templars over David's daily life:

> He committed himself to the counsel of religious men of all kinds, and surrounding
> himself with very fine brothers of the illustrious knighthood of the Temple of Jerusalem,
> he made them guardians of his morals by day and night.[48]

Another contemporary writer confirms David's strict observance of the
canonical hours:

> He was devoted to the divine offices, and each day he heard all the canonical hours, and
> also offices of the dead, without any interruption.[49]

Certainly by the thirteenth century it had become customary for a Templar
to act as almoner to the king's household, and this practice may have dated
from David I's time.[50]

It is perhaps curious in view of this alleged influence how seldom
Templars appear as witnesses to royal charters; no example survives earlier
than 1160.[51] But their earliest possessions in Scotland clearly date from
before this. Balantrodoch (now Temple, Midlothian) was the Templars'
chief preceptory in Scotland at least by the late twelfth century, but was
almost certainly granted to them by David I, possibly in 1128 or soon
after.[52] Another early acquisition was the church of Inchinnan
(Renfrewshire), which was expressly excluded from a grant of churches in
Renfrewshire to Paisley Abbey c. 1163, presumably having already been
granted to the Templars, probably by David I.[53] By the mid-twelfth century
they appear also to have had possessions in royal burghs, and to have
acquired small parcels of land in widely scattered parts of the country.[54] It is
uncertain when they acquired the estate of Temple Liston (now Kirkliston,
West Lothian), which was their other major possession in southern
Scotland. But there can be no doubt of the validity for Scotland of William
of Tyre's comment about the Templars' wealth c. 1185:

> It is said that they have immense possessions, both here [in the Holy Land] and across
> the sea, such that there is no province in the Christian world which has not conveyed a
> part of its property to these brothers; and they are said to have abundance equal to the
> wealth of kings.[55]

At an uncertain, but almost certainly later, point during David I's reign,
the other military order of the Hospitallers became established in Scotland
also. Much obscurity surrounds their early history in Scotland; it is
probable that in their early development and organisation their history was
similar to that of the Templars, though along more modest lines. A
fifteenth-century English Hospitaller cartulary records a tradition of their
earliest endowments in Scotland:

> David king of Scots gave the land of Torphichen. Fergus king of the Gallovidians gave
> the land of Galtway.[56]

These may well have been the Hospitallers' most substantial properties in Scotland before the fourteenth century, but like the Templars they also seem to have accumulated a large number of small parcels of land scattered over the length and breadth of the kingdom.[57]

David I's receptiveness to the Templars in particular reflects his attitude to wider spiritual trends of the times. David was much influenced by the Cistercian theologian Ailred of Rievaulx, and during his reign Cistercian monasteries were prominent among his many new monastic foundations. Ultimately can be detected the pervasive influence of St Bernard of Clairvaux, the great champion of early twelfth-century spirituality and of the crusading movement. Only one letter from St Bernard to King David survives, written probably in 1136, and couched in terms of warm admiration:

> For a long time I have honoured you and wished to meet you face to face, moved by the excellent repute of your name; I have desired it, and I have heeded the scripture: 'Lord, thou hast heard the desire of the humble; thou wilt prepare their heart, thou will cause thine ear to hear'.[58]

It is probable that David was the recipient of other letters from St Bernard's fertile pen which have not survived. Few subjects aroused Bernard's letter writing so much as the first great disaster which befell the Latin states in Syria, the fall of Edessa to Imad-ad-Din Zangi in 1144.

The news of the fall of Edessa came as a severe shock to the West. Less than fifty years had elapsed since the triumphs of the first Crusade, and it appeared now that these conquests might prove ephemeral. The eloquence of St Bernard and all his spiritual fervour persuaded King Louis VII of France and Emperor Conrad II of Germany to take the cross. His message, according to Ailred of Rievaulx, was not lost on the king of Scots, either:

> He [David] would have renounced the kingdom, laid down the sceptre, and joined the sacred army in the places of Our Lord's passion and resurrection, if he had not been dissuaded by the counsel of prelates and abbots, the tears of the poor, the sighing of widows, the desolation of the common folk, and the clamour and outcry of his whole kingdom; he was detained in body, but not in mind or will.[59]

No letter from St Bernard addressed directly to King David on the subject of the second Crusade has survived, but it is nontheless very likely that David's crusading longing belonged to the later years of his long life, when he had an adult son ready to succeed him. It is perhaps significant that from c. 1145 David's son Earl Henry is entitled 'king designate' (*rex designatus*), an unusual title which becomes easier to understand with the consideration that the king was discussing the possibility of leaving the kingdom at the time.[60] It was by no means uncommon for a man to set out on crusade late in life; the most notable example was Count Raymond IV of Toulouse, who was about 55 when he set out on the first Crusade, having vowed to end his days in the Holy Land.[61]

Had cares of state allowed David I to join the second Crusade, as he wished, probably many members of the Anglo-Norman families who were settling in Scotland at the time would have joined him. As it happened, Scottish participants again tended to be drawn from the 'barbaric' classes of society. Those Scots who were less susceptible than their king to the counsel of prelates and the groaning of widows travelled south to join an Anglo-Flemish fleet which assembled at Dartmouth in the spring of 1147. According to the eyewitness account of a member of this fleet, it consisted of Englishmen and Normans, 'with men of Cologne, Flanders, Boulogne, Brittany and Scotland'.[62]

The fleet was divided into three parts when it left Dartmouth; the Germans and Flemings travelled under their own commanders, while the remainder was further divided under the command of four constables. The Scots probably accompanied Saher de Archelle, one of the constables from England.[63] At the end of June 1147 the fleet arrived off Lisbon and joined the king of Portugal in besieging the city, which seemed at the time to offer a quicker return than that promised by the voyage to Jerusalem. The siege dragged on for some months, however, and some of the Englishmen began to regret that they had not followed their original intention and sailed on through the Meditteranean. To dissuade them from deserting, one of the English constables, Hervey de Glanville, made an impassioned speech to remind them of their loyalty. He praised the tenacity of the Normans:

> Who does not know that no man of the Norman race will refuse to persevere in works of virtuous toil?

After holding up the Flemings and Rhinelanders as examples of steadfastness, he shamed his hearers with a less flattering comparison:

> And who indeed would deny that the Scots are barbarians? Nevertheless, while in our company they have never transgressed the laws of duty and friendship.[64]

As a result of Glanville's persuasion, the English remained with the besiegers, and Lisbon surrendered to the Christian army on 24 October 1147.

The capture of Lisbon for the Portuguese was the only success of the second Crusade. The great army led by Louis VII to Syria foundered before the walls of Damascus, as the army of 1129 had done, and withdrew with considerable losses without even attempting to restore the county of Edessa. Few of the Frankish crusaders had any connection with Scotland. One who did was William de Warenne, Earl Henry's brother-in-law, who had taken the cross at Vézélay in March 1146, and who was captured by the Moslems during the retreat from Damascus in 1148.[65] His capture was noted in the *Chronicle of Melrose;* although this chronicle was not being kept contemporaneously until c. 1170,[66] the monks of Melrose may have had a special interest in the Crusades; they were Cistercians, and from 1148 to 1159 their abbot was Waldeve, whose father Simon de Senlis had gone to Jerusalem in the wake of the first Crusade, and whose mother Maud had married as her second husband Earl (later King) David, thereby bringing the honour of Huntingdom to the Scottish royal house.[67] A charter issued by Earl Henry as earl of Northumberland at Newcastle in 1147 suggests how the second Crusade loomed large in the consciousness of contemporaries; it is dated 'Michaelmas next after Louis king of France began the journey to Jerusalem'.[68] A confirmation issued by King David in the same year at Coldingham is dated 'the year from the Lord's Incarnation 1147, that is, the year in which the king of France and many Christians went to Jerusalem'.[69]

Clearly Scottish contemporaries were well aware of the events of these years; in view of the many close connections of the nobility of the two kingdoms of England and Scotland, this is not surprising. In England the weakness of Stephen's authority made the Crusade an attractive proposition. Taking the cross secured ecclesiastical protection for the acquisitions of those who had profited during the 'anarchy', while with the return of relative stability in the late 1140s, the second Crusade offered an outlet for the belligerence of those who had made fighting their livelihood in the 1130s and early 1140s. The absence of a strong king in England meant that those who wished to go on crusade were perfectly free to do so. None of these factors prevailed in Scotland; David I, a strong king, was dissuaded from taking part, and his councillors and nobility seem to have shown little enthusiasm. The Scots who went to Lisbon in 1147 were, like the Scottish participants on the first Crusade, 'barbarians'.

It may have been on their way to join the second Crusade that a group of particularly barbaric Scots was noted by a Premonstratensian monk from the diocese of Cambrai:

> In our own times in western Scotland not all of the people wear drawers (*feminalia*), but all the knights and townsfolk do wear them; the rest make do with a general covering, which is closed over at the front and back, but which underneath is open at the sides. This was related to me by certain clerics who had come from these parts. . . . And it was clearly seen that some of these people, who were travelling through our land on pilgrimage, were not wearing drawers.[70]

This description bears interesting comparison with that of Guibert de Nogent some fifty years earlier. These Scots, travelling through Flanders 'on pilgrimage' (*peregre*) in the mid-twelfth century, may well have been participants in the second Crusade, an event which was usually described by contemporaries as a pilgrimage. This passage also seems to be the earliest known example of speculation about what the Scotsman wears under his kilt.

Despite the failure of the second Crusade, enthusiasm for crusading remained lively in some quarters; in the years immediately following the

Frankish fiasco, an extraordinary venture was undertaken by the men of Orkney, which is very fully described in the *Orkneyinga Saga.*

It might appear to require some justification why the Orcadian Crusade of 1150-53 should be discussed in a Scottish context at all, since the Northern Isles were not a part of the Scottish kingdom in the twelfth century (neither, of course, were Man and the Hebrides). But the Scottish kings were interested in the affairs of the Northern Isles, and Orcadian politics were to some extent influenced by events in Scotland. There were Orkneymen in King David's army in the north of England in 1138,[71] and in the following winter John bishop of Glasgow seems to have been sent to Orkney by King David, and to have been well received by Rognvald and William, respectively earl and bishop of Orkney.[72] It was seventeen years since John had himself visited the Holy Land, but meeting him may perhaps have contributed to Earl Rognvald's later enthusiasm. John's mission may have been part of King David's policy of closer contact with Orkney, as shown in his treatment of Swein Asleifsson when the latter visited him in Edinburgh in the mid-1140s. A few years later Orcadians visited Malcolm IV at Aberdeen and were well received by him there.[73] It may be that the Scottish crown was at the time trying to extend its influence into the northernmost parts of the Scottish mainland, and possibly even into the islands themselves.

Be that as it may, the main influences which inspired and directed the course of Rognvald's pilgrimage were distinctly Norse rather than Scottish. He was persuaded to undertake the voyage by a Norwegian who had served in the Varangian Guard at Constantinople at the time of the second Crusade. Many of Rognvald's feats, such as the tying of knots on the east shore of the River Jordan, were in conscious emulation of the deeds of Sigurd Jorsalafara.[74]

In the summer of 1148 Earl Rognvald of Orkney met Eindredi Ungi, who persuaded him of the virtue of travelling to the Holy Land, from which he had recently returned; before that he had served as a Varangian at the court of the emperor Manuel II Comnenus, and he may have hoped to recruit the Orkneymen into the Varangian Guard. In the autumn of 1150 the Crusaders, led by Eindredi, Rognvald and Bishop William, assembled in Norway and sailed to Orkney, where they spent the winter. Possibly the 'Jorsalafarir' inscriptions at Maeshowe commemorate this visit.[75] In the summer of 1151 the pilgrims left Orkney and sailed round Scotland, probably by the east coast,[76] through the Channel and the Bay of Biscay, arriving at Galicia in October. After a short stay in Galicia, they sailed on round Portugal and Spain, through the Straits of Gibraltar, and on to Narbonne. About this time the earl and his friends, chiefly Bishop William and Erling Saki, parted company from Eindredi Ungi, who went straight on to Constantinople; if

Eindredi was chiefly interested in recruiting Varangians, he would have had little time for Rognvald's 'gallivanting . . . all over the Mediterranean Sea'.[77] The earl and his companions, however, were overcome by the seductive beauty of Ermingarde, daughter of Aimery count of Narbonne, and stayed in the city during the winter of 1151-52. Around Christmas they aided the people of Narbonne in capturing the castle of a certain Godfrey near Narbonne. In the early summer, regretting their parting from Ermingarde, they sailed away again, along the North African coast; in the course of this journey they encountered a saracen 'dromond' or massive galley, which they captured. They stopped briefly on Crete, then sailed on to Acre.

In August 1152 the pilgrims arrived at Jerusalem and the Jordan. The earl swam across the river and tied knots on the east bank in commemoration of his achievement, and in emulation of Sigurd Jorsalafara. After visiting the holy places, the pilgrims sailed to Constantinople in the autumn, where they wintered with Manuel Comnenus (emperor 1143-80). Here they were reunited with Eindredi Ungi. Manuel treated them with honour and offered them posts in the Varangian Guard, but Rognvald was reluctant to accept a position which would have made him subordinate to Eindredi; he, the bishop, Erling Saki and their followers decided to return to Orkney the following spring. They abandoned their ships (or possibly sold them to Manuel),[78] crossed in Greek ships from Durazzo to Apulia, and took horses to Rome. The summer of 1153 was occupied in the overland crossing from Italy to Denmark. They reached Norway in the autumn of 1153, and arrived home in Orkney before Christmas.[79]

Apart from the crusade of King Sigurd, this is probably the best-known of Scandinavian *Jorsalaferd;* its similarities to Sigurd's pilgrimage were not accidental, and the pattern was probably followed by other Norse pilgrims. It has been remarked that the twelfth century was 'la vrai période des Jorsalaferd'; expeditions which were not connected with a major Crusade or *passagium generale* summoned by the pope, but were more individualistic outbursts of Christian belligerence. In some ways they were similar to the raiding activities of the Scandinavian peoples before their conversion.[80] The *Jorsalaferd* added another dimension to the concept of crusading as it was understood in twelfth-century Scotland.

Scots, however, like Norsemen, continued to visit Jerusalem in the years following the second Crusade. John of Würzburg, a German pilgrim who visited Jerusalem in the 1160s, offered some observations on why the city had fallen so much into the hands of Franks and Italians to the exclusion of northern Europeans:

> Since only a few of our people remained . . . and very many of the others had with great haste and homesickness returned to their native land [Germany, after the first Crusade], the city has fallen entirely into the hands of other nations – Frenchmen, Lorrainers, Norman, Provençals, Auvergnats, Italians, Spaniards and Burgundians, who took part in the Crusade.[81]

But with the meticulous accuracy which characterises his work, he enumerates the many nations which maintain a pilgrims' chapel at Jerusalem:

> I have omitted many of the chapels and smaller churches which are maintained there by men of various nations and languages. For there are Greeks, Bulgarians, Latins, Germans, Hungarians, Scots, Navarrese, Bretons, English, Franks, Ruthenians, Bohemians, Georgians, Armenians, Jacobites, Syrians, Nestorians, Indians, Egyptians, Copts, Capheturici, Maronites, and very many others, whom it would take too long to tell.[82]

Is John of Würzburg here indulging in mere fanciful name-dropping, as was, for instance, his contemporary the Spanish rabbi Benjamin of Tudela, who included Scots among the many nations whose merchants maintained a hostel at Alexandria?[83] Arabic geographers of the twelfth century had only the vaguest knowledge about Scotland.[84] It is uncertain, but quite possible, that John of Würzburg should be taken seriously, since in many other respects his description of Jerusalem is notably accurate. Possibly his *Scoti* were Irish, though by the later twelfth century (and in all the writers cited above in this chapter) the term had usually come to mean Scots. If a Scottish pilgrims' chapel at Jerusalem in the 1160s is to be believed, it suggests something of the volume of pilgrim traffic to the Holy Land that such an institution could be maintained. Such an institution was not in existence in the 1120s, when the bishop of Glasgow lodged with the patriarch of Jerusalem,[85] so it must be assumed that it came into existence between then and the 1160s.

A few months before Earl Rognvald's return to Orkney in 1153, King David had died at Carlisle; he has been described as a 'cultivated and attractive man, son of the learned Margaret, patron and friend of Saint Ailred, founder and benefactor of over half the monasteries of Scotland'.[86] Since his son Earl Henry had predeceased him, he was succeeded by his grandson Malcolm, a boy of twelve. Despite his youth and the brevity of his reign, Malcolm looked beyond the bounds of his kingdom no less than his grandfather had done. In 1159 he accompanied Henry II's expedition against Toulouse, in the course of which he was knighted.[87] He returned to face a political crisis in Scotland; the anger shown by many of his nobility because of his participation in the English expedition suggests the kind of problems which may have helped to dissuade King David from joining the second Crusade as he had wished. Malcolm, however, was not to be intimidated, for c. 1164 he made a vow to go on pilgrimage to the shrine of St James the Greater at Compostella;[88] a vow which his untimely death in 1165 prevented him from fulfilling.

Malcolm continued his grandfather's policy of generosity to the military orders. He confirmed the Templars' existing liberties and probably granted them new privileges.[89] To the Hospitallers he granted a toft (or smallholding) in each of his burghs, which may have been the origin of the network of tiny holdings which this order accumulated throughout Scotland during the middle ages.[90] During his reign for the first time a Templar and a Hospitaller appear as witnesses to a royal act.[91]

Malcolm IV was noted for his piety, as was his youngest brother, David; the latter's respect for church property, even in times of war, was conspicuous.[92] Piety was a less notable trait in the middle brother, William, who succeeded Malcolm in 1165 and reigned for nearly half a century. The early years of William's reign were occupied in a struggle for the recovery of the northern counties of England, which his grandfather had acquired and his brother had given away. The result of this struggle was the king's capture in 1174, after which William's foreign policy was severely circumscribed until after Henry II's death in 1188.

William also found time to quarrel with the papacy during the late 1170s and early 1180s; as a result of a dispute over the bishopric of Saint Andrews, the king was for a time excommunicated, and was not restored to papal favour until 1182.[93]

Soon after his reconciliation with the papacy, William's relationship with the king of England began to improve also. It is possible that considerations of the state of the Holy Land played a part in this *rapprochement*. Heraclius, patriarch of Jerusalem, arrived in England early in 1185, and met Henry II at Reading; there he acquainted the king with the crisis faced by the kingdom of Jerusalem posed by the increasing power of Saladin (Salah-ad-Din Yusuf), who had united Syria and Egypt under his own leadership in an encircling ring round the Holy Land. Henry summoned a great council of his nobility to meet at London on 10 March 1185 to discuss ways of sending aid to the kingdom of Jerusalem, and among those whom he summoned were William king of Scots and his brother David.[94] A contemporary chronicler records that 'during this time many of the barons and knights of the kingdom took the cross from the hands of the patriarch of Jerusalem', but King William was not among them, and it is not certain that David was either. That notwithstanding, Henry was anxious to show favour to the Scottish brothers; the danger to the kingdom of Jerusalem meant that many of his leading fighting men would be absent from the kingdom for a time, and this consideration must have inclined Henry towards harmonious relations with his northern neighbours. Before the council broke up, he restored to King William his principal English possession, the honour of Huntingdon, and William transferred it to his brother David.[95]

This is an early example of how the affairs of the Holy Land could affect Anglo-Scottish relations, a phenomenon which was to be often repeated over the next century and more. But in 1185, help for the Holy Land was insufficient. Not enough foreign knights went to Jerusalem to dissuade Saladin from invading the kingdom in great strength in 1187. In a brilliantly succesful campaign he destroyed the army of the kingdom of Jerusalem at Hattin (4 July 1187) and forced the Holy City to surrender (2 October 1187).[96] The news of the fall of Jerusalem came as a profound shock to the West. Those who had failed fully to heed the warning given by Heraclius two years before now took the cross in huge numbers, and made real preparations for the long journey to win back Jerusalem.

NOTES

1. Cf. Runciman, *History of the Crusades,* i, 87-92, 98-100.

2. D. C. Munro, 'The Speech of Pope Urban at Clermont', *American Historical Review,* xi (1906), 231-41.

3. R. Somerville, 'The Council of Clermont and Latin Christian Society', *Archivum Historiae Pontificiae,* xii (1974), 55-90, at 71-2.

4. *MGH Script,* vi, 367.

5. *RHC Occ,* v, 16; *MGH Script,* vi, 213.

6. *RHC Occ,* v, 16; *MGH Script,* vi, 213-4.

7. Cf. *Annalista Saxo* (*MGH Script,* vi, 729); *Chronica de Origine Ducum Brabantiae* (*MGH Script,* xxv, 408).

8. *MGH Script,* xx, 249.

9. *RHC Occ,* iv, 125.

10. A. A. M. Duncan, 'The Dress of the Scots', *SHR,* xxix (1950), 210-12.

11. K. Hughes, *Celtic Britain in the Early Middle Ages* (Bury St Edmunds, 1980), 28-32, and plates I, II, and IV.

12. *ASC,* 232.

13. William of Malmesbury, *Gesta Regum Anglorum,* ed. W. Stubbs (RS, 1887-89), ii, 399.

14. *Itinera Hierosolymitana Saeculi IIII-VIII,* ed. P. Geyer (Corpus Scriptorum Ecclesiasticorum Latinorum, xxxviii, 1888).

15. Anderson, *ES,* i, 558.

16. *ASC,* 182.

17. Ibid., 189.

18. *King Harald's Saga,* ed. M. Magnusson and H. Pálsson (1966), 47ff.

19. K. N. Cigaar, 'L'Emigration anglaise à Byzance après 1066', *Revue des Études byzantines,* xxxii (1974), 301-42; M. de Waha, 'La Lettre d'Alexis Ie Comnène à Robert le Frison', *Byzantion,* xlvii (1977), 113-25; V. Laurent, 'Byzance et Angleterre au lendemain de la Conquête normande', *Numismatic Circular,* lxxi (1963), 93-6.

20. *Chron. Man,* i, 54.

21. *ASC,* 232.

22. William of Malmesbury, *Gesta Regum Anglorum,* ii, 402.

23. *RHC Occ,* iii, 366.

24. Orderic Vitalis, *Ecclesiastical History,* ed. M. Chibnall (Oxford, 1969-82), v, 58.

25. *Annals of Innisfallen,* ed. S. Mac Airt (Dublin, 1951), 262.

26. W. Douglas Simpson, 'The Augustinian Priory and Parish Church of Monymusk, Aberdeenshire', *PSAS,* lix (1925), 34-71, at 65.

27. *ASC,* 234.

28. *Chron. Fordun,* 224-5.
29. R. L. G. Ritchie, *The Normans in Scotland* (Edinburgh, 1954), 95-7.
30. Orderic Vitalis, *Ecclesiastical History,* v, 270.
31. William of Malmesbury, *Gesta Regum Anglorum,* ii, 310, 349.
32. *DNB,* s.n. 'Edgar Atheling'.
33. A. A. M. Duncan, *Scotland: the Making of the Kingdom* (Edinburgh, 1975), 127.
34. A. C. Lawrie, *Early Scottish Charters prior to 1153* (Glasgow, 1905), 19, 259.
35. Runciman, *History of the Crusades,* i, 92.
36. Ibid., ii, 92-3.
37. *Orkneyinga Saga,* ed. A. B. Taylor (Edinburgh, 1938), 299-300, 395.
38. Ritchie, *Normans in Scotland,* 175.
39. *Chron. Wyntoun,* ii, 176.
40. Symeon of Durham, *Opera Omnia,* ed. T. Arnold (RS, 1882-5), ii, 264.
41. Runciman, *History of the Crusades,* ii, 166-7.
42. A. W. Haddan and W. Stubbs (edd), *Councils and Ecclesiastical Documents relating to Great Britain and Ireland* (Oxford, 1883), ii, 16, 20-1.
43. *ASC,* 259.
44. *RHC Occ,* i, pt i, 595-6.
45. Ibid., 596.
46. Henry of Huntingdon, *Historia Anglorum,* ed. T. Arnold (RS, 1879), 251.
47. *ASC,* 259.
48. *Chron. Fordun,* 225.
49. Symeon of Durham, *Opera Omnia,* ii, 330.
50. 'The Scottish King's Household', *SHS Misc,* ii, 34-5.
51. *St. Andrews Liber,* 207; *RRS,* i, 218-9.
52. Cf. *RRS,* i, 98.
53. *Paisley Registrum,* 5-6; *RRS,* i, 98, 169.
54. *St Andrews Liber,* 124; cf. *Newbattle Registrum,* 85-6, 127-8; *Glasgow Registrum,* 37; *Midlothian Charters,* 18-9, 28-9; SRO RH 6/17.
55. *RHC Occ,* i, pt i, 521.
56. W. Dugdale, *Monasticon Anglicanum* (1st edn 1655-73), ii, 551.
57. *RRS,* i, 230; cf. *Newbattle Registrum,* 131-2; *Dryburgh Liber,* 156-7; *Paisley Registrum,* 379-80; cf. in general I. B. Cowan, P. H. R. Mackay and A. Macquarrie (edd.), *The Knights of St John of Jerusalem in Scotland* (SHS, 1983).
58. *RRS,* i, 289-90.
59. *Chron. Fordun,* 222.
60. Lawrie, *Early Scottish Charters,* nos. clxii-clxiv. David also corresponded with Suger, abbot of Saint Denis de Paris, one of Louis VII's chief councillors and regent for the king during his absence on the Crusade; *RRS,* i, 169.
61. J. H. and L. L. Hill, *Raymond IV, Count of Toulouse* (New York, 1962).
62. *De Expugnatione Lyxbonensi,* ed. C. W. David (New York, 1936), 102.
63. Ibid., 52-6; Saher de Archelle is mentioned in *Records of the Templars in England,* ed. B. A. Lees (British Academy, 1935), 24, 80, 99.
64. *De Expugnatione Lyxbonensi,* 106.
65. *Chron. Melrose,* s.a. 1147; cf. Suger of St Denis, *Vie de Louis VIIe,* ed. A. Molinier (Paris, 1887), 159.
66. *Chron. Melrose,* xi-xvi.
67. Cf. *Vita Waldeni* in *Acta Sanctorum,* August, i, 248-76; cf. D. Baker, 'Legend and Reality: the case of Waldef of Melrose', *Studies in Church History,* xii (1975), 59-82.
68. *RRS,* i, 159.

69. Lawrie, *Early Scottish Charters*, 139-40.

70. Migne, *PL*, cciii, col 730.

71. Anderson, *SAEC*, 189.

72. *Orkneyinga Saga*, 261-2.

73. Ibid., 273.

74. Ibid., 307.

75. *PSAS*, v, (1865) 247; *PSAS*, vi (1866), 78-82.

76. But cf. Snorre Sturlusson, *Heimskringla*, ed. E. Monsen (Cambridge, 1932), 155.

77. S. Blöndal, *The Varangians of Byzantium* (Cambridge, 1978), 154-7.

78. Ibid., 157.

79. The chronology here followed is that worked out by A. B. Taylor in his edition of *Orkneyinga Saga*, 285-304, 392-6; cf. A. B. Taylor, 'Studies in the Orkneyinga Saga', *Proceedings of the Orkney Antiquarian Society*, xi (1933), 48-9.

80. P. Riant, *Expéditions et Pèlerinages des Scandinaves en Terre sainte au Temps des Croisades* (Paris, 1865), i, 42.

81. John of Würzburg, *Description of the Holy Land*, ed. C. W. Wilson, trans. A. Stewart (PPTS, 1890), 41.

82. Ibid., 69.

83. *The Itinerary of Benjamin of Tudela*, ed. and trans. M. N. Adler (London, 1907), 76.

84. D. M. Dunlop, 'Scotland according to al-Idrisi', *SHR*, xxvi (1947), 114-18.

85. See above, p. 14.

86. C. N. L. Brooke, *Europe in the central Middle Ages* (1964), 381.

87. A. C. Lawrie, *Annals of the Reigns of Malcolm and William, Kings of Scots* (Glasgow, 1910), 40-1, 54-6.

88. *RRS*, i, 276-7.

89. Ibid., 281-2.

90. Ibid., 230.

91. Ibid., 219.

92. *Chronicles of the Reign of Stephen*, ed. R. Howlett (RS, 1884-9), iii, 296-300.

93. Duncan, *Making of the Kingdom*, 270-3.

94. *Chron. Benedict*, 335-6.

95. Ibid., 357; cf. Lawrie, *Annals*, 265-7.

96. Runciman, *History of the Crusades*, ii, 454-68.

2

Recovery and Defeat, 1188-1244

The first of the princes of the West to take the cross at the end of 1187 was Richard count of Poitou, quickly followed by his father Henry II and King Philip II of France.[1] The two kings quickly patched up their differences and made joint plans for a new Crusade. These included the levying of the 'Saladin tithe', a tenth of rents and moveables in all their dominions. Early in 1188 Henry crossed into England to supervise the collection of the tithe there, and sent Hugh du Puiset, bishop of Durham, to Scotland to demand a contribution from King William.

Roger Howden, the English chronicler who described the meeting between the bishop and the king of Scots, has left two slightly differing accounts of the events in question.[2] In one version, William offered Henry 4,000 marks for the restoration of Scottish royal castles still held in English hands, but King Henry demanded payment of the tithe in addition to this; William agreed to try to obtain the consent of his prelates and barons, which was not forthcoming. When Bishop Hugh arrived at Birgham on the Tweed he was met by William and his council, and was told that the prelates and barons would not pay the tenth even had William sworn it himself.[3] In the second version, the initiative in refusing to pay the tithe appears to come from William himself. It recounts how William met Bishop Hugh between Birgham and Wark and refused to let him enter Scotland to collect the tithe; instead, the king offered him 5,000 marks for the tithe and the redemption of his castles together, an offer which King Henry refused.[4] It has been observed that 'we do not know whether the resistance to English demands originated from the barons or from King William, whether King William was pushed into refusal by his magnates or was shrewdly exploiting the new political difficulties of King Henry'.[5]

It is unlikely that Scotland's refusal to pay the Saladin tithe in 1188 should be interpreted as 'a marked lack of enthusiasm for the recovery of Jerusalem after its fall'.[6] It is perhaps more likely that William, or his magnates, were anxious to get the best possible terms from Henry II in return for a contribution, and may have been justifiably suspicious of the sincerity of his crusading intentions. Within a few months renewed war had broken out between Henry and Philip II, which was only ended by King Henry's death at Chinon on 6 July 1189. It was only then that serious plans for the new Crusade were instituted, nearly two years after Saladin's conquest of the kingdom of Jerusalem. Within a very short time of Henry's death William had entered into fresh negotiations with the new king, Richard I, securing a 'promissory letter of King Richard to the king of

Scotland that he would restore to him all his rights'. On 5 December 1189 the two kings agreed to the 'Quit-claim of Canterbury', whereby Richard restored all royal castles in Scotland and the *status quo* that had existed before 1174 in return for 10,000 marks.[7] A few days later Richard crossed into France on the first stage of his journey to recover Jerusalem.

The agreement was admirably suited to the needs of both kings. Richard was desperately in need of finance for his Crusade, while the sovereignty of Scotland was of little use to him while he was in Palestine. On the other hand, a peaceful Scottish frontier during his absence was clearly important to Richard, while William was willing to pay a high price to secure the cancellation of the 'Treaty of Falaise' imposed on him in 1174. It is also possible that William may have been convinced of the genuineness of Richard's crusading intentions, in a way that he was not convinced of his father's.

The 'king's aid' agreed on at Musselburgh in 1189 to raise the 10,000 marks was the first tax of its kind raised in Scotland. Very little is known about how it was carried out or about popular reaction to it; one royal brieve commands the tenants of the abbot of Scone who have fled their land 'because of the aid' to return to their land until the aid has been paid.[8] But there is no evidence of widespread opposition to the aid, as there had been to Henry II's demands in 1188, and there is no evidence of Scots taking the cross on a large scale to avoid paying it.

Indeed, relatively few Scots are known to have joined the third Crusade. The most important Scottish nobleman who certainly took part was Robert de Quincy, who had risen to prominence early in the reign of William I and married Orabile, daughter of Ness son of William, a major landowner in east and south-east Scotland. On lands in Tranent which had come to him through his wife, he had probably been the founder of a hospital of Bethlehemite canons from Clamecy in central France, a daughter-house of the Church of the Nativity in Bethlehem.[9] It is unknown when he took the cross, but it may have been soon after hearing the news of the fall of Jerusalem. He appears to have been with the king and an impressive array of prelates and barons at Perth in April 1189,[10] and may thereafter have accompanied King William south to meet Richard at Canterbury in December 1189. If so, he probably crossed into France with Richard on 12 December, was with the king when he met King Philip at Vézélay in July 1190, and joined the march of the English army down the Rhône to Marseilles in August 1190. Here the land army joined up with the English fleet, which Richard had sent on in advance.[11] After wintering in Sicily and a spring campaign in Cyprus, Richard's forces did not arrive at Acre until June 1191.

They found the French army already there, helping the remnant of the army of the kingdom of Jerusalem in the siege of the city. The English arrival had a decisive impact on the siege, and Acre surrendered on 12 July.

Soon after King Philip retired to Tyre with Conrad of Montferrat, one of the claimants to the throne of Jerusalem, and at the beginning of August he set out for home. He had left some Saracen prisoners in Conrad's hands, and as soon as he had gone King Richard demanded that they be handed over to him. When, on 7 August, Conrad refused to surrender them, Richard arranged an embassy to go to Tyre, consisting mainly of followers of the king of France:

> And with them the king of England sent on his own behalf Robert de Quincy. They set out for Tyre on 8 August.[12]

A few days earlier Robert de Quincy had been entrusted with a still more responsible task. The two kings had agreed each to provide one hundred knights and fifty sergeants for the defence of Antioch until the following Easter (5 April 1192), and King Richard had appointed Robert de Quincy 'constable and leader' of the English knights.[13] Probably Robert set out with his knights for the defence of the North around the same time that Richard and the bulk of his army moved south from Acre (22 August) on his bold but ultimately unsuccessful attempt to recover Jerusalem.[14] Robert de Quincy probably stayed in the Holy Land until the autumn of 1192, and returned to the West along with the bulk of Richard's forces. He was back in Scotland not later than 1195, possibly by 1193,[15] and thereafter appears regularly as a witness to royal acts, as he had done before 1190.[16] Clearly this former Scottish justiciar had made a good impression on the English king, and emerged from the third Crusade with some credit.

Who accompanied Robert de Quincy on the third Crusade? It is not known whether any of his knightly tenants from Fife or East Lothian followed him to the Holy Land, though it is what one would expect. One Scot who took the cross and set out on crusade is Osbert Olifard of Arbuthnott, a former sheriff of Mearns; 'in the time of bishop Hugh' of Saint Andrews (1183-1188) he took the cross and desired to set out for Jerusalem, first leasing and setting in ferme the lands of Arbuthnott which the king had given him.[17] He does not appear to have returned to Scotland. It is likely that he took the cross on hearing of the fall of Jerusalem, and immediately set his lands in ferme to raise money for the Crusade. He may have accompanied Robert de Quincy and died on crusade.

It is possible that Alan son of Walter the Steward joined the third Crusade, and very likely at least that some of his knightly tenants in Innerwick (East Lothian) did so. The fourteenth-century historian John Barbour is alleged to have

> said that lord Alan Stewart, son of Walter, was in the expedition with Godfrey de Bouillon king of Jerusalem, in which the city of Antioch was captured.[18]

Since Alan son of Walter died more than a century later than Godfrey de Bouillon, this is clearly impossible; but it is not impossible that he joined the third Crusade. Two pieces of evidence indirectly support this possibility.

The Hospital of Saint Thomas of Acre, founded by English pilgrims on the third Crusade, held lands at Spittalhill in Symington (Ayrshire). As the area is in the heart of the Stewarts' great complex of estates in Kyle, it is likely that the grantor was one of the Stewarts; and if, as seems likely, the grant was made soon after the foundation of the Hospital of Saint Thomas of Acre, that points in the direction of Alan son of Walter. Thus, this may indicate a connection between the Stewarts and the third Crusade.[19]

Shortly before the departure of the Crusade, three of the Steward's knightly tenants in Innerwick, Robert de Kent, Robert Hunaud and Roland son-in-law of Nicholas de Côtentin, set their lands in Innerwick in tack to Kelso Abbey for an unspecified sum of money; the tack was to come into force at Martinmas after Kings Richard and Philip set off for Jerusalem, and was to be of thirty-three years' duration. The deed was in the form of a chirograph, and confirmed by Alan son of Walter and by King William.[20] Although the chirograph does not state explicitly that these knights of the Steward were raising money to go on crusade, it seems very likely since the money was required from the time of the departure of the crusading armies.

These considerations strengthen the possibility that Alan son of Walter joined the third Crusade; but it is by no means certain. The English exchequer rolls for Richard I's reign are full of references to persons absent on Crusade, including Robert de Quincy, but do not mention Alan son of Walter in that context.[21] An examination of the witness-lists of Scottish royal acts for the period of the third Crusade is inconclusive.[22] On the whole, the evidence suggests that Alan son of Walter might well have gone on Crusade, as some of his knights may have done, but certainty is impossible.

There is less reason to take seriously the suggestion that Earl David, King William's brother, joined the third Crusade. On examination, the evidence amounts to very little. One manuscript of John de Fordun's *Chronicle,* believed by its editor to derive from an early uncorrected version of his work,[23] persists in a curious mistake about the relative ages of David and William:

> William, his [Malcolm IV's] brother, and youngest of all the brothers, was made by them guardian of the kingdom against the king's will, while his elder and more worthy brother, David earl of Huntingdon, was fighting across the sea against the enemies of Christ and Saracens, as is more fully described in the history compiled on that subject.[24]

This manuscript appears to have been written in the late fifteenth century, but the tradition that David was absent on Crusade at the time when William was made king was clearly known to the chronicler Andrew de Wyntoun around 1400:

As some men saide, in Sarzenes
He trawylit, quhen Wilzam crownyt wes.[25]

This makes it clear that the story had a fourteenth-century source, presumably the enigmatic 'history compiled on that subject' mentioned in the Fordun manuscript. What that source was is impossible now to ascertain.

Neither Wyntoun nor Fordun in his main manuscript tradition takes the story seriously; but it resurfaces in two unhistorical works of the early sixteenth century. The first is the *Livre des trois filz de Roys,* a French romance published in Paris in 1504; in this, the sons of the kings of France, England and Scotland (called respectively Philip, Auffroy and David) wear a series of disguises and have a series of adventures against the Turks led by Fierebras, a figure from Carolingian romance.[26] The *Livre* may be of interest as a piece of propaganda for Christian unity against the Turks during the reigns of Henry VII and James IV, but it is not historical evidence for the twelfth century. Neither, for that matter, is the fabulous *History of the Scots* of Hector Boece; in this he sends Earl David off to the siege of Acre with 500 knights and makes him instrumental in the capture of the city, through the agency of a Scot called Oliver living amongst the Moslems. On his return journey Boece subjects David to such a series of shipwrecks and imprisonments that it is a wonder that he got back to Scotland alive.[27]

Such facts as are known are less romantic. Earl David cannot have accompanied King Richard across the channel in December 1189, as his marriage to a daughter of Ranulf earl of Chester took place, probably in England, on 26 August 1190.[28] By this time the English fleet had already set sail from Marseilles, and it would not have been easy for David to catch up with the Crusaders. Although his name appears frequently in the English exchequer rolls for the early 1190s, he is not mentioned as being absent on Crusade.[29] He is not mentioned in any of the English chronicles of the third Crusade, and the *Melrose Chronicle* (which admittedly has curious omissions) does not mention him as a crusader.[30] It seems highly unlikely that Earl David can have taken part in the third Crusade; but the problem remains of the origin of the persistent tradition that he fought against the Saracens, and that problem will remain unsolved until new evidence comes to light.[31]

A number of factors may have contributed to make the number of Scottish participants in the third Crusade relatively small. The project was closely associated with England, and in particular with Henry II. King William himself showed no inclination to go to Jerusalem, and this would have discouraged many of those closest to him from taking the cross; though he did not prevent Robert de Quincy, a former royal justiciar, or

Osbert Olifard, a royal sheriff, from joining the Crusade, and it is possible
that the king's Steward did so also. Perhaps the lack of a highly developed
machinery for propagating the Crusade was another factor; there was no
equivalent in Scotland of Archbishop Baldwin of Canterbury's preaching of
the cross in Wales in 1188.[32]

In the twelfth century, zeal for the Crusade depended largely on the
enthusiasm of individual rulers and leading churchmen: factors which for
various reasons were absent in Scotland in 1187. The election of Innocent
III as pope in 1198 was to change this situation. He was a great
organiser, determined to systematise the preaching and financing of the
Crusades which were to be the passionate interest of his pontificate. It may
be that the apparent upsurge in interest in Scotland for the wellbeing of the
Holy Land was due to the application of Innocent's administrative talents
to the problem of providing effective preaching of the cross in remote
parts.

Although the third Crusade had ensured the continued existence of the
kingdom of Jerusalem despite Saladin's success, it had failed to recover the
Holy City itself. In August 1198 Innocent III proclaimed a new Crusade to
achieve this objective.[33] His original intention seems to have been to
organise a *passagium generale* of the traditional, multinational type. Legates
were active in France in 1199, and in November of that year the count of
Champagne became the first great noble to take the cross.[34] Legates were
also active in the Rhineland in 1199, and in 1202 Innocent requested King
John of England to send a hundred knights to the Holy Land, hoping that
John would show the same interest in the Crusades as his brother had
done.[35] In the winter of 1201-2 a papal legate, John de Salerno, was active in
Scotland. In December 1201 he held a council at Perth, during which he
preached the cross; his preaching found a responsive hearer in the person of
David Rufus of Forfar, who took the cross. Before setting out for Jerusalem,
Rufus named the monks of Coupar Angus as his heirs and granted them his
lands of Kincriech; he set out to join the Crusade early in 1202 and did not
return.[36]

The legatine council at which David Rufus took the cross was attended by
an impressive array of prelates and barons: these included the bishops of St
Andrews, Glasgow, Aberdeen, Moray, Dunkeld, and Ross; the abbots of
Melrose, Arbroath, Kelso, Lindores, Kilwinning, Holyrood and Jedburgh;
the dean of Glasgow and archdeacons of Lothian and Glasgow; and, among
the laymen, Duncan earl of Fife and Gilchrist earl of Strathearn.[37] Another
leading layman who may have been present (though he does not witness any
document issued at the council) was Gilchrist earl of Mar. He had
converted the Celtic monastic *céli Dé* community at Monymusk into a house
of Augustinian canons regular,[38] and later was the principal witness to the

king's grant of custody of the Monymusk reliquary of Saint Columba to the monks of Arbroath;[39] his consent must have been required in this transaction. At some stage in the course of John de Salerno's legatine visit, the legate imposed a cess or tax on Earl Gilchrist, which he paid directly into the Roman *curia* using the Knights Hospitallers as banking intermediaries.[40] The reason for the cess imposed on the earl of Mar is not known; but it is probably safe to assume that the money was intended to be put towards Pope Innocent's projected new Crusade.

The much later *Book of Clanranald* states that Ranald son of Somerled 'received a cross from Jerusalem' before his death.[41] It gives the year of his death as 1207, though Ranald may in fact have died a few years earlier, perhaps soon after 1203, in which year he reconstituted Iona Abbey as a Benedictine monastery.[42] Although the phrase is ambiguous, it probably means that Ranald took the cross; if so, this may have happened around the time of his foundation of Iona monastery, and may reflect the activity of Cardinal John de Salerno in 1201-2. Considering that Ranald's island lordship was as closely connected with northern Ireland as with the kingdom of Scotland at this time, it is worth noting that John de Salerno seems also to have preached the cross in Ireland in 1202; and the Irish annals record s.a. 1204 that John de Courcy, leader of the English in Ulster, took the cross and went on Crusade.[43]

In the end the fourth Crusade was composed predominantly of the nobility of central France and a Venetian fleet. The pope may have hoped that a less internationally composed army, free from the national jealousies which had hindered the third Crusade, would have had a better chance of freeing Jerusalem. If so, he was entirely mistaken, for the most significant achievement of the fourth Crusade was the capture of the Christian city of Constantinople and the establishment of the Latin Empire in Greece.[44] The complex reasons behind this turn of events had more to do with the internal politics of the Eastern Empire and with relations between Venice and the Franks than with the aspirations of the relatively small number of crusaders from other parts of Europe. It is possible that David Rufus of Forfar 'may have finished up scaling the walls of Constantinople';[45] but for the non-French participants, who can have had no hope of carving out fiefs for themselves in the Eastern Empire, the deflection of the Crusade must have been a disappointment after they had set out to liberate Jerusalem.

In the years immediately following the fourth Crusade (1204), Innocent was much taken up with other troubles. In 1209 began the Albigensian Crusade against the heretics of Languedoc, which diverted resources which the pope might otherwise have been able to direct against the Ayubids in Syria. In 1212 occurred the bizarre phenomenon known as the 'Children's Crusade', an embarrassment to the church as no serious efforts were made to control or disperse it. Neither of these events seems to have made much impact in the British Isles.

They may have stirred Pope Innocent to take in hand the project of a new Crusade; from 1213 until his death three years later he worked unceasingly on the organisation of a fresh expedition to Palestine which would be under direct papal supervision. The fourth Crusade had been deflected by secular interests, and the Albigensian Crusade appeared to be going the same way, while the Children's Crusade had never had the support of the pope or church. Innocent was determined that this should not happen again.

On 19 April 1213 Innocent proclaimed the new Crusade in the bull *Quia maior,* which was sent to Scotland among many other places.[46] It has been remarked that 'This justly famous letter marks the apogee of papal crusading propaganda':

> Because at this time there is a more compelling urgency than there has ever been before to help the Holy Land in her great need and because we hope that the aid sent to her will be greater than that which has ever reached her before, listen when, again taking up the old cry, we cry to you.[47]

At the same time he notified the bishops and prelates of Scotland, as elsewhere, of the summons to a great council of the church to meet in Rome in 1215 to discuss the recovery of the Holy Land.[48]

Also in April 1213, Innocent appointed legates to preach the cross and to collect offerings and (for the first time) redemptions of crusading vows; one of the lessons of the fourth Crusade had been that adequate financing was required from the start to avoid heavy debts to the Italian maritime cities. In Scotland, he appointed the bishops of Saint Andrews and Glasgow as preachers and collectors.[49] The *Melrose Chronicle* describes how they tackled their new duties:

> In the meantime these pastors were to preach the word of life with all diligence, confirming waverers in the faith and stirring up those already confirmed; also they were to sign them with the sign of the cross in aid of the Holy Land of promise, which at that time the Saracens were abusing foully and indecently.[50]

The effects of their preaching are described in a fifteenth-century chronicle, possibly quoting a contemporary source:

> Thereupon a great and almost innumerable multitude throughout the whole of Scotland . . . were signed with the cross; few of them, however, were from among the rich and powerful of the kingdom.[51]

In a way, this follows an earlier pattern, where it has been seen that Scottish crusaders were generally regarded as barbaric and unwarlike beyond the bounds of their own land. Most of the participants in the Crusades of the twelfth century had been men of lesser status whose names are not known to posterity. But the use of papal legates and papally appointed collectors and preachers to promote the Crusade, was a new departure. William I's payment of 10,000 marks for the redemption of the Treaty of Falaise in 1189 can be seen as the earliest payment from Scotland towards the financing of a Crusade; but papal crusading finance of the thirteenth century was a different matter. The collection raised by Innocent in 1213 was purely voluntary, but in 1215 he returned to an expedient he had tried earlier, and at the fourth Lateran Council ordained a tax of a twentieth on ecclesiastical incomes.[52] The *Melrose Chronicle* was very well informed of the decisions of the fourth Lateran Council:

> It is firmly laid down by apostolic authority that everybody in every kind of ecclesiastical benefice, both lowly and prelates, should give a twentieth part of all ecclesiastical revenues in aid of the Holy Land, for the whole of the next three years, by the hand of those who are assigned to that task by the apostolic providence; except certain religious orders and those who are about to set out personally for the Holy Land.[53]

The chronicler goes on to describe how the pope and cardinals promised to pay a tenth of their revenues in contrast to the twentieth they demanded from other ecclesiastics; Innocent made generous private donations towards the Crusade, which was to be assembled and ready to set out from Sicily in June 1217. Among the two patriarchs and 412 bishops present at the Council was a Scottish contingent which included William Malvoisin bishop of Saint Andrews, Walter bishop of Glasgow, Brice bishop of Moray, Henry abbot of Kelso, and representatives of other Scottish bishops.[54]

Even before the fourth Lateran Council met, there was a flurry of crusading interest in the British Isles. King John, beset with troubles on all sides, took the cross in 1215, accompanied by some of his leading nobility.[55] Some of these had Scottish connections: Saher de Quincy earl of Winchester was son of Robert de Quincy, the former justiciar, and heir to the substantial de Quincy estates in Scotland; Ranulf earl of Chester was Earl David's brother-in-law; and John de Lacy constable of Chester was connected by marriage with Alan of Galloway.[56] The return of the clerics who had attended the Lateran Council would have provided a stimulus for them to prepare for the Crusade according to the pope's guidelines; but the renewal of the civil war in England and the events surrounding John's death in 1216 meant that there would be delays in the fulfilment of their vows. Innocent III also died in 1216, with his great design still unrealised, and was succeeded by Honorius III. Honorius continued his enthusiasm for the Crusade, but in the end there were few Crusaders ready to set out in the summer of 1217. In England the civil war dragged on through the summer of 1217, so it was not until the end of the year that the Crusaders were able to set about the fulfilment of their vows.

Part of the English contingent made rapid preparations, and was ready to set out by the summer of 1218. Ranulf earl of Chester, the earl of Salisbury, John de Lacy and others set sail on 3 June 1218, reaching Acre by mid-August, and arriving at the siege of Damietta in the Nile delta by the end of August.[57] Possibly in their company was the Scottish landowner William de Somerville, who appears as a witness to several royal acts, and who held lands in Clydesdale by c. 1200.[58] He was at Damietta along with John de Lacy, possibly in the company of Ranulf earl of Chester, for he witnessed a charter of John de Lacy issued at Damietta during the Crusade.[59] Earl Ranulf and the knights serving with him conducted themselves with distinction during the lengthy siege of Damietta; on 29 August 1219 Ranulf, the earl of Salisbury and their men came to the aid of the king of Jerusalem and the military orders in driving off an Egyptian attack which had come close to destroying the Crusaders' camp; and at the time of the fall of Damietta he strongly counselled acceptance of the terms offered by the sultan al-Kamil, which would have restored Jerusalem to the Christians in exchange for Damietta.[60] The city fell on 5 November 1219, and the terms were rejected by the papal legate as general commander of the Crusade. Earl Ranulf returned to England soon after, having spent two years with the army, and probably feeling slighted by the legate.[61]

Saher de Quincy's career during the fifth Crusade appears to have been rather different. Although the contemporary chronicler Oliver of Paderborn, followed by Matthew Paris, states that he sailed with Ranulf earl of Chester, this is unlikely; it appears that during the winter of 1218-19 he was having a ship built for himself in Galloway for the Crusade, and sailed to Bristol to have it fitted out during the early months of 1219.[62] He may not have arrived at Damietta until the late summer or autumn of 1219, because one English annalist implies that he arrived not long before he died; his death, by natural causes, took place before the walls of Damietta on 3 November 1219.[63] His companions mentioned in the same source, Robert fitz Walter, William de Harcourt and William earl of Arundel, may also have arrived at Damietta in the second half of 1219, a year after Ranulf earl of Chester and his companions.

Saher de Quincy did not live to see the triumph of the fall of Damietta. He fell ill at the end of October 1219 and lived only for a few days thereafter. He had time to summon his companions to his bedside and request them to take his heart and entrails for burial at Garendon before he died on 3 November. The rest of his body was taken to Acre for burial.[64] It is uncertain who were the companions who heard Saher's dying request; in one of two closely related accounts of the events, they are called his sons (*pueri*), while in the other they are called his attendants (*seruientes*).[65] If his sons were present, they presumably included Roger, his eldest surviving son (an elder son Robert having died in 1217), who married Helen, daughter of Alan of Galloway, and thus inherited one-third of the lordship of Galloway in addition to the de Quincy estates in Scotland and the earldom of Winchester; and also Robert the younger, who later married Helen, daughter of Llewelyn prince of North Wales, widow of Earl David's son John the Scot (died 1236).[66]

Saher de Quincy and William de Somerville could be counted among 'the rich and powerful of the kingdom' who were said to be exceptional among the 'great and almost innumerable multitude throughout the whole of Scotland' who took the cross. Of that multitude, very little is known; but the fortunate survival of a group of Gaelic poems casts light on the thoughts and fears of one little group of Crusaders from the *Gaidhealtachd* who joined the fifth Crusade and sailed to Damietta. Among them were the bards Muiredhach Albanach Ó Dálaigh and Gille-Brigde Albanach. The designation *Albanach* does not invariably mean a Scotsman, but can mean one who resides or has resided in Scotland. In the case of Gille-Brigde, he 'seems to have been a native of Scotland, whose woods he loved by birthright'.[67] Muiredhach Albanach, on the other hand, was active in Ireland before he was banished c. 1213,[68] though in a later poem he speaks of 'my own land . . . Scotland of the woods and the grass, of the feasts, the hills and the isles'.[69] After 1213 he came to Scotland and took service with Alwin earl of Lennox, who died c. 1217, and to whom Muiredhach addressed an elaborate praise-poem.[70] He probably departed on crusade shortly after Alwin's death. Some fifteen years after his exile, c. 1228, Muiredhach was allowed to return to Ireland, but he seems to have settled finally in Scotland, where his descendants became the hereditary bardic family of Mac Mhuiredhaich or MacVurich.[71]

The two poets seem to have had two other companions on the voyage, both of whom died on the return journey.[72] One of these was probably Aed mac Conchobhair Maenmuige, whose death, 'returning from the Jordan and from Jerusalem', is entered in the Irish annals s.a. 1224.[73] In a poem addressed to him shortly before setting out, Muiredhach Albanach wrote: 'Protect us in the hot land, gentle Lady Mary'.[74] The fourth companion cannot have been Cathal Croibhdearg Ó Conchobhair, who also died in 1224, because he died in Ireland in the habit of a Franciscan. He is traditionally thought to have been the companion mentioned in Muireadhach Albanach's poem *An foltsa dhuit, a Dhé Athair*, in which he describes how he has been newly tonsured along with a companion.[75] The shearing was presumably part of their initiation as pilgrims.

Gille-Brigde Albanach, in his poem *A ghilli, gabhus an stiuir*, describes the anxiety of the Crusaders as they sail from Acre towards Damietta in the autumn of 1218 or 1219:

Lad who takest the helm,
you travel often to unknown lands;
you have almost deserved anger;
many havens have you visited.

Let us make a hard decision;
these clouds are from the north-east;
let us leave the bases of the rough mountains of Greece;
let us strive to make Damietta.

These clouds from the east are dark
as they drive us from Acre;
come, Mary Magdalen,
and wholly clear the air.

Distress of one night or of two
would cause me no grief;
the whole season in distress
is a long stretch, great Mary.

Lady of the undulating hair,
you have kept us all the autumn
on the bright-edged Mediterranean;
O modest one with the yellow locks.

Brigid of the bright bosom,
though we have been sailing for some time,
our sailings here have been enough for me,
maiden of Europe, beloved one.

Take care as you voyage
to steer the helm aright;
if the ship carry us off,
on what beach, lad, will it land,
Lad who takest the helm?[76]

It appears that the travellers had reached Acre after a long voyage taking up most of the summer and autumn; either 1218 or 1219 may be meant. Leaving Acre to follow the main force of the Crusade, they were driven by an east wind as far as 'the bases of the rough mountains of Greece', probably the southern coast of Cyprus, before turning south towards Damietta. How long they remained with the Crusade is not known, but since the death of one of the pilgrims is entered in the Irish annals in 1224, it may be that they remained with the army right up to the evacuation of Damietta in 1221, and thereafter have made their leisurely way back through the Mediterranean.

Muiredhach Albanach's poem *Fada is chabhair a Cruachain* finds the little group of pilgrims in homesick mood, anchored off Monte Gargano in the Adriatic:

Help from Cruachan is far off
across the wave-bordered Mediterranean;
the journeying of spring separates us
from these green-branched glens.

I give God thanks . . .
up against Monte Gargano;
between Monte Gargano and the fair-ditched lands of Cruachan
the distance is not small.

It would be as the reward of heaven tonight,
if we could touch off Scotland of the lofty manors;
that we might see the haven . . .
or whiff the air of Ireland.[77]

The group may have left their ship in the Adriatic and travelled overland to Rome, as the Orcadian pilgrims of 1151-53 did.[78] Muiredhach Albanach seems to imply that the return journey from Rome to Scotland was made on foot, in a verse which he spoke 'at the head of Lochlong in Argyllshire when he sat down to rest himself when he returned thither from Rome':

As I sit upon the hillock of tears,
without skin on either toe or sole;
O King! – Peter and Paul!
Far is Rome from Lochlong.[79]

Shortly after he was allowed to return to Ireland, c. 1228, Muiredhach Albanach allows himself a final boast about his achievements as a pilgrim: 'I come . . . from over the bright-surfaced Mediterranean; I am going round the world'.[80] His and his companion's poems provide a unique insight into the mentality of Scottish crusaders, whose movements often have to be deduced from legal documents or from laconic references in chronicles.

Despite its initial successes, the fifth Crusade achieved no long-term benefits for the Latin states in Palestine. The papal legate Pelagius refused to negotiate even when the sultan offered very favourable terms in the summer of 1219, and as time wore on the Egyptians grew stronger while the Crusaders' army dwindled as Crusaders completed their vows and returned to the West. In the end their position within Damietta became untenable, and in 1221 the city was evacuated without the sultan having to make any concessions at all.[81]

Successive wars had failed to win back Jerusalem since its loss in 1187; that remarkable feat was, however, achieved by the excommunicate emperor Frederick II a few years later. The emperor's negotiations with sultan al-Kamil were successful to the point that they recovered control of Jerusalem, Bethlehem, Nazareth, Lydda, Toron and Sidon for the kingdom of Jerusalem by the Peace of Jaffa (18 February 1229); Frederick entered Jerusalem in triumph on 17 March 1229. Despite his personal unpopularity with the barons of the kingdom and the papacy, and concern over whether Jerusalem could be defended without adequate fortification and control of the castles of Transjordan, the city was to remain in Christian hands for a further fifteen years.[82]

Although Frederick's Crusade was not a multinational *passagium generale*, he was nothing if not cosmopolitan, and his entourage appears to have included one noteworthy Scot (certainly by name, and very likely by origin). This was Michael Scot, a translator and philosopher. A recent biographer has no doubt about Michael Scot's Scottish birth, and lays stress on his service with Frederick, which other writers have tended to minimise.[83] He may have joined the imperial service as early as 1220, as he was at Bologna when Frederick was passing through northern Italy to Rome for his imperial coronation. Up until his excommunication in 1227, Frederick was trying to procure ecclesiastical preferment for Michael Scot; in 1224 Scot declined the archbishopric of Cashel in Munster, 'being ignorant of the language of that country' (which suggests that he was Scottish rather than Irish), and in 1227 he had the right to hold two benefices in England and two in Scotland.[84] A passage in one of his books suggests that he had been with Frederick in the Holy Land:

> Since such places [as Crete and Romania] are very hot, the vines yield an odoriferous and very potent wine, as is evident in that of Crete, Malvisia, Cyprus and Damascus; since there fogs never rise, nor dark clouds nor thunderstorms.[85]

This information he has obtained, he claims, by personal experience. Michael Scot probably knew Arabic, which would have been useful to Frederick during the subtle negotiations with al-Kamil. Frederick II's Crusade was an unusual one, and the one Scot who took part in it (although his links with his own country were by this time tenuous) was no ordinary Scot.

The vulnerable position of Jerusalem following Frederick II's Crusade meant that fresh reinforcements of crusaders were constantly required to defend the precarious city and the kingdom, still menaced from Egypt. The most noteworthy Crusades of the period 1229-1244 were those organised by Theobald count of Champagne and Richard earl of Cornwall (1239-40 and 1240-1 respectively); these were in response to renewed preaching of the cross in France and England by Pope Gregory IX in 1239.[86] Earl Richard had taken the cross in 1235, and other nobles followed him a year later; among them were John the Scot, earl of Huntingdon and Chester, son of Earl David and nephew of Ranulf earl of Chester, and Gilbert Marischal, who had married Alexander II's sister Margaret.[87] Had John lived long enough, he would presumably have joined Earl Richard's expedition in 1240; but he died (it was rumoured, by poison) in the summer of 1237.[88] His death deprived Richard's Crusade of one of its wealthiest leaders, who would probably have drawn upon his great resources in Scotland and England for the trip to the East had he lived long enough. Another crusader at this time was Richard de Toni, treasurer of Angers and nephew of King

Alexander II of Scotland, who took the cross in the summer of 1238, resigned his benefices and received payments from them to enable him to fulfil his vows.[89] He probably joined Richard's small force, which arrived at Acre a few days after Theobald's departure; Richard achieved much by negotiation in the Holy Land, and when he returned to the West in May 1241 the kingdom of Jerusalem was at peace both with Egypt and with Syria.[90]

In Scotland itself, Crusaders were probably quite a common phenomenon in the first half of the thirteenth century. The 'General Statutes of the Scottish Church', drawn up in the mid-1220s, provided ecclesiastical protection for Scottish crusaders:

> We further decree, by authority of the Lateran Council, that those who have ritually taken the cross (*crucesignati riti*) are protected by the church, unless they have been cast away from ecclesiastical protection by their own misdeeds; concerning which the just judgement of the diocesan is required in every case.[91]

The taking of the cross had originally been a spontaneous act of the intending Crusader; but in the thirteenth century a rite was devised in which the cross was blessed by a priest before being sewn onto the clothes of a Crusader.[92] This passage suggests that this practice had spread to Scotland by the second quarter of the thirteenth century. The ceremony was normally carried out by a parish priest; but it could also be done by members of the new orders of friars, who were beginning to make their appearance in Scotland around this time, and who were to become increasingly important as time went on in the preaching of and collecting for the later Crusades.

That events in the Holy Land from the time of the fall of Jerusalem onwards were keenly followed in Scotland is clearly shown in the pages of the *Melrose Chronicle*. This document, the product of a great Cistercian monastery in southern Scotland, is full of information about the Crusades, much of it strikingly accurate. Its annal for 1187 contains meticulous details of Saladin's campaign in that year:

> The Turks, the enemies of God, profaned the church of Saint Mary of Nazareth, and killed many people; and the master of the Hospital was killed there with five knights and many others on the day of the apostles Philip and James [1 May]. Saladin king of Babylon with 80,000 knights and many followers invaded the land of the kingdom of Jerusalem on the Friday after the feast of the apostles Peter and Paul [6 June], and seized Tiberias by force. The king of Jerusalem with his army advanced against them within a day's journey of Tiberias; when they came to a high and rocky place, the king with the barons' advice judged it necessary to offer battle, because of the proximity of the enemy. And in that place King Saladin with his host and an infinite number of warriors attacked the Christians, who could not fight because of the rocky and inhospitable site, and beset them with all kinds of warfare. At last Tochedin [Taki-ad-Din], Saladin's nephew, prevented the king from fleeing and captured the wood of the Lord's cross; almost all the

rest were beaten, captured and led away in chains, or killed. Saladin at once had the Templar and Hospitaller knights separated from the rest and beheaded in his presence; with his own hand he slew Prince Reynald de Châtillon. It is said in truth that 230 Templars fell that day, in addition to the ninety killed on 1 May.[93]

All the details of this passage, including the name of Saladin's nephew, can be verified from Holy Land sources. Internal evidence suggests that the Melrose writer was copying a written source, possibly a letter.[94]

Of the third Crusade itself, the chronicler has less to say, ignoring Henry II's demand for the Saladin tithe and Robert de Quincy's participation in the Crusade. The death of an unnamed king of Jerusalem (in fact Henry de Champagne) is noted s.a. 1197, and s.a. 1204 there is a laconic note of crusading events:

> Seven bishops in the Holy Land renounced the Christian faith. Baldwin count of Flanders became the emperor of Constantinople.[95]

The *Chronicle's* interest revives with the summons of the fourth Lateran Council in 1213, the council itself,[96] and the capture of Damietta in 1219. In addition to annals for 1219 and 1221 noting the capture and loss of the city, the chronicler includes a copy of a letter sent from Herman de Salza, master of the Teutonic Knights, to a cardinal, giving his account of the Egyptian campaign. This is headed 'How Damietta was captured, A.D. 1219', and is incomplete as the *Chronicle* now stands, though probably part has been lost. On the loss of Damietta, the chronicler comments:

> It is not known whether this came about by the demerits of the Christians or by the judgement of God; especially since at that time divine service was being carried out in that city with splendid magnificence.[97]

The writer seems to find it difficult to understand how God can have allowed the city to be lost in spite of the institution of Christian worship there; the only possible explanation seems to be the demerits of the Christians and their negligent guardianship of the city.

The *Melrose Chronicle* contains a few subsequent incidents relative to the Crusades. S.a. 1223 it notes the death of King Philip II of France and his generosity in his will to the military orders and the king of Jerusalem. In the same year it notes the visit of the same king (John de Brienne) to London.[98] S.a. 1238, it notes the first rumours of the Mongol menace to the Holy Land;[99] this entry seems to have been added in a later hand, which was responsible for one of the most important passages about the Crusades in the *Melrose Chroncile*. This is the annal for 1244, which contains two contemporary letters extensively describing the loss of Jerusalem and the battle of Gaza in that year, the greatest disasters to befall the kingdom of Jerusalem since 1187. The first letter, dated Acre, 21 September 1244, is from the patriarch and queen of Jerusalem, the archbishop of Tyre, the bishops of Acre, Sidon and Lydda, the masters of the military orders, the constable of Jerusalem and the lord of Toron, and is addressed to Pope Innocent IV. It contains information found in no other source, and has been used by historians as a major primary source for the events which it describes.[100] It describes how the Khwarismians were driven westwards by the Mongols, and invaded the Holy Land at the invitation of Ayub, sultan of Egypt; on 11 July they seized Jerusalem, driving the garrison and citizens into the citadel. These appealed for help to Acre, and the lords at Acre requested an-Nasir of Kerak to negotiate a safe-conduct, which was done through a Dominican friar. On 23 August 6,000 Christians marched out of the city towards the coast, but due to the treachery of the Khwarismians, only some 300 arrived safely at Jaffa. The citizens who had chosen to remain in Jerusalem were all massacred, and the churches and holy places of the city desecrated. The letter ends with an appeal to the pope to do what he thinks best for the speedy succour of the Holy Land.[101]

The second letter was written after the destruction of the Christian army at Gaza on 17 October 1244. The author (probably the archdeacon of Tyre) tells two monks that if they seek information concerning the terrible events in the Holy Land, they should intercept the prior of the Hospital, who bears letters to King Louis IX of France with details of the losses sustained by the military orders and the knights of the kingdom of Jerusalem in the battle.[102] The two monks cannot be identified, but they may have been French Cistercians.

The events of 1244 reverberated in the West; they cancelled most of the gains of successive crusades since 1187. They also roused a new and great leader for the crusading movement, one whose appeals for renewed crusading efforts would be heard with sympathy in Scotland.

NOTES

1. *Chron. Richard I*, i, 32-3; *Chron. Benedict*, ii, 74-5.
2. Duncan, *Making of the Kingdom*, 234-5.
3. *Chron. Benedict*, ii, 44.
4. *Chron. Howden*, ii, 338-9.
5. Duncan, *Making of the Kingdom*, 235.
6. Ibid., 446.
7. *APS*, i, 108; Stones, *Anglo-Scottish Relations*, 12-17.
8. *RRS*, ii, 333-4.
9. A. Macquarrie, 'The Bethlehemite Hospital of Saint Germains, East Lothian', *TELAFNS*, xvii (1982), 1-10.
10. *RRS*, ii, 308.
11. Runciman, *History of the Crusades*, iii, 36.
12. Ibid., 43-53; *Chron. Benedict*, ii, 187.

13. Ibid., ii, 185.

14. Runciman, *History of the Crusades,* iii, 53ff.

15. *RRS,* ii, 370.

16. Robert de Quincy appears regularly as a witness to royal acts throughout the pages of *RRS,* ii; between pp. 308 and 369, however, his name appears only twice, once in an act (no. 300, pp. 317-18) which has been misplaced in the sequence, belonging to the period 1193 x 1195, and once in an act dateable 1189 x 1195 (no. 332, p. 337).

17. *Spalding Misc.,* v, 210-11. This is erroneously quoted in *RRS,* ii, 225, where 'Bishop Richard' should read 'Bishop Hugh'.

18. *Chron. Bower,* ii, 542.

19. W. J. Dillon, 'The Spittals of Ayrshire', *AANHSC,* 2nd ser., vi (1958-60), 12-42, at p. 39; W. J. Dillon, 'Three Ayrshire Charters', Ibid., 2nd ser., vii (1961-6), 28-38, at 32-4.

20. *Kelso Liber,* nos. 256, 260, 261; *RRS,* ii, 330.

21. *Pipe Rolls, 1191-1192,* 262 and passim.

22. Cf. n. 16 above. Alan son of Walter's name is not notably absent from documents which can be approximately dated 1189 x 1195 in *RRS,* ii; but it does not appear on any document which can be specifically dated to 1191 or 1192.

23. *Chron. Fordun,* xxix ff.

24. Ibid., 257.

25. *Chron. Wyntoun* (Laing), ii, 313.

26. *Le Livre des trois filz de Roys* (Paris, 1504); there is a copy of this edition in the British Library.

27. Hector Boece, *Chronicles of Scotland,* trans. J. Bellenden (STS, 1941), ii, 209-12.

28. *Chron. Melrose,* 47.

29. *Pipe Rolls, 1191-1192,* passim.

30. *Chron. Howden; Chron. Benedict; Chron. Richard I; Chron. Melrose;* the last-named work does not mention King William's meeting at Birgham with Hugh du Puiset in 1189.

31. The problem is discussed by Bishop Dowden in *Lindores Chartulary,* xxx-xxiv, and in Lawrie, *Annals,* 78-9; most recently it is discussed in K. J. Stringer, 'The Career and Estates of David Earl of Huntingdon' (Cambridge Ph.D. thesis, 1971), 44-7, and in Dr Stringer's forthcoming book, *Earl David of Huntingdon (1152-1219): A Study in Anglo-Scottish History* (Edinburgh, 1984).

32. *Giraldi Cambrensis Opera,* ed. T. S. Brewer (RS, 1861-91), i, 74-9.

33. H. E. Mayer, *The Crusades* (Oxford, 1972), 183 and n. 70.

34. Ibid., 185; Runciman, *History of the Crusades,* iii, 107.

35. Ibid., 109; *CPL,* i, 10.

47, *Coupar Angus Charters,* i, 24-6, 130-2. The words transcribed *iterum Ierlin* (p. 25) should probably read *iturus Ierusalem* (cf. p. 131).

37. *Kelso Liber,* 327-8; *Coupar Angus Charters,* 24-5.

38. *St Andrews Liber,* 374-6.

39. *Arbroath Liber,* i, no. 5; *RRS,* ii, 453-4.

40. *Le Liber Censuum de l'Eglise Romaine,* ed. P. Fabre (Paris, 1889), i, 232.

41. A. Cameron, *Reliquiae Celticae,* ed. A. Macbain and J. Kennedy (Inverness, 1892-4), ii, 156-7.

42. Ibid; *Chron. Man,* 152-3; *AU,* s.a. 1203; *Iona Inventory,* suggests that the Benedictine foundation might have been as early as c. 1200, but the sources seem to point towards 1203; cf. A. Macquarrie, *Iona through the Ages* (Isle of Coll, 1983), 15.

43. *Annals of Loch Cé,* ed. W. M. Hennessy (RS, 1871), i, 232-5.

44. The principal chronicle of the fourth Crusade is Geoffrey de Villehardouin, *La Conquête de Constantinople,* ed. N. de Wailly (Paris, 2nd edn 1874).

45. Duncan, *Scotland: the Making of the Kingdom,* 447.

46. The text is printed (among other places) in P. Labbé and G. Cossart, *Sacrorum Conciliorum nova et amplissima Collectio* (Venice, 1778), xxii, cols 956-62; translation in L. and J. Riley-Smith, *The Crusades: Idea and Reality, 1095-1274* (1981), 1·19-24.

47. Ibid., 118-9.

48. *CPL,* i, 38.

49. Ibid.

50. *Chron. Melrose,* 56.

51. *Chron. Bower,* i, 534.

52. Riley-Smith, *Crusades: Idea and Reality,* 124-5, 144-5.

53. *Chron. Melrose,* 60-1.

54. Ibid., 61.

55. *DNB,* xvi, 556-7; J. A. P. Jones, *King John and Magna Carta* (1971), 132-4.

56. K. J. Stringer, 'A new Wife for Alan of Galloway', *TDGNHAS,* xlix (1972), 49-56.

57. Matthew Paris, *Chron. Maior,* iii, 40-1; *Ann. Monast.,* ii, 289.

58. *Dryburgh Liber,* 162-3; *RRS,* ii, 42, 329, 361, 387.

59. *Pontefract Chartulary,* i, 36-7; G. W. S. Barrow, *The Anglo-Norman Era in Scottish History* (1980), 108.

60. Matthew Paris, *Chron. Maior,* iii, 53.

61. Ibid., 56.

62. *Cal. Pat. Rolls, 1216-25,* 185; *CDS,* i, no. 703, has the date 20 Dec. 1218, but 20 Jan. 1218/9 seems correct.

63. He is said to have died *postquam in terram sanctam venerat: Ann. Monast.,* ii, 292 (Ann. Waverley); Ibid., iii, 56 (Ann. Dunstable).

64. Ibid., ii, 292.

65. Ibid; Garendon Cartulary, British Library, MS Lansdowne, 415, f. 38r; G. G. Simpson, 'An Anglo-Scottish Baron of the Thirteenth Century: Roger de Quincy, Earl of Winchester and Constable of Scotland' (Edinburgh Ph.D. thesis, 1966), 16.

66. Ibid., 16 and Chapter 1, passim; cf. S. Painter, 'The House of Quency, 1136-1264', *Medievalia et Humanistica,* xi, (1957), 3-9.

67. G. Murphy, 'A Vision concerning Rolf MacMahon', *Éigse,* iv (1944), 79-111, at 94-5.

68. *Annals of the Four Masters,* ed. J. O'Donovan (Dublin, 1856), iii, 178-81.

69. O. Bergin, 'Unpublished Irish Poems, xxviii: a Palmer's Greeting', *Studies,* xiii (1924), 567-74, at 574.

70. W. F. Skene, *Celtic Scotland* (Edinburgh, 1880), iii, 117-9, 454-5.

71. D. Thomson, 'The MacMhuirich bardic Family', *TGSI,* xliii (1966), 276-304, at 279-80.

72. G. Murphy, 'Two Irish Poems from the Mediterranean in the thirteenth Century', *Éigse,* vii (1955), 71-7.

73. *Annals of the Four Masters,* iii, 214-5.

74. *Measgra Danta,* ed. T. F. O'Rahilly (Dublin, 1927), no. 69, p. 179.

75. *Annals of the Four Masters,* iii, 210-15; *Aithdioghluim Dana,* ed. L. McKenna (Irish Text Societey, 1939-40), i, 174-6.

76. Murphy, 'Two Irish Poems from the Mediterranean', 71ff.

77. Ibid.

78. See above, pp. 20-1.

79. D. Mackintosh, *Collection of Gaelic Proverbs* (2nd edn, Edinburgh, 1819), 190-1.

80. Bergin, 'A Palmer's Greeting', 574.

81. Runciman, *History of the Crusades,* iii, 151-70; Mayer, *Crusades,* 210-18.

82. Ibid., 219-30; Runciman, *History of the Crusades,* iii, 177-92.

83. L. Thorndike, *Michael Scot* (1965), passim, esp. 11-13, 32-9; G. Donaldson, *Who's Who in Scottish History* (Oxford, 1973), 13-4.

84. *CPL*, i, 97-8, 102; Theiner, *VM*, 23.

85. Thorndike,*Michael Scot*, 35.

86. Runciman, *History of the Crusades*, iii, 211-12.

87. Matthew Paris, *Historia Minor*, ii, 391.

88. Ibid., ii, 398.

89. *CPL*, i, 175.

90. Runciman,*History of the Crusades*, iii, 217-9.

91. *Aberdeen Registrum*, ii, 15.

92. J. A. Brundage, 'Cruce Signari: the Rite for Taking the Cross in England', *Traditio*, xxii (1966), 289ff., esp. 290-1.

93. *Chron. Melrose*, 45-6.

94. The MS of *Chron. Melrose* reads *dc*, i.e. 600, rather than *xc*, 90, the actual number killed (cf. Runciman, *History of the Crusades*, ii, 453).

95. *Chron. Melrose*, 52.

96. Ibid., 60-1.

97. Ibid., 72-3, 75.

98. Ibid., 76.

99. Ibid., 86.

100. Cf. Runciman, *History of the Crusades*, iii, 224-7.

101. *Chron. Melrose*, 91-5.

102. Ibid., 95.

3

The Loss of the Holy Land, 1245-1291

In December 1244, in thanksgiving for his recovery from a serious illness, King Louis IX of France took the cross. In him the Crusading movement found its greatest champion, a man whose moral qualities far outshone those of any of his contemporaries, and whose influence outside his own realm depended not on force, but on the strength of his saintly and ascetic character.[1] The nobility of France followed his example in taking the cross, and in turn noblemen all over Europe did the same. In Scotland, consciousness of the plight of the Holy Land was stirred not only by the accounts of terrible disasters which found their way into Cistercian chronicles, but also by the papal chancery. When Innocent IV wrote to the abbot of Dunfermline on 3 May 1245 awarding him the right to wear the mitre and ring, the preamble to the bull expressed the pope's hopes:

> That the daughter of Jerusalem should appear beautiful and well-appointed to the faithful, and terrifying to the heathen, like a fair castle decked out for war.[2]

In June of the same year met the council of Lyons, at which Innocent confirmed the summoning of a new Crusade. This council was attended by David de Bernham bishop of Saint Andrews, whose seal appears appended to the communiqué issued by the council on 17 July 1245.[3] It is not known whether it was he who brought to Scotland copies of the letters which found their way into the *Melrose Chronicle;* but there can be no doubt of the keen interest taken by the monks of Melrose in events in the Holy Land.[4]

In Scotland, the leading magnate who took the cross was Earl Patrick of Dunbar. He emerges as something of a larger-than-life figure in the pages of the *Lanercost Chronicle,* which often has little good to say about Scots. It records how on one occasion he burnt down his own kitchen to avoid disgrace when he discovered that the amount of food available was insufficient for the number of guests whom he was entertaining, and how at another time he appointed a pardoned thief to an office in his household, and how when the man attempted to murder him the earl offered him a purse full of money to go on a pilgrimage of expiation.[5] Even for a man of his wealth and munificence, the Crusade was an expensive undertaking which could not be entered into lightly. Accordingly, in 1247 Earl Patrick came to an agreement with his son Patrick and the monks of Melrose whereby the monks agreed to purchase his stud-farm at Lauder for 100 marks to be paid to him and a further twenty marks to be paid to his son when he should confirm the sale.[6] The earl's wife seems to have been concerned for Patrick's safety, for shortly before his departure to join the crusaders she founded a hospital of Trinitarian brothers at Dunbar.[7] This order had been founded during the pontificate of Innocent III for the express purpose of ransoming Christian captives from the hands of the infidel, and was intended to play a major rôle in the redemption of captive Crusaders. Statements that there were Scots among the order's earliest recruits c. 1199 are difficult to accept,[8] but it remains true that there were two houses of Trinitarians in Scotland, at Failford in Kyle and at Berwick, when Innocent IV issued a solemn confirmation of all Trinitarian property in 1247.[9] The countess of Dunbar's Trinitarian foundation at Dunbar must postdate the pope's confirmation of 1247, but also antedates the earl's departure on crusade the following year. It probably belongs to 1247, and so is an interesting reflection of the concern of a wife for the wellbeing of a departing Crusader; in the unhappy event of the earl's capture by the Muslims, the countess would have been in a strong position, as a benefactress of the order, to ask the Trinitarians to help procure her husband's release. Her charter states that she grants to the Trinitarians the house which she has founded at Dunbar and which had been enriched by gifts by Earl Patrick and Sir David de Graham and Thomas de Bernach, placing it under the custody of the master of the Trinitarian house at Berwick, who is to appoint a brother to be perpetual chaplain at Dunbar to celebrate divine offices for the living and the dead, and dispose of all the possessions of the house according to the statutes of the order. These statutes provided that one third of all income was to be used for the redemption of captives.[10]

Earl Patrick spent Christmas of 1247 with the king, and then set off to join the king of France. He probably followed the route across France and down the Rhone described by Louis IX's biographer Joinville;[11] but when he reached Marseilles in the summer of 1248 he fell ill and died before he could embark.[12] Matthew Paris has this to say about his death:

> Earl Patrick also died, who was regarded as the most powerful among the Scottish magnates. He died signed with the cross, in pilgrimage in the army of the king of France; it is believed that he took the cross in order to be reconciled with God and Saint Oswine.[13]

Probably Patrick had more important personal reasons for going on crusade than any supposed injury which he had done to Saint Albans' appropriated parish church of Saint Oswine at Tynemouth. He was a figure of such international renown that his death was noted in the Holy Land by a continuator of William of Tyre's history, who mentions simply that *le cuens Patris* died at Marseilles.[14]

It is not easy to know what other Scots joined the Crusade of Saint Louis. Patrick must have been accompanied by a retinue befitting his station, and the sale of his stud-farm indicates the sort of expenditure he was prepared to make on them. Companions he must have had, but none of their names survive in contemporary record. Boece states that Earl Patrick took 'David Lindsaye of Glenesk and Walter Stewart of Dundonald with ane grete novmer of chosin men to support King Lowis in the said iornaye'.[15] John Stewart, Walter's brother, is said to have died at Damietta in 1249.[16]

The Crusade followed a not-dissimilar pattern to that of 1218-21. The king began by besieging Damietta in Egypt, which fell on 6 June 1249; next spring the king marched up the Nile, to be defeated and captured at the Battle of Mansurah in April 1250. A report of the enormous scale of the disaster was conveyed to Matthew Paris at Saint Albans by the master of the Templars in Scotland, who, it seems, had been in Egypt:

> According to the statement of the master of the Templars in Scotland, the ransom of the king of France, captured by Saracens in Egypt, amounted to 40,000 pounds. The number of those killed was 60,000, and 20,000 from the Frankish army; this was in the year 1250. This was for a long time kept secret from Lady Blanche, the king's mother, and the whole baronage of France, lest in desperation they should refuse to consent to the ransom.[17]

The master of the Templars in Scotland was probably not a Scot himself, but the report of the disaster reaching the British Isles shook the population into activity. The earl of Gloucester took the cross in 1250, and was joined by Robert de Quincy,[18] younger brother of Roger de Quincy who held the de Quincy estates in Scotland and a share of the lordship of Galloway; Robert was married to the widow of John the Scot.

Another group of Scottish crusaders prepared to set out in 1250. On 11 September of that year Innocent IV mandated the bishops of Saint Andrews and Dunkeld to assign the sum of 400 marks out of the redemptions, legacies and gifts which they had collected for the Holy Land, to Sir Richard Giffard, who was setting out for the Holy Land with five knights. He further ordered that sums should also be assigned to other Scottish knights setting out on crusade at their own expense: Thomas Paynel, Adam de Lascelles and Adam de Pencaitland (*Penkethan'*).[19] This was done ostensibly at the request of King Alexander III, but must in fact have come from the regency in power at the time, headed by Alan Durward. Sir Richard Giffard was brother of Hugh Giffard, son of John Giffard; the latter's confirmation of a grant of lands in Haddington to the monks of Newbattle is witnessed by John de Pencaitland (*Penkatil'*), who may be the father of Adam de Pencaitland.[20] In an earlier generation, c. 1170, a Henry de Pencaitland (*Pencatl'*) appears as a witness to a de Quincy document,[21] and another document of Robert de Quincy dated 1170 is witnessed by both Henry de Pencaitland and Hugh Giffard.[22] Thus both Adam de Pencaitland and Richard Giffard were members of East Lothian families who had been connected with the Countess Ada at Haddington (d. 1178), and who also appear in a de Quincy connection. It is tempting to link their departure on crusade with that of Robert de Quincy in 1250, but there is no solid evidence for it. More certain is the connection of the Giffards with the faction led by Alan Durward during the minority of Alexander III (1249-57). The request for Giffard to be given sums from the papal collectors came at a time when Durward was in control of the regency, and Richard Giffard was among those restored to power along with Durward in a *coup d'état* in 1255.[23] Also among those restored to the council in 1255 were Alexander Stewart, who is stated (on no certain evidence) to have 'attended St Louis of France to the Holy War, and after the death of the earl of Dunbar, commanded the Scots pilgrims',[24] and Patrick, son of the crusader earl of Dunbar. Insofar as the Durward group was outward-looking, non-isolationist (as might be expected from Alan Durward's own wide travels), it might be expected that participants in Louis IX's first Crusade would come from this party, rather than from the seemingly more 'insular' Comyn faction.[25] On the other hand, a Templar knight who was acting as royal almoner was among those who were removed from office when Durward returned to power in 1255;[26] he may well have been English.

Successive Scottish governments from 1247 onwards were anxious that the crusading tax being levied in Scotland should be used for the benefit of Scottish crusaders only. A three-year twentieth on clerical incomes was ordained by the council of Lyons. On 30 May 1247 Innocent IV wrote to the bishop of Saint Andrews requiring him to prevent any molestation of Scots who had taken the cross, stating that Crusaders were to be free of the subvention ordered for the defence of the Latin Empire at Constantinople, which was tottering towards extinction.[27] On 23 October 1247 he appointed the bishop of Dunblane collector of the twentieth and redemptions of vows and offerings for the Holy Land, and ordered him to transmit 3,000 pounds *tournois* to two Crusaders, Peter de Courtenai and Walter de Joigny.[28] These men had no discernible connection with Scotland, but were both married to sisters of Simon de Montfort earl of Leicester.[29] Such a situation can hardly have been acceptable to Alexander II, who required to be mollified in the following year by an assurance from Pope Innocent that he should suffer no prejudice by the recent visit to Scotland of the Franciscan friar William de Batinches, sent to Scotland by the papal collector of the Holy Land subsidy in England, Scotland and Ireland.[30] On the same day (14 March, 1247/8) the pope wrote to the bishops of Saint Andrews and Glasgow, ordering them to collect and distribute redemptions of Crusaders' vows, legacies and gifts for the Holy Land to Crusaders who set out in person.[31] This must reflect pressure from Alexander II to ensure that the crusading contributions should not be transmitted outside Scotland, but should be used to subsidise native crusaders. Alexander II's attitude was continued by the Durward administration after his death. In September 1250 Innocent assigned the sums mentioned above to Sir Richard Giffard and his companions, probably on Durward's recommendation. On 4 September 1251 Innocent wrote a conciliatory letter to the *crucesignati* (that is, those who had taken the cross) of the kingdom of Scotland, explaining that the king of Scots had reminded him that the pope was once of the opinion that redemptions and offerings for the Holy Land from Scotland should be distributed among those of that kingdom who intended to cross the sea for that purpose; but more recently the pope had in fact granted the Scottish collection to the king of England and his subjects. The king of Scots, therefore, had besought the pope to see to the interest of his subjects, and the pope accordingly has confirmed his earlier grant to the crusaders of Scotland, which is not to be prejudiced by his subsequent grant to the king of England.[32] This probably reflects Durward's increasingly unco-operative attitude to Henry III which led to his being removed from power in December 1251, to be replaced by an administration more favourable to Henry III and reflecting the power of the Comyns in Scotland. It is unlikely that this *coup d'état* can have altered the destination of crusading contributions from Scotland; by the end of 1251 most crusaders had already departed, and the twentieth and other crusading monies were largely exhausted.

The evidence so far examined suggests a significant number of Scots taking the cross in the late 1240s and early 1250s; although some may have commuted their vow for a money payment,[33] many seem to have set out in person. Indeed, Scotland seems to have provided not only money and manpower for the Crusade, but other services as well. Matthew Paris reports that in 1248 Hugh de Châtillon, count of Saint-Pol, had a great ship built in Scotland, *ad Ilvernes scilicet in Muref*, i.e., at Inverness in Moray, so that he could boldly cross the sea with men from Blois and Flanders and the Low Countries, to join up with the forces of King Louis IX.[34] It has been pointed out that there was 'a substantial Flemish settlement in Inverness and the Moray Firth towns' by the mid-thirteenth century,[35] but it may also be significant to remember that Saher de Quincy had made use of Scottish shipbuilding during the Crusade of 1218.[36] More intriguing is the possibility that the count of Saint-Pol's ship may have sailed with some native passengers and crew as well as Flemings and Netherlanders. In this connection it is worth considering a curious tradition which has been preserved concerning Coinneach mac Mathghamhna, eponym of Clan Mackenzie, who lived in the mid-thirteenth century. As a young man he was banished by his father for repeating unpleasant predictions which

E

he learned from the singing birds (which he understood), joined a ship bound for France, and came to the favour of the French king. The king gave him a ship in which he travelled to distant lands, and everywhere he went he was able to understand the speech of that land. Finally, having grown rich as a result of his gift for languages, he returned to Kintail and was met by his father, who failed to recognise him and waited on him at table as a respected guest – thus fulfilling the birds' original prediction. 'To suppose that Coinneach mac Mathghamhna took part in the crusade of Saint Louis is of course a flight of fancy, but it may serve to illustrate how a historical personage could become the hero of a type of tale in existence long before his time.'[37]

There is no reason to doubt that Coinneach mac Mathghamhna did visit far-off lands and acquire a gift for languages in the mid-thirteenth century, and it is obviously tempting to connect this with the departure of the count of Saint-Pol's ship from Inverness in 1248; some Scottish crusading traditions relating to this period have even less foundation. One such example is a tall story in an early seventeenth-century French book concerning the origins of the Scots Guard of the French kings. It relates how, after capturing Damietta, Louis IX subjugated *le Roy des Arsacides, Prince Payen appellé le Vieil de la Montagne* (the 'Old Man of the Mountain', prince of the Assassins), and how a plot by the Assassins to kill Louis was foiled by the timely intervention of a group of Scottish crusaders.[38] The story was probably inspired by Joinville's description of Louis' meeting with Assassin envoys in 1250;[39] Joinville, however, implies elsewhere that Louis had not been greatly impressed by the Scots he encountered on crusade. He describes how sometime between his return from the Holy Land in 1254 and the death of his son Louis in 1260, the king said to the young prince:

> I beg you to make yourself beloved of the people of your kingdom; for indeed, I would prefer that a Scot should come from Scotland and govern the people of the kingdom well and faithfully, than that you were seen to govern them badly.[40]

The king's remark hardly seems to have been intended as a compliment to the Scots; however, like earlier crusaders, he implies that they were capable of good and faithful conduct.[41]

Despite the disaster at Damietta, the six years which Louis spent in the East (1248-1254) left the Latin states stronger and better able to resist Islamic attack than they had been earlier in the thirteenth century, consolidated within narrower bounds. The late 1250s and early 1260s saw the attention of the papacy and monarchies of Europe diverted elsewhere. In the 'Sicilian business' Henry III, with papal support, sought to have one of his sons placed upon the throne of Sicily following the death of Frederick

II, under the guise of a new Crusade; there was no support in Scotland for this adventure either from the Comyn administration or from the series of compromise governments which succeeded it from 1255 onwards.[42] The arrival in Scotland in 1257 of John of Acre, 'son of the king of Jerusalem', in company with his wife the queen dowager of Scotland, did nothing to promote crusading zeal in Scotland. John of Acre's father's claim to the kingdom of Jerusalem had never come to anything; John himself had relations with the royal families of France and Castile, and after his single visit to Scotland in 1257-8 he never returned to the land where his wife had her dowager estates.[43] Throughout the early 1260s Alexander III of Scotland was chiefly concerned with the problems of the Western Isles, which were not finally solved until the cession of the Isles to Scotland in 1266.

Interest in the Holy Land was kept alive, among other ways, by the military orders. The Templars in particular had continued to be the recipients of generous grants of land and churches, most notably the estate of Maryculter and a group of churches, including Aboyne, on Deeside.[44] At an uncertain date, probably in the thirteenth century, the Templars were given the estate of Temple Liston (now Kirkliston) in West Lothian; unlike Maryculter, there is no evidence that this was ever established as a preceptory, and it may have been administered as an outlying estate from the main preceptory at Balantrodoch.[45] It is uncertain how much else of the lands held by the Hospitallers in the later Middle Ages had formerly been Templar property.[46] By the early fourteenth century their income had risen to about two-thirds of that of the Templars, which suggests the receipt of continuing generosity.[47] A rare glimpse of this generosity in action is seen at an uncertain, but probably thirteenth-century, date when John de Colville granted the church of Ochiltree to the Hospitallers, a grant which ultimately proved transitory.[48]

But the influence of the military orders is shown also in other ways than by the generosity showered on them. The mobility of their members made them valuable in carrying news from one end of the known world to the other. It has been seen that Matthew Paris received information about the Crusaders' defeat in the Nile Delta from the master of the Templars in Scotland,[49] and it is possible that some of the material about Holy Land events embodied in the *Melrose Chronicle*, with its mention of Templar casualties, may come from Templar sources.[50] The so-called *Holyrood Chronicle*, probably in its present form compiled at the Cistercian monastery of Coupar Angus, has a lengthy, circumstantial, and seemingly highly original description of events in the Holy Land in 1266 which shows every sign of coming from a Hospitaller source.[51] This is worth quoting at length:

A.D. 1266. On Wednesday, the second day of the month of July [*lege* June], the sultan of Babylon took up a position before the city of Acre; he kept part of his army there for fifteen days, to the number of 200,000 men with arms and horses, and 400,000 foot-soldiers, and sent another part of his army into the land of Tyre and Sidon. He plundered the land of Acre and burned a large part of it; he also plundered the land of Tyre and Sidon, and burned a large part of it with fire. This sultan captured 3,000 Christians in these lands, and sent them to prison in Babylon; nevertheless, the said sultan called the lord of the land of Tyre his brother.

When fifteen days were over, he made his way with all his army towards the castle of Safed, and took up a strong position there. He caused the whole army of the law of Mohammed to come to him there, to the number of 104 score thousand men. He so pressed the Christians there that, on the day before the feast of Saint James the Apostle in the above year [24 July, 1266], the brothers [Templars] and guardians of the said fortress made a peace with the said sultan; which was namely that the brothers and guardians of the castle, with all the Christians who were in the castle, should leave with life and limb, and make their way to the city of Acre with their property, and hand over the castle to the sultan with everything pertaining to it. However, when the Christians came out of the city, the sultan ordered all the brothers and guardians, clerics as well as laymen, to be executed by decapitation, to the number of 1,700 men, besides women and children, and those who renounced the law of God and turned to the law of Mohammed.

Thereafter the sultan sent his army into the land of Tripoli and wasted and plundered a great part of that land, and took two castles by force, one of which was called Qulaiat and the other Arqa; and he sent 4,000 Christians from that land to prison in Babylon.

Then the sultan with all his army headed towards the land of Armenia and invaded it; part he burned with fire, and he destroyed the whole land except for the mountains. He killed the Christians of that land to the number of 40,000 men, imprisoned one son of the king of that land, called Leo, and sent him to Babylon, and killed another son of that king.

What more is there to say? This sultan at his pleasure subjugated to himself all lordship and power of the whole eastern land. And the sultan with all his army returned to Damascus.

And be it known that on the Friday before the feast of All Saints in the above year [29 October 1266], the brothers of the Hospital, the Temple, and other houses, and the commune of Acre, to the number of 7,000 men, went out at night, and took a great spoil from the Saracens; and the brothers of the Hospital sent their pigeon with letters about what they had done to their hospice. But a certain legion of Saracens beset them by an ambush in the mountains, and took the spoil from them by force, and killed 252 knights, both of the Hospital and of other [orders]; but they did not know the number of those killed. And this confusion of the Christians was done some two leagues outside the city of Acre.[52]

The very precise record of casualties where Hospitallers were involved, and the curious detail concerning a Hospitaller carrier-pigeon sent to Acre (which occurs in no other source for these events), together with the phrase 'knights, both of the Hospital and of other [orders]' (*milites tam de Hospitali quam de aliis*), all point to a Hospitaller source, very probably a letter like those incorporated in the *Melrose Chronicle* s.a. 1244. It is curious that a Cistercian monk at Coupar Angus should have considered these events worthy of record in his sparse chronicle, but have ignored the Scottish triumphs in the Western Isles and the struggle of the English crown against Simon de Montfort, which were happening at the same time.

Still, it has been pointed out that 'these events of 1266 caused great concern in Europe. According to the Chronicle of Limoges, it was the execution of the Christians at Safed that caused Louis IX to undertake the last crusade.'[53] These campaigns of Sultan Baibars Bunduqdari were steadily making more and more serious inroads into the Christian territories in Syria; in 1267, realising that his previous Crusade had gained no more than a respite for the Latin states, Louis IX took the cross for the second time; in the following year Antioch, the first city to have been captured by the first Crusade in 1098, fell to Baibars after a Christian occupation lasting 170 years.

Already in the West preparations for the new Crusade were under way. Ivo, a Dominican friar at Ayr, was collecting money for the aid of the Holy Land in the early 1260s; he and successive collectors had difficulty recovering sums of money which had been lodged with the canons of Whithorn in 1261.[54] In 1264 Cardinal Ottoboni de Fieschi was sent to the British Isles to mediate between Henry III and his Montfortian enemies, and later to preach the cross;[55] but, according to Clement IV's letters of 5 May 1265, the Crusade which he was first sent to preach was against the rebels fighting against King Henry.[56] Ottoboni's legatine mission may not have had much impact in Scotland, and may not have been the main reason for the large number of Scots who eventually joined the Crusade in 1270. Indeed, as long ago as 1263 Urban IV had licensed the bishop of Saint Andrews to preach the cross, and had issued instructions for the protection of *crucesignati* in Scotland.[57] There was opposition in Scotland to Ottoboni's financial demands, not surprisingly since the 'crusading tenth' collected in Scotland was to be assigned to the needs of the English royal household.[58] According to the chronicler Fordun, probably relying on a thirteenth-century Scottish version of the events, Ottoboni demanded a subsidy of four marks from each parish, and six marks from each cathedral church, in Scotland for his expenses alone; had it been forthcoming, this would probably have amounted to much more than the 2,000 marks whose export to England was later forbidden by King Alexander III.[59]

Ottoboni's relations with King Alexander did not get off to a good start. Early in his stay in England, the legate wrote to the king notifying him of the purpose of his visit and apologising that he would be unable to visit Scotland in person; subsequently he sent his chaplain, Master Maurice, to Scotland, in the hope that his counsels would prevail with the Scottish king.[60] In this he was disappointed, for he later wrote to the king complaining that his messenger had not been well received, and that:

> Furthermore it is said that your highness has issued an edict against us, that no-one should obey or attend our foresaid messenger concerning these things which pertain to us and to our office.[61]

By October 1266 the pope was seriously considering turning Ottoboni's legatine mission into a crusading one, and he ordered the legate to preach the loss of Ashtod, Safed and Caesarea, and the dangerous plight of the Holy Land.[62] Thereafter the legate's visit became increasingly directed towards the preaching of a new crusade to the Holy Land. Probably in the summer of 1267 Ottoboni issued a powerful general letter exhorting people to join a forthcoming *passagium generale* against 'the unclean dogs, blasphemous enemies of the cross and name of Christ', who were infesting the land where his blood had been shed.[63] He may have hoped to divert the belligerence of the participants in the English civil war into a channel more suitable for the advancement of Christendom, but in fact many of those who took the cross seem to have had motives of their own; many of Lord Edward's followers in 1270 had acquired lands of disinherited rebels, and were using the protection granted to *crucesignati* to avoid litigation over them.[64]

Neither this motivation, nor the unpopular legate Ottoboni, can have been responsible for the substantial number of Scots who took the cross. It seems, indeed, that Henry III was anxious for the crusading subsidy from Scotland, but less interested in Scottish manpower. Fordun states that Ottoboni demanded the release of the large procuration which Alexander III had arrested in 1266, and in 1268 demanded that the Scottish bishops, with two abbots and two priors, should attend his legatine council in London. The bishops sent only two of their number with one abbot and one prior, and the Scottish clergy as a whole refused to abide by the new constitutions which the council laid down.[65] Although our sources for these events are poor, probably Fordun is again to be trusted.

> Pope Clement wrote to the clergy of Scotland, that they should pay the tenth penny from all their ecclesiastical income to the king of England; which the king and clergy with one voice and one heart refused to do. But in the following year [1269] Henry king of England again sent his messengers to Scotland to ask for the tenth penny. The clergy, however, protested as before, appealed to the pope, and sent clergymen to his court.[66]

Alexander III had already refused a clerical tenth towards Henry III's household needs in 1266, and it must have been wishful thinking to expect him to surrender it three years later. Henry's sons, Edward and Edmund, took the cross soon after Ottoboni's legatine council in 1268;[67] but it seems that enthusiasm for the crusade in Scotland was fired from quite a different source.

Louis IX took the cross at the end of 1267, and news of this must soon have reached Scotland. It is possible that he may have sent a letter to Scotland inviting the Scots to join his project, similar to the letter written by Philip IV to Robert I in 1309, inviting him to join a projected crusade.[68] Hector Boece, although his *History* can hardly be regarded as authoritative for this period, states that he did:

Attoure, he [Alexander III] send to King Lowis, as his ambassatouris affoir desyritt, ane thousand armytt men with the Erlis of Carrik and Athoill, and mony uthir nobill capitanys, quhilkis war all slayne in Aphrik throw excessyve heit and pest.[69]

Boece also states that Alexander resisted English demands for money, promising to send men instead. More reliably, Fordun also associates the two Scottish earls with Louis IX's expedition to Tunis:

A.D. 1271 (*recte* 1270). Louis king of France, after he had captured a great island, called Barbary, in fighting against the Saracens, together with Louis, his first-born son, died, and many Christian people were with him. Among them were David earl of Atholl and Adam earl of Carrick, and many other Scots and English nobles.[70]

The *Melrose Chronicle* provides firm contemporary evidence that the earl of Atholl died in the company of Louis IX in 'Barbary', while Bower's *Scotichronicon* states that he died at Carthage on 6 August 1270.[71] One Scottish knight, Ingram de Balliol, was attached to Louis IX's household during the north African campaign, and thereafter was associated with Louis's son Philip III, at Messina in Sicily.[72] It is clear that Scottish participation in the last of the Holy Land crusades was not simply a northern extension of English activity, but involved associations with both French and English leaders. Some Scots are found involved in Lord Edward's activities in the Holy Land following Louis' death, and some, apparently, both there and in the campaign against Tunis. An examination of the activities of individual crusaders, which is possible in greater detail for this Crusade than for any other, will show the complexity of Scottish involvement.

David de Strathbogie, earl of Atholl, first appears as earl of Atholl in 1264; he was 'an Aberdeenshire baron descended from the earls of Fife; his title to the earldom is unknown'.[73] He was married c. 1267 to Isabella, sister of Richard de Dover.[74] On 23 April 1270 he had letters of protection for four years from all plaints and pleas of the English crown, presumably on behalf of his wife's lands in England.[75] He must have set out for the Holy Land immediately thereafter, because the *Melrose Chronicle* states that he died in the army of Louis IX:

After the land of Barbary had been subjugated to the king of France, while that king was returning home together with the king of Navarre, they both died on the way; and with them died David earl of Atholl in that pilgrimage.[76]

Bower's date for his death, 6 August 1270, at Carthage, may well be right, and if so shows that Bower was using a thirteenth-century source independent of Fordun or the *Melrose Chronicle*. David may have been one of the first of the crusaders to succumb to heat and disease; the army had arrived before Tunis on 18 July, and was immediately struck by disease. Louis himself died on 25 August.[77]

Adam de Kilconquhar, earl of Carrick, appears also to have been descended from the earls of Fife. He came to the earldom of Carrick by marriage with Marjorie, daughter of Niall earl of Carrick; but his control of the earldom may not have extended beyond his wife's demesne lands, for the last Celtic earl had appointed his nephew Lachlan as leader of the men of Carrick and *ceann cineil* or head of kin.[78] But he must have had some followers, and some of them may have come from Carrick. There is no record of his having obtained letters of protection from Henry III to cover his absence on crusade; unlike the earl of Atholl, he seems to have had no lands in England. Fordun states that he was with Louis IX in the campaign against 'Barbary' along with the earl of Atholl, and Boece (for what it is worth) also links him with David de Strathbogie as joint leader of the Scottish host.[79] If they are correct, he and the remnant of the forces of both earls must have joined up with Lord Edward's army in Sicily in the autumn of 1270 and proceeded to Acre the following spring. The *Melrose Chronicle* states that he died at Acre in the year after the death of David earl of Atholl:

> Adam de Kilconquhar, earl of Carrick, died at Acre, whose wife, the countess of Carrick, Robert de Bruce the younger thereafter took as his wife.[80]

The death of the earl of Atholl is placed s.a. 1269 in the *Melrose Chronicle,* and that of the earl of Carrick s.a. 1270; in fact, they appear to have died in 1270 and 1271 respectively.

Robert de Bruce the elder, lord of Annandale, must have been one of the oldest crusaders to set out, having been born c. 1210. His active career in politics continued until his death in 1295. He had been active on the royalist side against Simon de Montfort during the 1260s.[81] Unlike his son, he did not set out with Lord Edward in the summer of 1270, but instead sailed with his brother, Lord Edmund, in March 1271; he had letters of protection from Henry III dated 19 October 1270, stating that he was setting out with Edmund the king's son to the Holy Land.[82] Edmund joined his brother in the Holy Land in the summer of 1271, and he and Robert de Bruce probably remained there until the autumn of 1272. On his return journey, late in 1272 or in 1273, Robert de Bruce visited the Cistercian monastery of Clairvaux, where he paid his respects at the shrine of Saint Malachi; he issued a charter granting the lands of 'Esticroft' (probably in Annandale) to the monks of Clairvaux for the provision of lights at the shrine of St Malachi, an Irish saint who had cursed one of Bruce's ancestors.[83] The witnesses to this charter may represent the lord of Annandale's retinue on crusade:

> These witnesses: Sir Adam de Torthorwald, at the time steward of Annandale; Sir Robert de Herries; Sir William de Saint Michael, knights; Master Adam de Kirkcudbright; Sir William de Duncorry; William de Corri; Adam Hendeman; Richard de Crispin; William de Ayr, clerk; and others.[84]

Their number – four knights, three squires (presumably), and two clerics – suggests that going on crusade in a manner befitting one's station was an expensive business.

Absent from this list is the name of *Robert de Bruce the younger*. He was born probably in the 1240s, and would have been in his twenties when he joined Lord Edward's army; Fordun described him as 'an extremely handsome and elegant young knight' at the time of his return from crusade.[85] He had letters of protection from Henry III dated 10 July 1270, immediately before the departure of the fleet.[86] Having left Scotland before his father, he does not appear to have returned in his company either, if the elder Robert's charter was indeed issued at Clairvaux. Fordun describes how the young widow of Adam de Kilconquhar, Marjorie countess of Carrick, met him soon after his return to Scotland, and soon after she had learned that she was a widow, imprisoned him at Turnberry, and married him by force. This was probably in the summer or autumn of 1273, as their first son was born on 11 July 1274, and christened with his father's name of Robert.[87]

At least three, possibly more, members of the widely ramified Balliol family took part in the Crusade of 1270-72. *Alexander de Balliol* was the son of John Balliol the elder, and elder brother of John Balliol who later became king. He was heir to the Balliol estates of Barnard Castle and Galloway, and of Bailleul in Picardy. On 12 May 1270 he had protection from Henry III during his absence on crusade with Lord Edward.[88] Earlier he had been loyal to Henry III and Lord Edward, and had been rewarded by them with the grant of Thackthwaite, part of the barony of Multon, in 1267.[89] After his return from crusade in 1272 he succeeded to the senior estates of his family, and died in 1278.[90]

Eustace de Balliol was a brother of the elder John de Balliol, and so an uncle of the above Alexander. He was married to the heiress of Linton, and had protection as a crusader with Lord Edward on 20 February 1270.[91] He died without issue in 1274.

Ingram de Balliol was probably the son of Eustace de Balliol, lord of Red Castle (Lunan, Angus). His presence on the Crusade was entirely in a French context. His name appears in 1269 on a list of 'knights of the household of the king [Louis IX] for the journey to Tunis'.[92] He survived the disaster at Tunis, and withdrew with the remnant of the French army to Sicily in the autumn of 1270; at the end of August 1270 he received a gift of 290 pounds *tournois* from King Philip III at Messina.[93] It is not known whether he sailed from Sicily to the Holy Land with Lord Edward, though it is possible that King Philip's gift may have been for that purpose. He succeeded to the Red Castle estates in the mid-1270s, and died in the late 1290s. It appears that the Red Castle branch of the Balliol family still had connections with the French crown as late as 1291.[94]

Another Balliol, *Hugh de Balliol*, is less certain to have been a participant in the Crusade of 1270-72. He was the eldest son of John de Balliol and Dervorgilla of Galloway, elder brother of Alexander and nephew of Eustace de Balliol (both of whom are mentioned above). In company with his uncle Eustace, he had leave to go overseas for one year from December 1268;[95] this may have been simply to visit the Balliol estates in Picardy. No letters of protection for the Crusade survive for Hugh de Balliol, but he died in 1271,[96] and this, together with his association with his crusading uncle, has prompted a recent writer to comment that 'it is probable that he also died on crusade'.[97] Circumstantial evidence − his previous record of royalist service during the English civil war and his association with his uncle, a known crusader, during the twelve months before the crusade − make it likely that Hugh was a crusader, and that his death, like that of the earl of Carrick and others, took place in the Holy Land; but it is impossible to be certain.

John de Vescy, lord of Alnwick and Sprouston (near Kelso), came from a family whose Scottish connections went back to the reign of William the Lion.[98] In the summer of 1270 he obtained protection as a crusader going to the Holy Land with Edward the king's son, and the right to lease manors which he held in chief of the English crown.[99] Earlier he had paid off debts owed to Guy de Châtillon count of St-Pol, a member of another eminent northern French crusading family.[100] After his return from the Crusade, he was one of the leaders of the Scottish army sent to expel English raiders from the Isle of Man in 1275.[101]

Other persons with Anglo-Scottish surnames joined the Crusade of 1270, but they are less easy to identify. *Henry le Walays* (Wallace) may be identifiable with the Henry Walays who was steward of the de Lacy manor of Pontefract in 1264, but Henry was also a common Christian name among the Wallace family who were tenants of the Stewarts in Renfrewshire.[102] Likewise *Richard de Glen*, another crusader, appears frequently as a member of the archbishop of York's household, but a person of this name is also mentioned as a 'tenant in chief of the royal dignity of Scotland'.[103] Three members of the de Mowbray family, called John, Ralph and William, had crusaders' letters from Henry III,[104] and it is possible that one of them at least was Scottish. A Trinitarian hospital was founded at Houston (Prestonkirk) by Christiana Fraser, widow of Sir Roger de Mowbray, 20 January 1268/9 x 26 January 1271/2, and it is possible that she was the mother of one of the Mowbray crusaders;[105] the countess of Dunbar's Trinitarian foundation at Dunbar (1247 x 1248) provides another example of a Trinitarian house being founded by the family of a departing crusader.[106]

Documents and indirect evidence throw up other tantalising possibilities. *Adam de Folkerton*, from near Lesmahagow, 'left the land of Scotland' some years before 1279, and did not return; it is possible that his departure was connected with the Crusade of 1270-72.[107] If he obtained the crusaders' protection from the English crown, the record has not survived; but if he did not hold lands in England, he may have had no reason to do so.

Gordon family tradition records that a member of this family joined the second Crusade of Louis IX, but there is doubt as to his identity. The sixteenth-century historian John Ferrerio calls him 'William Gordon', but no person of this name appears on record.[108] The Gordons were benefactors of Kelso Abbey, and their lineage is well attested in the Kelso cartulary.[109] At the time of the Crusade of 1270, the main line was represented by a female, Alicia de Gordon, who married one *Adam de Gordon* (whose lineage is uncertain, though he may have been a relative), who predeceased her.[110] Some time in the second half of the thirteenth century this Adam de Gordon granted his peat bog in Fawnes (Berwickshire) to Dryburgh Abbey, and died a few years later.[111] If Ferrerio's story of a Gordon crusader at this time is correct, then it may well have been Adam de Gordon who joined the Crusade, and his grant to Dryburgh, possibly to raise money, may have been made shortly before his departure. The Gordon crusader is said to have died in Africa, which would place him in the company of the earl of Atholl at Tunis. There is no record evidence that Adam de Gordon joined the Crusade, though he must have died around that time.

David de Lindsay is said to have 'joined the crusade of St Louis in 1268, and died in Egypt'.[112] He had been a member of the king's council appointed to safeguard English interests in 1255, along with Bruce and Durward;[113] as such, he can perhaps be seen as a member, with them and the earl of Dunbar, of the more outward-looking section of the Scottish nobility. He may have taken the cross in 1268 and set out with the Scottish earls two years later. He cannot have died in Egypt, since those crusaders who survived the disaster at Tunis either returned home or proceeded to Acre with Lord Edward. Perhaps North Africa is meant, but the name of Egypt has been substituted by confusion with Louis IX's earlier Crusade; Boece mentions a 'David Lindsay of Glenesk', a rather anachronistic-sounding title, on the Crusade of 1248.[114] There may be confusion between members of two different generations here. Very little is known of David de Lindsay's career. He appears as a witness to several charters, and the piety of his family is suggested by a grant to Newbattle by his son William de Lindsay, in return for 'pious works' for the souls of David de Lindsay and his wife Margaret.[115] His death seems to have occurred around the time of the Crusade.

We are on more certain ground with *Alexander de Seton*. The family of de Seton was settled at Seton in East Lothian from the mid-twelfth century. The Christian name Alexander was common in this family, and there are well-documented Alexanders in the generations preceding and following that centred around 1270. The crusader Alexander was son of Saher de Seton, and possibly father of another Alexander de Seton who joined the Knights Hospitallers and was preceptor of their Scottish estates in the 1340s.[116] He may have had connections with the de Vesci family, which could account in part for his presence on the Crusade.[117] He is not known to have had any lands in England, and his name does not appear among those who had protection from Henry III to go on crusade. He was at Acre in 1271, but it is not known whether he had previously been at Tunis with the earls of Atholl and Carrick, or whether he sailed to Sicily with Lord Edward in the late summer of 1270. Probably his presence on the Crusade would not be known at all were it not for a cautionary tale recounted in the *Melrose Chronicle*. This describes Lord Edward's only military exploit in Palestine, a raid across Mount Carmel up to the walls of the fortress of Qaqun in the Plain of Sharon; but his troops were insufficient to besiege the fort, so having attacked a bedouin caravan and captured its livestock, they set off back towards Acre. They all returned safely,

> except for one esquire, called Nicholas, of a certain knight of Scottish origin whose name was Alexander de Setun. The esquire became separated from the Christian army when he went to relieve himself, carrying his lord's shield on his back on his horse, and was immediately captured by a few pagans who lived beside the way along which the Christians were travelling unseen by the pagans, whom the Christians would have killed if they had seen them. But the esquire who was thus abducted by the pagans was never seen again by Christians from that day onwards.[118]

Nothing can be deduced from this about the family of the unfortunate esquire Nicholas, except that like his master he was probably Scottish.

There is no real evidence to support the assertion that Walter Stewart, earl of Menteith, 'is said to have gone to Egypt under Louis IX of France'.[119] The only grounds for this assertion is the fact that his effigy at Inchmahome priory shows him with his legs crossed, which was once erroneously thought to indicate a crusader.[120] Likewise it is difficult to credit the statement that 'James, fifth hereditary high Steward . . . is said to have joined the earls of Carrick, Athole, and other Scots lords in an expedition to Palestine'.[121] For this assertion there seems to exist no evidence at all.

Despite these red herrings, there is still enough evidence to show a substantial Scottish contingent on the Crusade, part of which seems to have been associated with Lord Edward, and part with the Crusade against Tunis. This makes Boece's story of a French invitation for the Scots to join them, similar to the one received in 1309, seem very likely. This explains why there is not an exact correspondence between grants of protection issued by the English government and the actual number of Scots who did join the Crusade. The English expedition did not visit North Africa on its route to the Holy Land, yet there is some evidence that there were Scots there. If the English crusade was inspired by the royalist victory in the civil war and influenced by Cardinal Ottoboni, these factors cannot explain the number of Scots who had no territorial interests in England or loyalty to Henry III; especially since Ottoboni's mission was greeted with hostility in Scotland. What may have happened is that a strong Scottish contingent, led by the two earls, responded to an invitation from Louis IX to join him. These followed him to Tunis, where many of them perished, and the survivors withdrew with the French to Sicily in the autumn of 1270. There they were joined by the English expedition under Lord Edward, which included a number of Anglo-Scottish landowners with royalist connections. When they sailed to Acre the following spring they were joined by part at least of the Scottish remnant under the earl of Carrick, who died at Acre. The return journey seems to have been even more diverse. The lord of Annandale visited Clairvaux, while his son seems to have returned to Scotland separately. Lord Edward himself did not return to England until 1274, by which time many of the Scots must have already arrived home.

This was the last of the great European crusades. Despite the attempts of Popes Gregory X and Martin IV to preach a new crusade after the failure of Louis IX's second expedition, this was not achieved even by the Second Council of Lyons in 1274. Pope Gregory informed Alexander III and his bishops of the new council on 13 April 1273;[122] and a year later the council opened, though the number of the Scottish contingent is uncertain.[123] Despite the unfavourable reports of his advisers on the chances of a new crusade,[124] Gregory pressed ahead with the project and set about a new collection of an ecclesiastical tenth to finance it. Perhaps he was aware of the problems which had faced Ottoboni as far as Scotland was concerned; this time Scotland was to have a papal collector of its own. Master Baiamund de Vicia, canon of Asti and chaplain to the cardinal of St Eustachius, was a minor papal bureaucrat whom the pope selected to collect the crusading tenth from the Scottish church for six years, in person and by sworn sub-collectors; the pope also enjoined him to write frequent reports on his progress.[125] Baiamund arrived in Scotland in 1275 and held a council at Perth at which he announced that the collection would be calculated not according to the 'old taxation', but according to the true value of the lands in question.[126] It is not clear what earlier taxation can have been meant, though there had been intermittent crusading levies from early in the thirteenth century. Baiamund's hard line did not last very long, for the Scottish clergy persuaded him to return to the *curia* to ask for a return to the old taxation, 'but he returned to Scotland without success'.[127] Money was forthcoming in Scotland, but not in sufficient quantities to satisy the papacy. Baiamund's accounts have survived, and they show discrepancies as well as an unwillingness to contribute.[128] Despairingly, Baiamund asked to be relieved of the task in April 1282; but the pope refused, and ordered him to proceed against defaulters.[129] It seems that in the interval King Alexander had intervened and placed an arrestment on the money to be exported through Italian bankers; and it came to the pope's notice that Baiamund had used the arrest as an excuse for lending the money at interest.[130] Already in 1282 Baiamund had been under suspicion, for a new collector, Geoffrey de Viçano, was sent to the British Isles, and in 1284 the pope instructed him to put pressure on Baiamund to hand over the money received.[131] Alexander's reluctance to allow the money to be transmitted is understandable, as the only likely beneficiary would be Edward I; in May 1284 Martin IV granted the tenth from Scotland to Edward should Alexander's consent be forthcoming, in which case Edward would be responsible for financing Scottish crusaders.[132] Alexander probably knew enough about Edward's dealings with Wales and in Gascony to know that a request for money in aid of the Holy Land could hardly be taken at face value. But on the death of Martin IV and succession of Honorius IV in 1286, Edward still had influence with Christ's vicar, who confirmed the grant of the tenth from Scotland, and also allowed Edward's request to select crusaders from Scotland personally, 'as having practical experience of the country' – in other words, Edward was allowed to use ecclesiastical revenue from Scotland, raised specifically for the relief of the Holy Land, to maintain a pro-English faction among the Scottish governing class.[133] It is hard to conceive that either the pope or the king of England can have imagined that Alexander would have allowed them to carry out such a preposterous arrangement; but Alexander died in the same year, and thereafter abuses of crusading finance continued to multiply, without a strong hand to prevent the export of money. As recently as July 1285 he had been able to forbid the export of sums of money through Italian banking houses,[134] but thereafter the transfer of money may have gone ahead unhindered, to the benefit of Edward I.[135] When Nicholas IV became pope in 1288, he showed faith in Edward's intention of going again to the Holy Land; in January 1290 he ordered a new assessment of the true value, including Scotland with England, Wales and Ireland as due to pay the tenth to Edward,[136] and in the summer of the same year he reached agreement with Edward that the king should set out by the summer of 1293.[137]

In March 1290/91 a general exhortation was sent to all the faithful, urging them to take the cross.[138] The pope had just learned of the death of the sultan Qalawun, who had died on 10 November 1290,[139] and felt that the time was right to strike a blow against the enemies of the kingdom of Jerusalem: the bishops of Scotland were commissioned to preach the cross with a view to a crusade leaving in the summer of 1293, and to grant indulgences accordingly.[140] Edward, having achieved his aims against the Welsh, may have been sincerely motivated to return to the Holy Land. Collectors for a new tenth were appointed, the Scottish collectors being the bishops of Carlisle (John de Halton) and Caithness (Alan de St Edmund, an Englishman who figures largely as in favour with Edward I of England in the various transactions after the death of Alexander III);[141] clearly Edward was still anxious to milk the Scottish church for his own purposes as far as possible, and in view of the weakness in Scottish central government following Alexander III's death, he was able to secure favourable appointees as collectors.[142]

But if he had intended to sail to the Holy Land again, two events in 1290-1 prevented him from doing so. In October 1290, news reached the Scottish guardians of the death of the queen at Orkney, throwing Scottish affairs into greater confusion; and the bishop of St Andrews was writing to Edward asking for his help in resolving the situation.[143] In May 1291 Acre fell to the new sultan, al-Ashraf Khalil, shortly followed by the remnant of the Christian cities of the Palestinian mainland, Tyre and Beirut.[144] The kingdom of Jerusalem was effectively at an end, and there was no territorial base from which to attempt the recovery of the Holy City. In future, the recovery of the Holy Land would be a subject of much pious talk, but very little constructive action.

NOTES

1. Louis' character is described in John de Joinville, *Histoire de Saint Louis*, ed. N. de Wailly (Paris, Société de l'Histoire de France, 1868).

2. *Dunfermline Liber*, 128-9.

3. Duncan, *Making of the Kingdom*, 294.

4. See above, pp. 41-3.

5. *Chron. Lanercost*, 54.

6. *Melrose Liber*, 204-5.

7. *Yester Writs*, no. 14.

8. R. Brunschvig, *La Berbérie Orientale sous les Hafsides* (Paris, Institut d'Etudes orientales d' Alger), i, 455-6; J. Mesnages, *Le Christianisme en Afrique: Eglise Mozarabe – Esclaves Chrétiens* (Paris and Algiers, 1915), 17-18.

9. Paris, Archives nationales, L 947.

10. *Yester Writs*, no. 14; Cowan and Easson, *MRHS*, 107.

11. Joinville, *Histoire*, 43-5.

12. *Chron. Lanercost*, 54.

13. Matthew Paris, *Chronica Maiora*, v, 41.

14. 'Histoire d'Eracles', in *RHC Occ.*, ii, 436.

15. Boece, *Chronicles*, trans. Bellenden, ii, 229.

16. *SP*, i, 12.

17. Matthew Paris, *Chronica Maiora*, vi, 521.

18. Ibid., v, 98-9.

19. *CPL*, i, 261.

20. *RRS*, ii, 315-6.

21. *Newbattle Registrum*, 64.

22. SRO GD 241/254.

23. *CDS*, i, no. 2013.

24. *The Story of the Stewarts* (Edinburgh, 1901), 61.

25. Cf. D. E. R. Watt, 'The Minority of King Alexander III of Scotland', *TRHS*, 5th ser. xxi (1971), 1-24.

26. *CDS*, i, no. 2013.

27. *CPL*, i, 232.

28. Ibid., 237, gives an abstract which omits the crusaders' names; Theiner, *VM*, 48, gives the full text.

29. F. M. Powicke, *King Henry III and the Lord Edward* (Oxford, 1947), i, 201, 207.

30. *CPL*, i, 243; Theiner, *VM*, 49.

31. *CPL*, i, 243; Theiner, *VM*, 50.

32. *CDS*, i, no. 1806.

33. *CPL*, i, 232.

34. Matthew Paris, *Chronica Maiora*, v, 93.

35. Duncan, *Making of the Kingdom*, 585.

36. See above, p. 36.

37. W. Matheson, 'Traditions of the Mackenzies', *TGSI*, xxxix-xl (1942-50), 193-228, at 221-3.

38. *Papers relative to the Royal Guard of Scottish Archers in France* (Maitland Club, 1835), 74.

39. Joinville, *Histoire*, 160-4.

40. Ibid., 7.

41. See above, pp. 6, 10, 18.

42. See Duncan, *Making of the Kingdom*, 564.

43. Watt, 'Minority of King Alexander III', 18-19 and nn. 107-8.

44. *Kelso Liber*, 191; *Aberdeen Registrum*, ii, 272-3.

45. At the time of the suppression of the Templars in Scotland (1312) there were only two preceptories, at Balantrodoch and Maryculter; *Spottiswoode Miscellany*, ii, 1-16.

46. See in general I. B. Cowan, P. H. R. Mackay and A. D. Macquarrie, *The Knights of St John of Jerusalem in Scotland* (SHS, 1984).

47. *Report of Philip de Thame*, 129, 201.

48. *Melrose Liber*, i, 288-91.

49. See above, p. 49.

50. See above, pp. 41-2.

51. *Chron. Holyrood*, 173-7.

52. Ibid.

53. Ibid., 177, n. 2.

54. *CPL*, i, 384-5, 423.

55. Ibid., 426-32 and passim.

56. Ibid., 427.

57. Ibid., 394.

58. Ibid., 433; Theiner, *VM*, 99.

59. *Chron. Fordun*, 303-4.

60. 'The Letters of Cardinal Ottoboni', ed. R. Graham, *EHR*, xv (1900), 87-120, at 90.

61. Ibid., 117-8.

62. *CPL*, i, 436.

63. 'Letters of Cardinal Ottoboni', 113.

64. Cf. B. Beebe, 'The English Baronage and the Crusade of 1270', *BIHR*, xlviii (1975), 127-48.

65. *Chron. Fordun*, 303-4.

66. Ibid., 304.

67. *Chron. Rishanger*, 58-9.

68. *APS*, i, 459.

69. Boece, *Chronicles*, trans. Bellenden, ii, 229.

70. *Chron. Fordun*, 304.

71. *Chron. Melrose*, 144; *Chron. Bower*, ii, 101.

72. M. Bouquet and others, *Recueil des Historiens des Gaules et de la France* (Paris, 1738- in progress), xx, 308; Paris, Archives Nationales, J475/77.

73. Duncan, *Making of the Kingdom*, 585, and cf. 635.

74. *CDS*, i, nos. 2455, 2531.

75. Ibid., no. 2557.

76. *Chron. Melrose*, 144.

77. *Chron. Bower*, ii, 101; Runciman, *History of the Crusades*, iii, 292.

78. *RMS*, i, 508-9.

79. *Chron. Fordun*, 305; Boece, *Chronicle*, trans. Bellenden, ii, 229.

80. *Chron. Melrose*, 146.

81. On his career, see G. Donaldson, *Who's Who in Scottish History* (Oxford, 1973), 18-9.

82. *CDS*, i, no. 2575.

83. Troyes, Archives départementales de l'Aube, 3 H 332; edited in Migne, *PL*, clxxxv, pt ii, cols 1759-60 and in A. Macquarrie, 'Notes on some Charters of the Bruces of Annandale', *TDGNHAS*, 3d Ser., lviii (1983), 72-9, at 76-7.

84. Ibid.

85. *Chron. Fordun*, 303-4.

86. *Cal. Pat. Rolls, 1266-72*, 480.

87. *Chron. Fordun*, 304-5.

88. *Cal. Pat. Rolls, 1266-72*, 426, and cf. 628.

89. J. Wilson, 'A Balliol Charter of 1267', *SHR*, v (1908), 252-3.

90. I am indebted to Mr G. Stell for this and other information about the Balliol family.

91. *Cal. Pat. Rolls, 1266-72*, 411, 441.

92. Bouquet, *Recueil*, xx, 308.

93. Paris, Archives nationales, J475/77.

94. *Cal. Close Rolls, 1288-96*, 170.

95. *Cal. Pat. Rolls, 1266-72*, 308.

96. Ibid., 615.

97. W. B. Hedley, *Northumberland Families* (Newcastle, 1968-70), i, 207.

98. *RRS*, ii, 99, 124, 424; cf. Duncan, *Making of the Kingdom*, 253-5.

99. *Cal. Pat. Rolls, 1266-72*, 439, 480.

100. *CDS*, i, no. 2456.

101. Duncan, *Making of the Kingdom*, 582.

102. *CDS*, i, nos. 2363, 2559; Barrow, *Kingdom of the Scots*, 352-3.

103. *Cal. Fine Rolls, 1272-1307*, 316; *Cal. Pat. Rolls, 1266-72*, 589; *Register of Walter Giffard, Lord Archbishop of York, 1266-79*, ed. W. Brown (Surtees Society, cix, 1904).

104. *CDS*, i, no. 2558.

105. J. Bain, 'Notes on the Trinitarians or Red Friars', *PSAS*, x (1887-8), 27-8.

106. See above, pp. 47-8.

F

107. *Kelso Liber*, 155.
108. *SP*, iv, 510.
109. *Kelso Liber*, 106-9.
110. Ibid., 87, 89.
111. *Dryburgh Liber*, 140-1.
112. *SP*, iii, 8. This gives as its authority for the statement Dugdale's *Monasticon*, but without volume or page number; I have not been able to trace the exact reference.
113. *Cal. Pat. Rolls, 1247-58*, 421.
114. Boece, *Chronicle*, trans. Bellenden, ii, 229.
115. *Newbattle Registrum*, 137-8.
116. Cowan, Mackay and Macquarrie, *Knights of St John*, xxxii-xxxiii; *Melrose Liber*, 199.
117. Ibid., 255.
118. *Chron. Melrose*, 145-6.
119. *SP*, vi, 130.
120. F. H. Groome, *Ordnance Gazetteer of Scotland* (1882-5), s.v. Inchmahome; see E. S. Prior and A. Gardner, *An Account of Medieval Figure Sculpture in England* (Cambridge, 1912), 594, on the subject of cross-legged effigies.
121. *Story of the Stewarts*, 64.
122. *CPL*, i, 446.
123. Duncan, *Making of the Kingdom*, 291.
124. Runciman, *History of the Crusades*, iii, 338-42.
125. Theiner, *VM*, 104; *CPL*, i, 449.
126. *Chron. Fordun*, 306.
127. Ibid.
128. 'Bagimond's Roll', ed. A. I. Dunlop, *SHS Miscellany*, vi (1939), 1ff; cf. Ibid., v (1933), and x (1965), for other fragments of the roll.
129. *CPL*, i, 465.
130. Ibid., 469.
131. Ibid.
132. Ibid., 473-4.
133. Ibid., 479-80.
134. Ibid., 481.
135. *SHS Miscellany*, vi, 1ff.
136. *CPL*, i, 509.
137. Ibid., 527.
138. Ibid., 533.
139. Runciman, *History of the Crusades*, iii, 411-12.
140. *CPL*, i, 533.
141. Dowden, *Bishops*, 238-9.
142. *CPL*, i, 554.
143. Nicholson, *Later Middle Ages*, 35.
144. Runciman, *History of the Crusades*, iii, 412-23.

4

In Search of New Horizons, 1291-1410

The fourteenth century is often though of as 'the Age of Chivalry', and this is reflected in a continuing interest in and appeal to the ideal of the Crusade long after the reconquest of Jerusalem had ceased to be a practical possibility. Warfare in the east was still carried on by the Lusignan kings of Cyprus and by the Hospitallers in Rhodes; but the knights of western Europe had other outlets of sacred belligerence open to them which attracted increasing attention. The Teutonic Knights in Prussia began their campaign against heathen Lithuania in the late thirteenth century, and after the fall of Acre transferred all their military interests there.[1] And the *Reconquista* in Spain began to attract knights from northern Europe in increasing numbers from the late 1320s onwards as Alfonso XI renewed the war against Granada. The concept of the Holy War against the heathen continued, but the energies of fighting men were directed in different ways, all of which can still be termed crusades. At the same time, the fourteenth century contrasts with the high Middle Ages in that it was a period of large-scale protracted wars between European nations. The long reigns of Louis IX and Henry III (who is described in one Scottish chronicle as 'the most peace-loving king of England'[2]) gave way to those of ambitious, aggressive successors. England in particular contributed to a breakdown of international stability with the bloody wars provoked by Edward I and Edward III. It might seem surprising that with so much war going on knights should have had time to embark on crusades at all; but the protracted wars of the fourteenth century gave rise to a new type of professionalism among soldiers, a class of fighting men who made warfare a career rather than a feudal obligation.[3] These men had to be kept occupied in times of truce or peace, and the crusading ideal was a device often used to keep them busy when there were no domestic wars to be fought.

When news of the fall of Acre reached Scotland in the summer of 1291, the governing classes were preoccupied with the problem of the succession and were in no position to consider taking part in a new crusade. Despite his declared intention of returning to the Holy Land in 1293, Edward I soon became distracted by problems nearer to home. John Balliol, chosen king of Scotland by Edward in succession to Margaret, proved less amenable to Edward's pressure than had been hoped; and in the summer of 1294 Edward's relationship with Philip IV of France reached a crisis which made war seem inevitable. The Franco-Scottish alliance of the following year and open war between England and Scotland in 1296 meant that the affairs of the Holy Land had to be again pushed into the background. Edward I was the favourite of the papacy and the champion of the Crusade, at least until the pontificate of Boniface VIII; but that pope was hostile to Edward's designs on Scotland, and perhaps showed less interest than some of his thirteenth-century predecessors in the recovery of Jerusalem. While he was pope (1295-1303), there was no chance that Edward would aid papal policy by going to the rescue of the Holy Land, even had he not been distracted by affairs in France and Scotland.

During the early 1290s, however, Edward was able to take advantage of papal favour and the lack of central authority within Scotland to exact the Holy Land tenth from Scotland and apply it to his own uses. The principal collector of the tenth from 1292 onwards was John de Halton, bishop of Carlisle, whose *Register* gives a detailed account of his proceedings in the collection.[4] In August 1294 Halton was at Kelso, sending out demands to various religious houses for sums due for the aid of the Holy Land; Halton seems to have intended to use religious houses as agents of collection and bases where moneys could be stored, and it had been observed that he had, at least until 1296, a measure of success in doing this.[5] At the very beginning of his pontificate, Boniface was still sufficiently favourable towards him to believe that Edward's reception of the cross was sincere, and confirmed to Halton that the grant of the tenth for Scotland made to Edward by Nicholas IV was still to be paid through Italian bankers.[6] The bishop of Carlisle made another visit to Scotland in the summer of 1295,[7] but thereafter he probably found it difficult to raise any revenue, particularly as hostility to the English deepened in 1297. Halton's *Register* does not record any more visits to Scotland before he was relieved of the duties of collector in February 1300/1. At this time his procurators informed the collectors appointed to succeed him that the bishop had collected four years of the tenth from Scotland, presumably for the years 1291, 1292, 1293 and 1294. Although he had been able to continue collecting from the Isle of Man, and had gathered the full six years' tenth there, only the four years' fruits from Scotland had been collected.[8] Years later, Halton recorded that Scottish religious houses still owed very large sums towards the tenth for six years confirmed by Boniface.[9]

While Edward was taking advantage of the crusading tax as a useful source of additional income, he also found the crusading ideal useful for diplomatic purposes, portraying himself as the champion of the movement for the recovery of Jerusalem, being hindered in his purpose by the rebellious Scots. In March 1303 Edward wrote to the patriarch of Constantinople and to the khan of the Tartars, assuring them of his intention to return to the business of the Holy Land, 'for whose success we hope, above all the other business of the world'.[10] The Plantagenets were a dynasty with a long history of crusading zeal; of Edward I's predecessors,

Henry II, Richard I, John, and Henry III had all taken the cross, and Richard and Edward himself had actually been on crusade, while Henry II and John had died within a short time of taking the cross and before their vows had been fulfilled. Henry III had been allowed to commute his vow when Edward agreed to go in his place. Richard earl of Cornwall, Henry III's brother, had been in the Holy Land in 1240-1. With such a distinguished record, it was impossible for the papacy to ignore the demands of the Plantagenets in respect of Scotland, especially when Edward I was continuing to express his intention of returning to the Holy Land. Scottish propagandists who were opposed to English ambitions towards Scotland had to bear in mind the impeccable record of Edward and his ancestors, which was for long periods able to turn papal hostility against Scotland.

The response of anti-English clergy was to go on the offensive. While Scotland was without clear leadership, and appeals to patriotic or nationalist feeling were not totally respectable *per se,* what was needed was an appeal to wider concepts with a general validity to the medieval mind. In using the analogy of the Holy War, Robert Bruce's propagandists found a concept with wider appeal.[11] But even before the rise of Bruce to prominence as a patriotic leader, a section of the clergy had been using its influence against Edward I and his innovations in 1296 by 'falsely asserting that to fight against Edward I was more justified than fighting against the Saracens'.[12] Ten years later, when Robert Bruce renewed the war by having himself crowned king of Scotland, Edward sent letters to the pope complaining that the bishop of Glasgow was going about encouraging the people to join Bruce's rebellion, which, said the bishop of Glasgow, was 'just as meritorious . . . as to go in the service of God to the Holy Land'.[13] The same accusation was levelled at bishop Lamberton of St Andrews: he preached to the people that it was no less meritorious to fight for Robert Bruce against the English than to go to the Holy Land to fight against pagans and saracens.[14] Bruce may well have seen himself as a champion of Christian ideals as he watched his men being ferried across Loch Lomond in the summer of 1306:

> The King, the quhilis, meryly
> Red to thaim, that war him by,
> Romanys of worthi Ferambrace,
> That worthily our-cummyn was,
> Throw the rycht douchty Olyver.[15]

The 'Roman de Fierebras', of which Barbour tells us that Bruce recited a version to his captains,[16] recounts how a small number of Charlemagne's Christian knights were bottled up in a castle by the infinitely superior pagan forces of King Lavyne, the sultan of Babylon, and his son Ferambrace; they were in the end rescued by Charlemagne:

> And wan the naylis, and the sper
> And the croune that Jesu couth ber;
> And off the croice a gret party
> He [i.e., Charlemagne] wan throw his chevalry.[17]

The comparison between his own vastly outnumbered forces and the might of England would not have been lost on Bruce's audience.

Towards the end of 1308 Philip IV of France, who already had designs on the wealth of the Templars, wrote to a number of European sovereigns notifying them of his intention of organising a new crusade. A London annalist was clearly aware of the contents of Philip's letter to Scotland:

> In this year [1308] the pope caused a crusade of the faithful to be preached throughout Christendom in aid of Cyprus and Armenia against the Saracens . . . At the same time King Philip of France wrote letters to King Edward of England, inviting him to attend his *parliamentum*. Likewise he wrote to Robert de Bruce, tyrant of Scotland, not styling him with the title of king, but greeting him as his dear friend . . . Neither, however, crossed over to France.[18]

The annalist does not state explicitly that Philip's letters directly concerned the Crusade, but seems to imply that he was anxious to mediate between Edward and Robert, which, taken together with Clement V's pursuit of a new crusade, would fit well with an invitation to join a crusade. Oliver des Roches, Philip IV's envoy to Robert Bruce and the bishop of St Andrews, had a safe conduct to go to Scotland issued by Edward II on 4 March 1309, and may well have been bearing the letter described by the London annalist.[19] A fortnight later, on 17 March, the barons of Scotland issued a courteous reply to the king of France's invitation that they and their lord King Robert should join his proposed crusade. The surviving Scottish copy is damaged, but its message is fairly clear, and it ends with a promise of help for the Holy Land when the war with England is over:

> If then the kingdom of Scotland returns to its pristine freedom, when the tempests of war have been suppressed and security and peace restored . . . then your majesty will have not only our lord the king, but also the inhabitants of his kingdom with all their strength, for your cherished project in divine service.[20]

This same message appears in the famous 'Declaration of Arbroath' of 1320. Its appeal both to national and to cosmopolitan values should not be seen as a contradiction or a puzzle, but the two should rather be seen as complementary. The assertion that the Scots wished to fight for the cross is, in a sense, an assertion of nationhood; it is an assertion that they wished to be like their European neighbours, and play their rightful part in the defence of Christendom – if only they would be left free to do so.

The Declaration is at pains to convince the pope that English assertions of crusading zeal are little more than humbug. He is warned not to believe 'the stories of the English', and is informed of the real reason why 'the borders of Christendom grow narrower every day':

> They claim that they cannot go to the aid of the Holy Land because of the wars which they have with their neighbours; but more truly the cause of their impediment is that they reckon to find greater usefulness and less resistance in fighting their smaller neighbours.

In conclusion, the Declaration asserts the Scots' own willingness to do what their selfish neighbours would not:

> But how gladly would our lord the king and we ourselves go thither [to the Holy Land] if the king of the English would leave us in peace, He knows from Whom nothing is hid.[21]

Towards the end of 1323 Thomas Randolph, earl of Moray, arrived in Avignon to negotiate with Pope John XXII; among other things he was anxious to impress on the pope his own crusading fervour, asking for a crusader's licence and indulgence to cross the sea in aid of the Holy Land.[22] Although he did not immediately achieve this objective, Randolph must have impressed the pope considerably, for he wrote apologetically to Edward II to tell him that he had conceded to Bruce the royal style in letters;[23] and on 31 August 1324 he wrote to Randolph, 'in whose labours to foster peace between England and Scotland the pope hopes and trusts', granting him an indult to visit the Holy Sepulchre, notwithstanding the sentences which stood against him, together with a crusader's indulgence, the latter to be valid upon his reconciliation with the Church.[24]

The Scots were probably right to dismiss English pretensions as humbug; but were their own professions of crusading fervour the same? Thomas Randolph never fulfilled his vow to visit the Holy Sepulchre, and there is no evidence that he commuted his vow. But as the remarkable reign of Robert I drew to a close, there was a final expression of crusading zeal on the part of the dying king himself which is as striking in its own way as any of Robert's achievements, as a genuine outpouring of piety and chivalrous spirit.

As he lay ill at Cardross, probably with leprosy, Robert sensed that his end was near; he sent letters to all his lords, summoning them to his deathbed, where he made his will. This involved (says Barbour) conspicuous generosity to many different religious orders, and regret for the amount of Christian blood that had been shed in the long wars that he had waged:

> I thank God that has me sent
> Spas in this liff for till repent.
> For throu me and my warraying
> Of blude thar has beyne gret spilling.[25]

According to Barbour, he regarded his infirmity as a punishment for this crime; and so he had long ago resolved in his heart

> Off my synnys till savit be
> Till travell apon Goddis fayis

(i.e. to strive against the enemies of God). Now, being struck down by sickness,

> That the body may on na wis
> Fulfill that the hert can devis,
> I wald the hert war thidder sent.

The story as told by Jean le Bel, who had previously fought against Bruce's army, is almost identical. Le Bel states that Bruce summoned James Douglas to his deathbed and said to him,

> I have vowed that : . . I would go and fight against the enemies of our Lord and of the Christian faith,

once his wars were over and his country at peace. But now that his body cannot do as his heart desires,

> I wish to send my heart instead of my body, to acquit myself and my vow . . . Carry my heart to the Holy Sepulchre, where our Lord was buried.[26]

The only difference is that Barbour states that Bruce made this speech to all the nobles present, and asked them to choose one of the number

> On Goddis fayis myne hert to bere,

and that they chose Douglas; according to le Bel, Bruce made a direct request to Douglas that he would undertake the task. The difference is a small one, and perhaps adds to the authenticity of the story, as it is clear that the two writers agree so closely yet still seem to be independent of each other. They both agree that Douglas and the king were both pleased with the arrangement; and the chronicler Froissart (following le Bel) attributes these words to King Robert:

> Now God be praised; for I will die more at peace now, when I know that the most worthy and strongest man of my kingdom will carry out for me what I can no longer do myself.[27]

But what do we know of the character of Sir James Douglas himself? He has been portrayed as a model of chivalry, always gallant and courteous.[28] But it would be perhaps more realistic to see him as a man of his time and occupied in the rough business of that time. Barbour had obvious reasons for polishing up his character into 'the good Sir James' who appears in his verses; but there is evidence which suggests that he also possessed elements of a rough soldier. By the time of the king's death in 1329, Douglas had been fighting almost continuously from his teens, and had probably become so inured to fighting through a quarter of a century that he had little skill or experience at anything else. On occasions he could be blunt and contemptuous of the rules of chivalrous conduct: during the border campaign of 1327, when the English invited the Scots army to descend from their strong position and do battle on open ground, Douglas is said to have sent back the message that he had come to England to burn and slay, and that if the English had any objection, it was up to them to do something about it.[29] His conduct after the battle of Bannockburn, when he pursued the fleeing Edward II with such vigour that

> He leit thame nocht haf sic laseir
> As anys wattyr for to ma,[30]

is perhaps fairly typical; and it is probably significant that it was to Douglas that the king's dying commission was entrusted, rather than to Randolph, who was an accomplished diplomat and statesman. Without wishing to deny his obvious qualities, it is important to view Douglas realistically as a man of his age and one accustomed to warfare. It is easy to understand why he was pleased to undertake the king's request, as it gave him an opportunity to continue his career overseas.

What was it that King Robert asked Douglas to do? According to Barbour, Bruce simply called for a brave knight

> On Goddis fayis myne hert to bere,

without directing him to any specific location. But Douglas's objective is clearly stated in the safe conduct issued to him by Edward III's government on 1 September 1329:

> Since the noble man, James lord of Douglas in Scotland, is about to set out for the Holy Land in aid of the Christians against the Saracens, with the heart of Robert king of Scotland, recently deceased . . .[31]

The safe conduct was accompanied by a letter of recommendation to Alfonso XI king of Castile, asking him to receive Douglas favourably should he pass through his domains on his journey; clearly Douglas intended to stop in Castile on his way to the Holy Land, and it seems that he had heard of the young Alfonso's intention of renewing the war against Granada. But these letters make it quite clear that his intention *was* some king of military expedition in the East. Barbour perhaps suppresses mention of the Holy Land as his objective because his hero never got there, but le Bel says that Bruce himself spoke of a longing to fight *oultre mer,* a term used to mean the Holy Land. Only the English writer Geoffrey le Baker mentions Granada as King Robert's objective:

'I have vowed to God,' he said, 'that I would fight against the enemies of Christ in person; which, since I cannot do so living, I beg you to carry my heart against the enemies of the name of Christ in the lands of Granada.'[32]

But this must surely be an *ex post facto* explanation of how he came to be there. Part of the confusion surrounding Douglas's objective arises from the letter which Robert is reputed to have sent to his son from Cardross while he lay dying, asking his protection for the monks of Melrose, where he bequeathed his heart for burial.[33] It has been convincingly shown that this letter is a forgery concocted at Melrose some seventy years later,[34] which cannot in any sense be regarded as evidence of where Robert I wanted his heart to be buried. There is no reason whatever to doubt Bower's statement that the king intended the Holy Sepulchre to be the final resting place of his heart, confirming the words of the only contemporary documents, the safe conduct and letter of recommendation issued by Edward III in 1329.[35]

It is certainly possible that Douglas intended to fight a few battles along the way in Spain, and then planned a peaceful pilgrimage with the king's heart to the Holy Sepulchre. But le Bel is quite explicit that his pause off the Flemish coast was intended to gather fighting recruits to go to the Holy Land; Douglas, he says, inquired if anyone 'on that side of the sea was preparing to go to the Holy Land of Jerusalem'.[36] On the way through the Mediterranean Douglas would certainly have had to stop in Cyprus, where he could have taken service with the Lusignan king of Cyprus. There he could have learned in detail of the situation in the Holy Land, and made a final decision about the practicability of a crusade in the Holy Land.

Throughout the autumn and winter of 1329-30 Douglas made his preparation for the journey. He was planning for a long absence, for his safe conduct from Edward III was for seven years' duration from 1 September 1329.[37] He assembled a body of knights and men at arms as his companions, some of whose names are known to us. Le Bel says that his train included a knight banneret, six other knights, twenty esquires, and other retinue.[38] Barbour mentions the knights William de Sinclair, Robert Logan, William Logan, and William Keith among his companions; le Baker mentions a certain Thomas de Lavingtone (probably Livingston), who was possibly one of the esquires and later became a Carmelite friar.[39] Possibly Simon Lockhart of Lee was one of the knights; tradition associates the 'Lee Penny' with a fourteenth-century crusade in which one of the Lockharts of Lee participated, and Simon Lockhart was a supporter of Bruce's cause from 1306 onwards.[40] Before his departure, Douglas celebrated his family's saint's day, the feast of St Bride (1 February 1330) at Douglas Park, and made a pious endowment to the monks of Newbattle, in whose abbey there was an altar of St Bride; they were in return to celebrate a sung mass annually on that feast at that altar, and afterwards serve a meal for thirteen

poor folk in honour of Sir James.[41] From there, he and his retinue went to
Berwick[42] in spring, to await 'la bonne saison pour mouvoir qui vouloit
passer outre mer', and set sail, probably in March or April.

The first port of call for which we have information was Sluys (*l'Escluse*)
in Flanders. Douglas waited there seeking news of the prospect of a crusade,
and encouraging anyone who might wish to join him on his voyage to
Jerusalem. Le Bel was vastly impressed by the lordly hospitality he offered
on board his ship, 'as if it was the king of Scotland' in person; Douglas
feasted all his visitors from silver vessels, with a choice of wines and
spices.[43] In all this there was a propaganda value; it was as if the victorious
King Robert himself were making a triumphant procession across Europe
on his way to the Holy War.

According to le Bel, it was at Sluys that Douglas heard of the renewal of
war between Castile and Granada; but we know from his safe-conduct that
Douglas was intending to visit Castile *en route* anyway. He had little choice,
for there was no other way for a Scottish ship to get to the Holy Land except
by the Spanish coast and the Straits of Gibraltar. Barbour says that he sailed
between Cornwall and Britanny,

> . . . . . . and left the Grunye of Spanhye
> On north half hym.[44]

Grunye is probably to be identified with Corunna in Galicia; but it is
unlikely that Douglas would have sailed straight across the Bay of Biscay
without following the coast. This consideration lends credence to the
Spanish oral tradition which states that Douglas made a landing at
Santander on the north coast of Spain; in 1879 Joseph Bain was shown a
grey stone on the heights above Santander, called the rock of 'El Dugla', a
brave Scot who came to Spain centuries earlier to fight against the
Saracens.[45]

Le Bel states that Douglas landed in Spain at 'Valence la Grande', i.e.
Valencia; Barbour is more likely to be correct in saying that his arrival was
at Seville on the Guadalquivir.[46] Alfonso XI of Castile was projecting a
renewal of the war against Granada in the summer of 1330, and to this end
concluded a truce with the king of Portugal and moved to Cordoba (higher
up the Guadalquivir), where he assembled his forces.[47] It was decided that
the campaign would be directed against the Moorish stronghold of Teba de
Hardales; and it was felt that the campaign had good chance of success
because of the internal condition of the Moorish kingdom. The king of
Granada, Muhammad IV ibn Ismail, was a minor, and the affairs of the
kingdom were left largely in the control of a Moroccan mercenary leader,
'Uthman ibn Abū'l Ula (called in the Spanish sources Don Osmin); it was
rumoured in Castile that Muhammad never ventured out for fear that he

would be assassinated as his father had been, and 'Uthman was able to act virtually as king himself.[48] In the midst of these warlike preparations, Douglas and his troops arrived at Seville, and were soon summoned (presumably to Cordoba) to the presence of King Alfonso. The king offered to take them on as mercenaries, but Douglas refused, saying that he was 'intill his pilgrimage/On Goddis fais'; however as he knew that the Castilians were fighting the Moors, he would join him voluntarily.[49] Douglas was introduced to men skilled in the warfare of the region, and also met numbers of English and other foreign knights who were flocking to King Alfonso's banner. One of the foreign knights, who had heard of Douglas's exploits in the Anglo-Scottish wars, expressed surprise that his face was so free of scars, despite all the battles he had fought; clearly Sir James was something of an international celebrity.[50]

Alfonso with his army and the foreign knights marched into Granada and laid siege to Teba, probably in early August 1330. 'Uthman with a relieving force advanced as far as the Guada Teba and encamped some way from the town across the river. There was a series of skirmishes, in the course of one of which the besieged sallied forth and burned one of the Castilian siege engines; and some of the Christian forces left the camp. The army was being weakened by desertions and by 'Uthman's skirmishing tactics, and a more decisive engagement was required to break the deadlock. The Spanish Chronicle of King Alfonso XI (which nowhere mentions Douglas or his forces) describes the battle: 'Uthman divided his forces in two, sending half his army to the Guada Teba to engage the besieging forces, while keeping the rest in ambush ready to make an assault on the Christian camp and the siege works. Alfonso was warned of the ruse by his scouts, and also divided his forces, remaining in the camp himself while part of his army went to drive off the attack at the river. The Moors at the river were driven back all the way to their own camp, while 'Uthman with his own part of the army advanced on the siege works, only to find them heavily guarded by the king and his troops, 'Uthman turned back to the aid of his own retreating men, and fell upon the Christian knights who were pressing them; so Alfonso detached 2,000 knights to rescue the Christians, and the day was won for Castile. The siege was renewed with vigour; and although 'Uthman appealed to the besieged not to surrender, Teba capitulated at the end of August 1330.[51]

This battle agrees remarkably well with Scottish and other accounts of the fight in which Douglas lost his life. Fordun gives the date of his death as 25 August 1330, and Bower adds that he lost his life *apud Castrum Tibris* – at the castle of Teba.[52] Barbour states that Douglas was placed at the head of the foreign knights serving Alfonso, and that after routing the Saracens, he and the ten or so men who were with him turned back towards the Christian camp; one of his knights, Sir William Sinclair, was surrounded by Saracens, and as Douglas rode up to the rescue, he was himself caught up and surrounded by the enemy.[53] Douglas, Sinclair, and Robert and Walter Logan were all slain; they were caught by the troops of 'Uthman retreating from the unsuccessful assault on the siege camp to the rescue of the other half of his army which had been routed by Douglas and the Spaniards. Fordun also states that the Moorish army was divided, and that after routing one part of it, Douglas caught sight of 'another sultan' whose troops joined battle and killed him.[54] But it was not a reckless suicide charge which cost Douglas his life (the story of throwing the king's heart into the midst of his foes is a later invention — Barbour states that the casket containing the heart was found beside Douglas's body);[55] it was a simple tactical error which cost dearly. He and his men advanced too far from the rest of the attackers, and were isolated and easily cut down when 'Uthman and his division came up; the help that Alfonso sent came too late.[56] Le Bel states that 'it was great harm and default by the Spaniards',[57] but it is more likely that his unfamiliarity with the tactics and warfare of the Reconquista was what caused Douglas's death.

The Scottish crusade of 1330 had come to a premature and tragic end in its first major battle. Douglas and three of his knights were dead, while another knight, Sir William Keith, had been wounded earlier. Douglas's body and the king's heart were recovered from the field; the former was disembowelled and boiled, so that the flesh could be buried in consecrated ground in Spain while the bones were brought back for burial in the church at Douglas. King Robert's heart also abandoned the road to Jerusalem, and found its last resting place in Melrose Abbey; there was no-one left to take it to its intended destination.

Despite its failure as a crusade against the Holy Land, Douglas's venture did have some success in restoring Scotland to papal favour; in August 1331 John XXII wrote to the bishop of Moray mandating him to release from excommunication all those who removed the heart of King Robert from his body, and carried it with Sir James Douglas against the infidels in Spain.[58] Douglas gained nothing but praise and admiration from his enemies because of his heroic death fighting for the faith; le Bel had fought against him, and le Baker was fervently anti-Scottish, but both unite with Scottish writers in praising the acts of his last year.

There is, however, another more practical aspect of the Crusade of 1330 which is worth exploring. Scotland and England had been at war since 1296, and in the course of over thirty years a new generation (of whom Douglas was one) had grown up in an atmosphere of intermittent war and constant hostility and vigilance. What was a man like Douglas to do in a time of peace, when his whole life had been devoted to fighting? This crusade can be seen in part as a device for pacification, a way of getting the incorrigible belligerents out of the country to do their fighting elsewhere when the country was looking forward (in this case, mistakenly) to a long period of peace.

But largely due to the expansionist designs of Edward III all hopes of a new crusade against the Holy Land were to be disappointed for a further generation. In 1332, two years following Douglas's death in Spain, there was a renewal of war between Scotland and England. Meanwhile relations between England and France were deteriorating; Scotland and France were allies, and 'in 1336 the French galleys which had been assembled at Marseilles for a proposed crusade were transferred to the Channel ports'.[59] After high hopes and early successes during the early 1330s, Edward's chances of lasting success in Scotland declined, with Scottish recovery and increasing tension between England and France. In 1338, perhaps partly at least to save face after his recent reverses in Scotland, Edward III led an army across the Channel and into France to pursue his claim to the French throne, and so began the 'Hundred Years' War'. Throughout the 1340s and '50s there was warfare on both fronts, though in Scotland this was curtailed by David II's capture at Neville's Cross in 1346; not until the Treaty of Brétigny in 1360, three years after King David's release from captivity, was there a general pacification in France and a genuine chance to launch a new crusade against the Holy Land.

The principal motivating force behind the new Crusade came from the young King Peter I (de Lusignan) of Cyprus. From the time of his accession in 1359 until his murder ten years later at the hands of his own knights Peter strove ceaselessly to recover the mainland part of the kingdom of Jerusalem; his dynasty had never abandoned the title of kings of Jerusalem, but only Peter himself tried to make that title effective. His character has received different interpretations, but there can be no doubt about his burning desire for the recovery of the Holy Land.[60] From 1362 to 1364 he travelled widely in Western Europe seeking recruits in Italy, France, England, Germany, the lands to the east of the Empire, and elsewhere. In the autumn of 1363 Peter visited Edward III in London, at the same time that David II was making a pilgrimage to the shrine of Our Lady of Walsingham in Norfolk:[61]

> When he heard on his journey that the king of Cyprus was in London, he hastened at great personal trouble to see him; and the king of Scotland came to London so quickly that he had not yet departed. Thus these two kings met and rejoiced greatly together; and the king of England invited them twice to dinners at the Palace of Westminster. And so the king of Cyprus took his leave of the king of England.[62]

David's anxiety to meet the king of Cyprus is understandable, as he is known to have himself been interested in the ideals of chivalry and

Christian warfare. Bower states in his eulogy of King David that he always had an ambition to go on crusade which was prevented by his untimely death:

> This king also, after great striving, decided to go on a journey to the Holy Land against the ferocity of the pagans, and [having appointed guardians for the Kingdom] to end this present life in the land of promise. Indeed, towards this pious end he showed great and special favour and friendship to his knights and esquires, of whom at that time there were many, who had enlisted and engaged in work of that kind; and he gave and granted to them wide possessions and military honours.[63]

Although Bower states that it was death which prevented him fulfilling his desire, the financial demands of Edward III towards David's ransom must also have been a contributing factor. The brief vernacular chronicle known as the *Brevis Chronica* confirms David's crusading ambitions in terms similar to Bower's:

> Eftir his hame cuming [in 1357] he began and guvernit the realme richt weill and nobilly, and purposit to have gane to the Haly Land to fecht aganis the Turkis; but he deyt in the meynetyme . . .[64]

Bower's statement that many of David's knights and squires were recruited for the crusade, and that David showered favours and generosity on them, is of particular interest. It may be possible to point to specific instances of this crusading desire and the king's resulting favour. What seems almost beyond doubt is that this crusading fervour among the king and his knights and esquires was due largely to the influence of King Peter of Cyprus, and was directed towards his crusading schemes of the mid-1360s.

Among the Scottish knights who joined the crusade of King Peter were the brothers Norman and Walter Leslie. They had previously been on the Baltic crusade in Prussia in 1356 in company with Sir Walter Moigne and others,[65] and so were perhaps receptive to the crusading ideal. On 25 November 1363 (which must have been quite soon after King David's meeting with Peter of Cyprus), a safe conduct was issued for Walter de Leslie and eight horsemen going through England or across the sea;[66] and in the summer following the two brothers were together in Florence. They acted as witnesses to a compact between the signory of Florence and the English 'White Company', a band of mercenaries who had been made unemployed by the Treaty of Brétigny and had spent the following years fighting and plundering in Italy.[67] The Company agreed to serve the community of Florence against Pisa, having previously been employed by the Pisans against Florence; there is nothing to link the two Scots directly with this disreputable band, and it is most likely that they were used as a neutral party in the negotiations which led to the compact.[68] Attempts by the papacy to reduce the menace of the 'free companies' which plagued Italy after the cessation of hostilities between England and France, by persuading the mercenaries to join King Peter's crusade, met with little success.[69] It is likely that the Leslie brothers were in Italy for that purpose anyway, and that their encounter with the White Company was purely incidental.

Other Scots joined King Peter's crusade. William de Ramsay and David de Berclay, each accompanied by six men and horses, had safe conduct to go to the Holy Land on 5 December 1363, ten days after the safe conduct issued to the Leslies.[70] A safe conduct was issued to Walter Moigne and Laurence Gelybrand, going to the Holy Land with twelve horsemen and four servants, late in 1365; Moigne had previously served in Prussia in company with the Leslie brothers, and earlier had been captured alongside his king fighting at Neville's Cross.[71] The date of issue of the safe conduct in *Rotuli Scotiae* is too late to allow the knights time to reach Alexandria by the date of its fall (10 October 1365), but it may have been issued earlier and wrongly dated, or else the party may have set off intending to join the Cypriot forces after the start of the campaign.[72]

The writer who provides the most detailed account of the campaign against Alexandria, the poet-historian Guillaume de Machaut, was aware of the presence of a Scottish element in the crusading army. Peter's fleet set sail from Rhodes on 4 October 1365 and five days later arrived off Alexandria, totally surprising the defenders; the following day a vigorous assault was launched on the walls of the city, which met with stout resistance at first. One group attacked the Customs Gate, and was repulsed by a shower of stones from the walls:

> There was a knight from Scotland, who was not killed by the lumps [of stone], as he kindled up a fire in the gateway without stopping; he was killed, slain and undone by a great stone.[73]

Although the Scots knight's death dismayed those around him,

> Because they had enough there both of wounded and of those left behind [i.e. dead],

the attack was pressed on until the defences crumbled, and the attackers poured into the city. Alexandria had fallen to the Crusaders less than twenty-four hours after their arrival before its walls.

However, the continuance of the campaign was to be less glorious than this bright start. First of all, the victors pillaged and massacred throughout the city; and the following day, gathering their booty, they retreated to their ships, led by the English, who had had enough of fighting. Peter tried in vain to restrain them, and to persuade them to stay and defend the newly won city against the Egyptian army which was soon to be advancing from Cairo; he reminded the retreating troops that the emperor of Constantinople and the Hospitallers of Rhodes had promised to send reinforcements, and when that failed, he appealed to the soldiers' honour:

What shall the Venetians do, the Genoese and Germans, French, Scots and Spaniards, Bohemians and Hungarians? I certainly have no doubt that they will not run away, who seek to come to honour.[74]

Machaut seems to imply that these were the nationalities who were prepared to stand firm while the rest, notably the English and Cypriots, wished to evacuate with the booty as quickly as possible. It is perhaps a pleasing reflection that after more than 250 years of crusading warfare the Scots were still noted for their steadfastness. It is also of interest to note that the Scot who met this death beneath a hail of stones at the customs-house gate at Alexandria was not the only one of his nation present at that conflict, and that some of his compatriots sailed away with Peter I the following day, helpless in the face of mass desertion and an advancing Egyptian army. No attempt was made to hold Alexandria, and the Egyptians were able to reoccupy the city almost as the last of the Crusaders were boarding their galleys and sailing for Cyprus. Peter's great Crusade was over almost as soon as it began, with nothing achieved but plunder and butchery.

It is possible (though by no means certain) that the Scottish knight killed in the assault on the customs-house gate was none other than Norman Leslie. The Coupar manuscript of the *Scotichronicon* mentions the presence of the brothers Leslie at the storming of Alexandria in passing, under the annal for 1427, while describing James I's visit to Inverness in that year:

He [James I] arrested Alexander of the Isles, and his mother the countess of Ross, daughter and heiress of Walter Leslie earl of Ross and, after the death of his brother Norman Leslie, duke of *Leygaroch* in France; they had captured the city of Alexandria by force of arms in the time of the last King David.[75]

Norman Leslie was dead soon after the capture of Alexandria, since on 11 February 1366/7 King David confirmed a charter granted by his widow.[76] But it is equally possible that it was one of the other Scottish knights who perished beneath the walls of Alexandria, and that Norman died soon after.

The second half of the fourteenth century was a period in which 'chivalrous' knights carried out exploits of war against the heathen in a more independent spirit than had been the case in the age of the great Crusades of the twelfth and thirteenth centuries. These knights would travel about the Christian world, and mostly about its frontiers, attaching themselves to the cause of an institution (such as the Hospitallers or the Teutonic Knights) or a kingdom (such as Castile or Cyprus) for limited periods of time, usually at times when wars between nations were in a period of temporary abeyance; they were to all intents and purposes mercenaries or soldiers of fortune. There is a splendid epitome of the career of such a soldier in the description of the knight in the General Prologue to Chaucer's *Canterbury Tales*.[77] There have been a number of interpretations of Chaucer's intention in painting the picture of his knight, which need not concern us here.[78] But it is worth noting that there were Scots of the fourteenth century who had careers similar to the one described by Chaucer, if not so bloody or varied. We do not know of any Scots who joined Alfonso XI for the siege of Algeciras, though there was considerable English participation;[79] nor do we know of Scots serving in North Africa or Turkey. We have plenty of evidence, however, for Scots serving in Prussia with the Teutonic Knights against Lithuania, and the level of Scottish interest in the Northern Crusade in the later fourteenth century is one of the most striking features of the period.

During the later fourteenth century, up to their decisive defeat at Tannenberg (15 July 1410), the Teutonic Knights pursued an expansionist policy on the south Baltic shore; although its aim was indistinguishable from any secularist expansionism (their aim was to unite their Prussian and Livonian territories by the conquest of Samogitia in Northern Lithuania), the Knights were able to wage the campaign as a crusade, because Lithuania was a pagan duchy.[80] Consequently, they were able to enlist support and recruits throughout the Christian world, and especially in northern Europe; the battlefields of the Baltic shore became a training ground for the youthful chivalry of the age.[81] Many of the most distinguished soldiers of the day, including Marshal Boucicaut of France and Henry, earl of Derby (later King Henry IV of England), served in Prussia; Guillaume de Machaut, historian of the capture of Alexandria, joined King John of Bohemia on a crusade in Prussia, and urged young knights to seek renown in the Baltic wars.[82]

In Scotland, where there was a resumption of hostilities with England during the 1330s and '40s, it was not until the second half of the century that interest in the Prussian crusade began in earnest. It is possible that the Black Death, with the social disruption resulting from it, distracted men from the crusading ideal; but on the other hand, the mortality of the late 1340s left its survivors more prosperous than they had been before the plague, when the same wealth was distributed among a smaller number of people, and (with the thought of death on all sides, and the chance of evading death by meritorious works available) gave nobles resources with which to undertake crusades and motives for doing so. Further, during David II's later years there was a large measure of *rapprochement* with England, which opened up foreign battlefields to Scottish soldiers. Thus in 1356 the brothers Norman and Walter Leslie, with Walter Moigne and Thomas Bisset, had a safe conduct to go to Prussia with twelve horsemen, passing through England on the way.[83] Walter Leslie had returned to Great Britain by the following October,[84] when he was again seeking safe conduct to cross the sea (to an unspecified destination) with horsemen and servants.[85] In February 1362, David II requested a safe conduct from the English king for David de Berclay, squire, going with twelve men and twelve horses through England to Prussia.[86] After his return to Scotland from Prussia, David de Berclay may have joined the crusade against Alexandria, as he had a safe conduct to go with six men and six horses to the Holy Land in December 1363; this was shortly after David II's meeting with King Peter of Cyprus, and less than a fortnight after the issue of a safe conduct to Walter Leslie which, as we have seen, took him to Alexandria.[87] The death of David II in 1371 did not stop the flow of Scots to the Northern Crusade, despite the troubled state of the kingdom under the first two Stewart kings. In November 1378 Adam de Hepburn had a safe conduct to go with ten knights and ten horses to Prussia.[88] Of course, where we rely on the evidence of English safe conducts, we have no way of knowing the full number of Scots adventurers who joined the Crusade in the North; the names which survive may be only a small fraction of the total.

During the 1380s, there was a renewal of Anglo-Scottish fighting, which included French intervention on the Scottish side, and ended after the Scottish victory at Otterburn (5 August 1388); Richard II was also faced by serious opposition in England which contributed towards pacification on the Borders.[89] Knights from both England and Scotland took the opportunity of a new truce to set out for Prussia to earn glory and spoils in the fighting there. Thus when Henry earl of Derby wintered at Königsberg in 1390-91, he found a Scottish knight there, with whom he got on so well that he gave him a new year's gift of cloth.[90] Perhaps they had both been on the *reysa,* or expedition, against Duke Jogailo of Lithuania which had besieged Vilnius (Wilna) without success in the late summer of 1390.[91] Relations between Scots and Englishmen serving with the Teutonic Knights at Königsberg were not always so cordial. In 1391, after the departure of the earl of Derby (April 1391) and around the time of the summer *reysa* of Frederick, margrave of Meissen, the Prussian chronicler Wigand von Marburg recounts a sorry tale of events in Königsberg:

> Meanwhile there was dissension on the part of the English and Scots. Indeed, the Scot Sir William de Duclos was killed near the high point of the bridge; he defended himself manfully when he fell with one leg into a hole, and was killed there together with one of his houshold.[92]

This was Sir William Douglas of Nithsdale. His murder was also recorded by another contemporary Prussian annalist, John von Posilge:

> Also a lord from Scotland, the lord of Douglas, was slain by the English at Königsberg, so that there was conflict between the French and the English, so that the table of honour was not held at Königsberg; and in this way the master [of the Teutonic Knights] and the visitors arose, and went forth upon a *reysa.*[93]

The *reysa* in question was probably the summer campaign of 1391, in which the margrave of Meissen took part. Among the French knights staying at Königsberg who were offended at the incident was the famous knight John Boucicaut, later marshal of France; according to Boucicaut's anonymous biographer,

> When many foreigners had arrived in the town of Königsberg . . . a valiant Scottish knight, called Sir William de Douglas, was there slain by the treachery of certain Englishmen.

Although he was not personally acquainted with Sir William Douglas, Boucicaut (who probably had reasons of his own for disliking the English wherever he met them) took up the quarrel, 'Although there was a great abundance of noblemen from Scotland there', who were all so terrified of the English that they raised no complaint.[94] Boucicaut challenged the English to fight him over the offence, but received the reply that it was none of his business; the perpetrators expressed themselves willing to fight the Scots over the rights and wrongs of the matter, but would have nothing to do with an interfering Frenchman. According to Boucicaut's biographer, it was while things stood thus that the grand master died and was succeeded by a new grand master who immediately led out the *reysa* into Lithuania; in fact the master Conrad Zöllner von Rothenstein died in 1390, and was succeeded in 1391 by Conrad von Wallenrod; the summer expedition into Lithuania usually set out in mid-August.[95] In defence of William Douglas's companions, it is likely that Boucicaut's very partisan biographer has exaggerated their timidity in order to glorify his own hero. The French account agrees with the Prussian historians that it was the summer campaign (almost certainly of 1391) which finally put an end to the dissension between the English and Scottish volunteers. The outline of the story is fairly clear; accounts in Scottish chronicles disagree only in detail. Bower states that Douglas was chosen admiral over 240 ships going to fight the pagans, and that he was himself honoured at the head of the *mensa honoris* of the grand master; the number of ships certainly, and the place at the head of the table probably, are exaggerations, and Bower is probably also wrong to state that the murder took place *super pontem de Danskin in Spruza,* since the other sources all agree that the place was Königsberg (the natural starting-point for a raid into Lithuania) rather than Danzig. Bower adds some circumstantial details about the quarrel between Douglas and the English knight, whose name he gives as Clifford; this man has not been identified certainly, as this noble English house had extensive ramifications. Boece's account of the story is based upon Bower's.[96]

Although Bower's figure of 240 ships must be an exaggeration, there is good reason to believe the statement in the life of Boucicaut that there were plenty of Scottish knights in Prussia in the early 1390s. As well as the reference to a Scottish knight who had a gift from the earl of Derby, there is also a receipt, in fragmentary form and imperfectly dated, whereby Sir James Douglas (possibly one of the Douglases of Dalkeith) acknowledged himself bound for a certain sum of *Prutencialis monete* to Sir Robert Stewart (of Durisdeer), which he promised to repay at Danzig next Easter, failing which he would not bear arms without Sir Robert's permission.[97] Although the precise date of the document is uncertain, Sir Robert Stewart's *floruit* was about this time, and it is possible that the two knights were among those who accompanied Sir William Douglas of Nithsdale to Prussia. Nor were these the last Scots to fight with the Teutonic Knights. About 1400, Sir John de Abernethy, with two servants and harness, had permission to go to *Sprucia* for one year.[98] And at the disastrous battle of Tannenberg in 1410, where the expansionist ambitions of the Knights were finally extinguished, there was present at least one Scot: 'le bastard d'Escoce, qui se appelloit comte de Hembe', survived the battle and carried back a report of the massive losses the Knights had suffered to the French writer Ingram de Monstrelet, who reported them in his chronicle.[99] The 'comte de Hembe's' report stated that the grand master (Ulrich von Jungingen) and the Knights and others from many nations, totalling 300,000 Christians, invaded Lithuania and defeated the 'king' and his army, killing the admiral of Lithuania and the constable of Sarmach (= Samogitia?), and 26,000 others. But the king of Poland (Jogailo, who had some years before been baptised and become King Wladislaw IV of Poland as well as grand-duke of Lithuania) reassembled an army and inflicted a defeat on the Knights, killing 60,000 including the grand master; but their victory was not without cost, as they lost 10,000 Poles and six-score thousand Saracens (i.e. Lithuanians). Obviously neither army approached the size described by the 'comte de Hembe'; but Tannenberg was such a grave defeat for the Teutonic Knights that they were never again able to pursue an expansionist policy in the Baltic. The number of foreign recruits dwindled immediately, and in fact there is no record of any Scots visiting Prussia for many years after 1410; the Northern Crusade was effectively at an end. Besides, with Jogailo's marriage into the Polish royal family and conversion to Christianity,[100] it was increasingly difficult for the Teutonic Knights to present their war against Lithuania as a crusade after 1386.

The mysterious 'comte de Hembe' must have had some connection with France for his report of the battle of Tannenberg to be included in a French chronicle; possibly he was fighting with the Scots on the French side in the Hundred Years' War. But the name of his county is confusing, and it has probably undergone corruption; perhaps in origin it was a Scottish place-name which the French found difficult. Also, the early fifteenth century was not a period in which the title 'bastard of Scotland' was the exclusive property of a single person. Robert II had left some two dozen illegitimate children in a remarkably philoprogenitive career. The 'comte de Hembe' may well have been one of them, but he cannot now be certainly identified.

Thus one of the major outlets of crusading aggression was closed to Scotland. It had been popular while it lasted, offering the same spiritual rewards as the pilgrimage to the Holy Land without involving the same amount of travel. The Holy Land had not altogether lost its attraction, though; Sir Alan de Wyntoun, a relative of the chronicler Wyntoun, had died in the Holy Land after 1347,[101] while Sir Patrick Dunbar, father of George Dunbar, earl of March, had gone *ad partes Jerosolimitani* (*sic*) in 1356, and died in Crete.[102] But after the failure of the Crusade against Alexandria in 1365, interest in the Holy Land waned. There is no record of any Scottish participants in either the Barbary crusade of 1390 or on Boucicaut's disastrous crusade which ended at Nicopolis in 1396.[103] Two Scottish brothers, Alexander and David de Lindsay, enrolled in the 'Order of the Passion', a new crusading order founded by Philip de Mézières, who had been chancellor to Peter I of Cyprus and an enthusiastic supporter of his crusading ambitions.[104] The Order of the Passion was founded in 1395 to be the core of a new crusading army; but although Philip de Mézières had visions and schemes of international crusading armies launching many-pronged attacks on their heathen enemies (schemes in which he envisaged Scottish participation), these remained crusades on paper only.[105] The Crusader of the fourteenth century had increasingly become an individual seeking personal satisfaction who attached himself to an institution encamped on one of the frontiers of Christendom; the days of the *passagium generale* had faded as society became increasingly complex and the number of distractions grew. Periodically, however, in the century that followed men of exceptional vision were to look back to the great days of the Crusade, and attempt to revive the spirit of the past.

NOTES

1. Cf. E. Christiansen, *The Northern Crusades* (1980), esp. 132-3.

2. *Chron. Fordun,* 305.

3. Cf. T. Jones, *Chaucer's Knight* (1980), esp. Ch. 2.

4. *The Register of John of Halton, Bishop of Carlisle, A.D. 1292-1324,* ed. W. N. Thomson, with an Introduction by T. F. Tout (Canterbury and York Society, 1913).

5. Ibid., 15-21: cf. D. E. Easson, 'Scottish Abbeys and the War of Independence: a Footnote', *Records of the Scottish Church History Society,* xi (1951), 63-74.

6. *Reg. Halton,* 62-3.

7. He was at Jedburgh in July 1295: *Reg. Halton,* 13, 42-6.

8. *Reg. Halton,* 150-63, shows his accounts on demitting office.

9. Ibid., 300

10. Rymer, *Foedera,* i, pt. ii, 949

11. A. D. Macquarrie, 'The Ideal of the Holy War in Scotland, 1296-1330', *IR,* xxxii (1982), 83-92, at 83-4.

12. *Chron. Lanercost*, 165-6.

13. Palgrave, *Documents*, 347-8.

14. Ibid., 330.

15. John Barbour, *The Bruce*, ed. W. M. Mackenzie (1909), 46-7.

16. Cf. Ibid., 399, 506-11: cf. also M. D. Legge, 'Quelques Allusions littéraires', *Mélanges de Langue et de Littérature Mediévales offerts à Pierre le Gentil* (Paris, 1973), 479-83, at 482, and L. Brandin, 'La Déstruction de Rome et Fierabras, MS Egerton 3028, Musé Britannique, Londres', *Romania*, lxiv (Paris, 1938), 18-100, at 55-99: this is probably the text of the romance known to Barbour, or something very similar.

17. Barbour, *Bruce*, 46-7.

18. *Chronicles of the Reigns of Edward I and Edward II*, ed. W. Stubbs (Rolls Series, 1881-3), i, 226.

19. Rymer, *Foedera*, ii, pt. i, 68.

20. *APS*, i, 459.

21. The text of the Declaration of Arbroath is edited in *APS*, i, and by Fergusson; the text here is taken from *A Source Book of Scottish History*, ed. W. C. Dickinson, G. Donaldson, and I. Milne (2nd edn. Edinburgh, 1958), 151-4.

22. Rymer, *Foedera*, ii, pt. ii, 541. There is an abstract in *CPL*, ii, but this is unclear and in places misleading.

23. Cf. G. W. S. Barrow, *Robert Bruce*, (Edinburgh, 1976), 354.

24. *CPL*, ii, 239.

25. Barbour, *Bruce*, 365ff.

26. *Chron. le Bel*, i, 79ff.

27. *Chron. Froissart*, i, 35ff.

28. I. M. Davis, *The Black Douglas*, (London, 1974), passim.

29. *Chron. le Bel*, i, 63.

30. Barbour, *Bruce*, 243.

31. Rymer, *Foedera*, ii, pt. ii, 770.

32. Geoffrey le Baker, *Chronicon Galfridi le Baker de Swynebroke*, ed. E. M. Thompson (Oxford, 1889), 41-2.

33. *Melrose Liber*, ii, 329.

34. A. A. M. Duncan, 'The Acta of Robert I', *SHR*, xxxii, (1953), 1-39, at 18-22.

35. *Chron. Bower*, ii, 300.

36. *Chron. le Bel*, i, 83.

37. Rymer, *Foedera*, ii, pt. ii, 770.

38. *Chron. le Bel*, i, 83.

39. Barbour, *Bruce*, 373-4; *Chron. le Baker*, 41.

40. This charm-stone is described in *PSAS*, iv, 222: a version of the legend surrounding it is recounted in F. M. MacNeill, *The Silver Bough*, i, *Scottish Folk-lore and Folk-belief* (Glasgow, 1957), 94.

41. *Newbattle Registrum*, 100.

42. Barbour (p. 369) states that he sailed from Berwick: le Bel does not name the place from which he sailed, but Froissart, whose account is almost wholly dependant on le Bel, states that Douglas sailed from Montrose (*Monrois*, i, 37). Froissart clearly had a source for this statement, independent of le Bel; but he was writing long afterwards, and it is hard to see why Douglas and his companions should have gone north to Montrose when Berwick would have been a more natural starting point. Cf. le Bel, i, 83. I presume that *mouvoir* here means 'to persuade, encourage'.

43. *Chron. le Bel*, i, 83.

44. Barbour, *Bruce*, 369.

45. *CDS*, iii, p. xxxvii.

46. *Chron. le Bel*, i, 84; Barbour, *Bruce*, 369.

47. 'Crónica del Rey Don Alfonso el Onceno', *Crónicas de los Reyes de Castilla*, i (Madrid, Biblioteca de Autores Españoles, vol. lxvi, 1919), 173-392, at 224ff: the chronology of the Crónica is confused. It dates the assault on Teba to 'the twentieth year of the reign of King Don Alfonso . . . A.D. 1329'. But Alfonso succeeded in September 1312. Juan de Mariana, *Historia General de España*, ed. H. M. Gutierrez de la Pēna (Barcelona, 1839) iii, 451-3, gives an account which is drawn from the *Crónica* and gives the date of the assault as August 1330. As 'Uthman ibn Abu'l Ula died the following year, 1331, this is certainly the correct date.

48. *Crónica*, loc. cit: cf. D. W. Lomax, *The Reconquest of Spain* (London, 1978), 165-7; J. N. Hillgarth, *The Spanish Kingdoms* (Oxford, 1976), i, 428-9; 'Uthman's career is mentioned also in C. E. Duforcq, *L'Espagne Catalane et le Maghrib au XIIIe et XIVe Siècles* (Paris, 1966), 384-7 & nn. 458, 469.

49. Barbour, *Bruce*, 369-70.

50. Ibid., 370-1.

51. *Crónica*, loc. cit; and cf. the closely related but less detailed account in *El Poema de Alfonso XI*, ed. Yo Ten Cate (Madrid, Revista de Filologia Española, anejo lxv, 1956), 97-101.

52. *Chron. Fordun*, 353: *Chron. Bower*, ii, 301-2.

53. Barbour, *Bruce*, 372-3.

54. *Chron. Fordun*, loc. cit.

55. Barbour, *Bruce*, loc. cit.

56. Barbour says 'he had nocht with him atour ten'; le Bel says that the Scots outran the Spaniards, and so became separated. le Baker, quoting an eyewitness, states that Douglas's body bore five wounds.

57. *Chron. le Bel*, loc. cit.

58. *CPL*, ii, 345; Theiner, *VM*, 251.

59. Nicholson, *Scotland: the Later Middle Ages*, 135-6.

60. Cf. A. S. Atiya, *The Crusade in the Later Middle Ages* (London, 1938), 330ff; *A History of the Crusades*, ed. K. M. Setton (Madison, Wisconsin, 1969-in progress), iii, 353ff; Runciman, *A History of the Crusades*, iii, 441ff; for an exaggeratedly hostile view of Peter's career, cf. Terry Jones, *Chaucer's Knight* (London, 1980), passim.

61. Rymer, *Foedera*, iii, pt. ii, 723.

62. *Chron. Froissart*, i, 467.

63. *Chron. Bower*, ii, 380. The words in square brackets appear only in the Coupar Angus group of MSS of Bower.

64. *Chron. Wyntoun* (Laing), iii, 337.

65. *Rotuli Scotiae*, i, 797.

66. Ibid., 875.

67. On the Italian background, cf. J. Temple-Leader and G. Marcotti, *Sir John Hawkwood (l'Acuto): Story of a Condottiere*, trans. Leader Scott (London, 1899), esp. 30-1.

68. For the text of the agreement cf. G. Canestrini, *Documenti per Servire alla Storia della Milizia Italiano dal XIII secolo al XVI* (Florence, Archivio Storico Italiano, xv, 1851), 57-60: 'presentibus domino Gualterio Leseli de Schotia, et Normanno de Leseli de Schotia fratre suo'.

69. Temple-Leader and Marcotti, *John Hawkwood*, 51; Canestrini, *Documenti*, 85-6.

70. *Rotuli Scotiae*, i, 877.

71. Ibid., i, 678, 797, 901.

72. The date given in Ibid., 901, is 15 October 1365, five days after the fall of Alexandria; but the date given in Rymer, *Foedera*, iii, pt. ii, 788, is 20 March 1365/6. Unless they set out before the issue of the safe conduct, they must have been very late starters.

73. Guillaume de Machaut, *La Prise d'Aléxandrie*, ed. L. de Mas Latrie, (Geneva, Société de l'Orient Latin, Série historique, I, 1877), 86.

74. Ibid., 105.

75. *Chron. Bower*, ii, 488 n.

76. *Aberdeen Registrum*, i, 167: for a résumé of his career, cf. *Scots Peerage*, vii, 270-1.

77. *The Works of Geoffrey Chaucer*, ed. F. N. Robinson (Oxford, 1957), 17.

78. Jones, *Chaucer's Knight* is the most recent and hostile interpretation of this character. Cf. Chaucer, *Works*, ed. Robinson, 652, and the articles cited there, esp. A. S. Cook, 'The Historical Background of Chaucer's Knight', *Transactions of the Connecticut Academy of Arts and Sciences*, xx, (1916), 161-240; J. M. Manly, 'A Knight ther was', *Transactions and Proceedings of the American Philological Association*, xxxviii (1907), 89-107.

79. P. E. Russell, *English Intervention in Spain and Portugal in the Time of Edward III and Richard II* (Oxford, 1955).

80. E. Christiansen, *The Northern Crusades* (1980), passim, esp. 251-3.

81. Jones, *Chaucer's Knight*, 49-55.

82. W. Calin, *A Poet at the Fountain: Essays on the Narrative Verse of Guillaume de Machaut* (Lexington, Kentucky, 1974), 211; cf. A. Prioult, 'Un poète voyageur: Guillaume de Machaut et la *reise* de Jean l'Aveugle, roi de Bohême, en 1328-9', *Lettres Romanes*, iv, (1950), 3-29.

83. *Rotuli Scotiae*, i, 797.

84. Ibid., i, 814.

85. Ibid.

86. Ibid., i, 869.

87. Ibid., i, 877: a similar safe conduct was issued on the same day to William de Ramsay, going with six knights and six horses to the Holy Land.

88. Ibid., ii, 13.

89. Nicholson, *Scotland: the Later Middle Ages*, 193-9.

90. *Expeditions to Prussia and the Holy Land made by Henry Earl of Derby in the Years 1390-1 and 1392-3*, ed. L. T. Smith (Camden Society, new series, ii, 1894), 111.

91. Ibid., introduction; Christiansen, *Northern Crusades*, 158.

92. 'Die Chronik von Wigand von Marburg', *Scriptores Rerum Prussicarum*, ed. T. Hirsch, M. Toppen, and E. Strehlke (Leipzig, 1861-74), i, 644.

93. 'Johanns von Posilge Chronik des Landes Preussen', *Scrip. Rerum Pruss.*, ii, 172.

94. *Le Livre des Faicts du bon Messire Jean le Maingre dit Boucicaut*, in *Collection Complète des Memoires Relatifs à l'Histoire de France*, ed. M. Petitot, tomes vi-vii (Paris, 1819), vi, 431ff.

95. Christiansen, *Northern Crusades*, xiv, 164.

96. *Chron. Bower*, ii, 416; Boece, *Chronicles* (trans. Bellenden), ii, 354.

97. *HMC Eleventh Report*, Appendix iv, 210: cf. Ibid., 205, 211.

98. *CDS* iv, no. 593.

99. *La Chronique d'Enguerrand de Monstrelet*, ed. L. Douët-d'Arcq (Paris, Société de l'Historie de France, 1857-62), ii, 75-7.

100. Christiansen, *Northern Crusades*, 158-60, 219-222.

101. *Chron. Wyntoun*, ii, 479.

102. *Chron. Fordun*, ann. clxxvii, 375-7; Sir Patrick Hepburn of Hailes, one of whose relatives had gone to Prussia in 1378, had a safe conduct to go to the Holy Land with twelve men and horses in 1381; Rymer, *Foedera*, iii, pt. ii, 131; *Scots Peerage*, ii, 137.

103. Cf. J. Delaville le Roulx, *La France en Orient au XIVe Siècle: Expéditions du Maréchal Boucicaut* (Paris, Bibliothèque de l'Ecole d'Athènes et de Rome, fasc. xliv, 1886); A. S. Atiya, *The Crusade in the Later Middle Ages* (London, 1938).

104. N. Jorga, *Philippe de Mézières* (Paris, 1896), 491.

105. Ibid., 471, 503.

5

The Long Decline, 1410-1472

The Battle of Tannenberg in 1410 effectively brought the Northern Crusade to an end; and in the fifteenth century a taste for 'chivalry' was less marked than it had been in the previous century. There were few of the great personalities, men like King Peter I of Cyprus, Philip de Mézières, or Marshal Boucicaut, to attempt to revive the crusading spirit of earlier generations. The Great Schism in the western church, by splitting the church, had effectively deprived the crusading movement of leadership.[1] Even the Hospitallers at Rhodes, trying to hold their island possessions at the eastern extreme of the western church, were caught up in the controversy and weakened by it.[2] Early fifteenth-century Scotland was in no position to aid the crusading movement; there had been an increase in internal unrest since the death of David II in 1371, and although the Albany governors were perhaps able to restore some measure of order, there was a constant threat of renewed war with England. From 1418, there was an increase in Scottish participation on the French side in the Hundred Years' War which was to continue all through the reign of James I.[3] Some of the fiercest fighting in the whole of that long struggle happened during the years from 1415 onwards, when Henry V renewed the war and won his spectacular victory at Agincourt.

In such a climate, there was no prospect of a united Christian crusade to recover the Holy Land, or even to push back the Turks from what they had already gained. Concern for the Holy Land was usually confined to pious hopes for an improvement in the situation in the west (which could hardly have been less conducive to a crusade), or to a peaceful pilgrimage to the Holy Land. This latter was becoming more common in the later middle ages; as the aggressive crusade became more and more impracticable, the peaceful pilgrimage became increasingly fashionable.

One of the first Scots to go on such a peaceful pilgrimage in the fifteenth century was the distinguished soldier of the Hundred Years' War, Sir John Stewart of Darnley. According to the early sixteenth-century *Extracta e variis Cronicis Scocie*, he founded a collegiate church of the Virgin at Orléans, and thereafter went on pilgrimage to Jerusalem.[4] He was killed in defence of Orléans against the English in 1429.[5]

He was followed some ten years later, by the heart of King James I himself. Possibly James modelled himself on his famous predecessor Robert I, or perhaps the decision to send his heart on pilgrimage to Jerusalem was taken after his death. Whatever the reason, this pilgrimage was much less spectacular than the Crusade of his predecessor, and attracted much less notice; not even the contemporary chronicles, Bower's *Scotichronicon* and the *Liber Pluscardensis,* note the fact. The names of the bearers of the king's heart to the Holy Sepulchre are not even certainly known, and the fact itself would not be known but for its chance mention in the Exchequer records of James II. There it is recorded that an unnamed knight of St John of Jerusalem came from Rhodes, bearing the heart of the late King James, which he returned to the Carthusian monastery at Perth for burial, and received two payments of twenty pounds in 1444 and ninety pounds in 1445 for his expenses. It has been suggested that the bearer was possibly Sir Alexander Seton of Gordon, who went on pilgrimage to the Holy Sepulchre and died in the east before 30 September 1440. He lodged precious metals and jewels with a Florentine merchant at Bruges on his outward journey, presumably as surety for a loan; it seems that when he died he bequeathed his goods to the Hospitallers, and the grand master of Rhodes had recourse to litigation through his Venetian procurator at Bruges for their recovery.[6] This does not make it certain that Seton was the bearer of the king's heart, although it is very possible, as he set out for the Holy Land shortly after James's death and at the time of his own had some connection with the Knights of Rhodes, while one of the knights returned the king's heart to Scotland. Seton is known to have been a loyal supporter of James I.[7] An alternative possibility is that the bearer may have been Sir Herbert Herries of Caerlaverock, who had safe conduct to go to the Holy Land on 14 March 1438/9.[8] Possibly he and Alexander Seton of Gordon went in the same company. Herries was one of the embassy who had conducted James I back to Scotland in 1424,[9] and in the following year he was one of the jurors at the trial of Murdoch duke of Albany;[10] he had been knighted by the king at his coronation,[11] and so one might expect a career of loyalty to James I.

All these visitors to the Holy Land in the early fifteenth century were peaceful pilgrims, and one would perhaps expect a transition increasingly from belligerent pilgrimage (of the kind which continued sporadically in the fourteenth century) to peaceful pilgrimage. But that is only part of the story. Some Scots were found fighting against the Turkish menace well into the middle years of the century. The Campbell family history known as the *Black Book of Taymouth* asserts that Sir Colin Campbell of Glenorchy (1400-1480) was 'maid knicht in the Isle of Rhodos', and family tradition points to a charm-stone which Sir Colin 'woir when he fought in battell at the Rhodes agaynst the Turks, he being one of the knychtis of the Rhodes'.[12] Sir Colin was known as *Colin dubh na Roimh* because he 'wes thre sundried tymis in Rome'.[13] The tradition is so firmly rooted that it can hardly be disbelieved that Sir Colin was widely travelled in the Mediterranean, visiting Rome and fighting at Rhodes; but there is reason to doubt whether he was a knight of St John. His name never appears in the records of the Knights now preserved in Malta; he never seems to have sought promotion to any of the material benefits which the Order held in Scotland, though members of the order who had served at Rhodes were entitled to do so. His names does not appear, as a witness or in any other capacity, in any document connected with the preceptory of Torphichen or any other property of the Hospitallers in Scotland. *Argumentum ex silentio* can never be conclusive, but the complete absence of Sir Colin's name from these sources calls for explanation. A further curiosity is that he was at least three times married,[14] while the Hospitallers were a celibate religious order. He can hardly have joined the order as a widower, as his three certain marriages were all contracted after 1448, by which time Sir Colin was about forty-eight and hardly likely to be embarking on a chivalrous career in the Mediterranean; if, as seems more likely, Sir Colin's service at Rhodes came before he was married, he must have apostatised from the order in order to marry. This is unlikely in view of the honourable place he occupies in Campbell family tradition. So one is led to the conclusion that Sir Colin fought with the Knights of Rhodes in his youth (before 1448), but was not himself received into full membership of the order; the assertion that he was a Knight of Rhodes may spring from a misunderstanding of the nature of Hospitaller knighthood in later family tradition, or from some honour that was conferred on him during his service, other than reception into the knightly fraternity.

There is a contemporary example of another Scot in this position, who fought as a layman at Rhodes and was rewarded for his service by the grand master John de Lastic. In 1442 he was granted a pension out of the payment which the preceptor of Torphichen made annually to the common treasury at Rhodes; the magisterial bull conferring the pension on him was copied into the cartulary of St Giles Church, Edinburgh, where his name appears as 'Diguerus le Scot'.[15] In the magisterial registers in Malta for 1454 there appears a confirmation of this pension in favour of 'Duguethus le Scot'.[16] It has been pointed out that this name looks very like the Aberdeenshire surname of Duguid, a family which has branches in Auchenhove (Lumphanan) and Udny.[17] Probably we should read his name as 'Duguid the Scot', a name formed like 'Duns Scotus', where a man is identified by his surname followed by a term denoting his nationality. The preceptor of Torphichen at the time was brother Andrew de Meldrum, who returned from Rhodes to Scotland in 1433.[18] Udny, where the surname Duguid is common, is only five miles east of Old Meldrum; the Meldrum family had first become tenants of the Hospitallers for their properties in Ellon in 1345,[19] and in the fifteenth century members of the family became knights of the order, and Andrew de Meldrum rose to be preceptor of Torphichen.

It seems likely that 'Duguethus le Scot' was a member of his household from a neighbouring part of Aberdeenshire who stayed on in Rhodes after Andrew returned to Scotland in 1433, making a career for himself but never becoming a brother of the order, though achieving sufficient distinction to be granted a pension when he retired from active service and returned to Scotland in 1442. In the confirmation of his pension in 1454, he is described as servant of the grand master, who served the order for many years by land and sea, with manly striving against the infidels.[20]

His career, perhaps, helps us to understand better what was Sir Colin Campbell's relationship with the order of St John. Both fought with the knights at Rhodes without ever becoming members of the order (perhaps through inability to prove the necessary degree of nobility required for admission); Duguethus was granted a pension of twenty gold *écus* annually, while Sir Colin was later described as *eques auratus apud Rhodos*.[21] The two cases are very closely contemporary.

Nor were these two alone among Scots who fought in the East as the Turkish menace pushed ever nearer to, and finally overran, the walls of Constantinople. A papal letter of 1455 mentions Alexander Preston, canon of Glasgow, who 'went lately with a notable company to the Holy Land to fight against the infidels, and whose father and many others of his kinsmen have fought against the infidels in the lands of the infidels and been made knights';[22] later it was said that he 'has been fighting for about a year with twelve archers and more fighting men against the infidels'.[23] In 1461 the pope made an appeal in favour of two Scots, Richard Murray and Peter Hunter, because they 'for more than six years fought in Turkey for defence of the Catholic faith against the Turks, exposing their bodies to bloodshed, and have consumed all their goods in the said defence, so that they have become so poor that they cannot return to their native parts without the alms of the faithful'.[24] Relaxations of penance were offered to any who gave alms towards their repatriation.

There may have been Scots fighting within the walls of Constantinople as well. The Genoese captain Giustiniani, who commanded a mercenary company in Constantinople at the time of the siege (1453), had with him a siege engineer skilled in countermining, whose name is given as 'Joannes Grandus' (i.e. John Grant), and who is called a German in the Greek sources. But Grant is hardly a German name, and it has been suggested that he may have been a Scottish Grant who had served as a mercenary in Germany before enlisting with Giustiniani.[25]

Perhaps with the return of more stable conditions in the second half of the fifteenth century there was also a revival of interest in the defence of Christendom, made keener by the inexorable advance of the Turks. The papacy still called for contributions to go to the aid of the Holy Land and the kingdom of Cyprus,[26] and during the pontificate of Pius II (1458-1464) it made a last genuine effort to organise a crusade against the Turks under papal leadership. Long before becoming pope, Aeneas Sylvius Piccolomini had visited Scotland, and in his writings has left a vivid account of life in Scotland seen through a traveller's eyes.[27] When he became pope, he was remarkable for the sincerity with which he pursued his ambition for a new crusade. Having taken the cross himself, he died at Ancona in the summer of 1464, when about to set out; and it is significant that the crusading armies which disbanded on the news of his death were nearly the last forces which seriously attempted to set out on a papally summoned crusade. Apart from the pope's own small force at Ancona, there was also a small Burgundian army which marched to Marseille under the leadership of Anthony, grand bastard of Burgundy. When they learned of the pope's death, they first postponed their departure and then returned to their homes.[28] But it would be wrong to regard the Burgundian initiative in this last abortive crusade as other than sincere. Since the participation of Duke John the Fearless at Nicopolis in 1396, Burgundy had been regarded as the natural leader of the crusading movement.[29] The dukes had built up over the years a wide network of alliances embracing much of Europe and even extending beyond. Duke Philip the Good and many of his courtiers, organised into the prestigious order of the Golden Fleece, took crusading vows at the elaborate 'feast of the pheasant' in 1454, on receiving news of the fall of Constantinople; they wrote to Louis XI of France expressing their intention and asking for his co-operation.[30] In the end, relations between France and Burgundy remained in such a climate of suspicion that only the modest expedition under the bastard Anthony in 1464 set out (even it got no further than Marseille); and in the next year Burgundian troops marched into France. There had been a chance, while Pius II lived and Philip the Good was not preoccupied elsewhere, that a new crusade might materialise. That chance was lost.

Even the death of Pius II, followed less than three years later by that of his friend and supporter Philip the Good, did not altogether end Burgundian interest in the revival of the Crusades. Philip's son and successor, Charles the Bold, shared his father's ambition of territorial expansion but lacked his grasp of the realities of political and military power. He continued his father's anti-French policy, and this inevitably led him into difficulties with France's staunch ally, Scotland. It is curious that the resolution of difficulties between Burgundy and Scotland in the late 1460s helped to revive an interest in Scotland in eastern Christendom.

The Scottish parliament, in the face of worsening relations between France and Burgundy, in January 1466/7 forbade Scottish merchants to trade at Flemish ports.[31] Over the next eighteen months the effect of this embargo was felt so much that in September 1468 the town of Bruges resolved to send its own legation to Scotland in an attempt to get the ban lifted. One of the leaders of the embassy was a prominent citizen descended from the great Adorno family of Genoa, Anselm Adornes. [32] He was able to befriend the Boyds, who were still in power, and he also seems to have won the admiration of the young king James III. On 15 January 1468/9, having been knighted by the king's own hand, Adornes was created a member of the king's council. [33] James, young and impressionable, was probably at this time reading the 'Travels of Sir John Mandeville', which he had had copied in the king's chapel in 1467; [34] and Adornes was already probably planning the expedition which in the next two years was to take him to North Africa, the Holy Land, and the lands around the eastern Mediterranean.

On 19 February 1470, Anselm Adornes left Bruges on his Mediterranean voyage, which was to last for more than a year. He has left a splendid account of his travels in the *Itinerarium* written down by his son John, which Anselm dedicated in 1471 to James III of Scotland. [35] The itinerary begins with an introduction addressed to James III. John Adornes condemns those who have no interest in countries other than their own, or who through their ignorance regard other lands as inferior to their own; such errors are not made by well-travelled men with experience of other lands. Several classical *savants* are cited as examples of well-travelled and experienced men, and also Marco Polo, whose writings the author had read and greatly admired. He goes on to explain that Anselm Adornes had developed a thirst for knowledge of foreign lands, and especially of the holy places of Christendom. This desire had daily increased until the day when James III had honoured him with the belt of knighthood, when he could present himself as a true knight, as one in a thousand. His voyage was undertaken to enhance the glory of the king of Scotland, which, while already considerable, has now been further augmented; Adornes missed no opportunity to expound James's power, virtue and nobility among the barbarous and distant nations he had visited. Now, they admire James more than any other western prince, and his subjects more than any other nation. At the end of his travels Adornes requested his eldest son John to write down an account of his journey and to dedicate it to the king of Scotland, in order to make the king aware of the ways and lands of the infidel. The dedicatory introduction nowhere mentions the crusading spirit; its emphasis throughout is on how men can improve themselves by increasing their knowledge and understanding of foreign lands, condemning chauvinist bigotry and promoting tolerance.

The dedication is followed by a table on contents or sketch itinerary. Between this and the first chapter is a brief note explaining to James that it was decided to start the book with a description of Rome, omitting the lands traversed in between, as James's own subjects go often to Venice, Pisa and Milan for commercial purposes, and often to the court of Rome, which is included because of its sanctity and importance.

The remainder of the manuscript is an exact and detailed account of the journey, describing the places visited, the way of life of their inhabitants, and the character of their rulers. A careful note is taken of the date of departure and arrival and the length of time engaged on any stage of the journey. Particular stress is laid on the site of the Holy Land, which reflects Anselm's piety; his father had had a traditional devotion to the Holy Sepulchre, reflected in the building of the Adornes' church of Jerusalem at Bruges.[36] This conservative piety must be set alongside the enlightened tolerance of the introduction, which pervades the book; although Adornes' description of Islam is reasonably accurate, he is in no doubt that the faith of Muhammad is 'that perfidious sect', even though it embraces all of Libya, most of Asia, and (most recently) a substantial part of south-eastern Europe. His interest in Islam is more concerned with superficial aspects of cult than with doctrinal differences, though he shows some interest in the law of Muhammad. John Adornes even attempts to reproduce the Arabic alphabet, slipping up by remarking that the Arabs do not write, as we do, from right to left, but rather from left to right (*sic*)! Certain individuals attracted particular attention from Adornes in his narrative, including 'Uthman king of Tunis. He also devotes a lengthy chapter to 'the Sultan of Cairo, his men, money and Mamaluks', in which he comments on the quality of Egyptian coinage, and attempts to draw a picture of an Arabic gold coin. But the description of the holy places of the Holy Land, starting with the monastery of St Catherine of Mount Sinai and ending with Adornes' departure from Beirut, occupies one-third of the whole book, and was clearly for the Adornes family the climax of their journey and the main reason for travelling in the first place. After leaving the Holy Land they returned to the west *via* Cyprus, Rhodes and Southern Italy. Adornes expressed admiration for the work of the Knights of Rhodes in holding at bay the mass of Turkish might at Rhodes and in the Aegean archipelago; and he commented on the system of promotion among the brothers, whereby the young knights undertake military tasks, while the older ones receive benefices when they have reached a fitting age. Had Adornes' *Itineratium* been intended to promote a new crusade, though, one would have expected more information about the strength and organisation of the Knights, who must have been at the spearhead of any new crusade; but the description of the island is short, and as much concerned with agricultural produce, native peoples and sightseeing as with the grand master and his knights. The last twenty pages of the manuscript contain short descriptions of all the towns in Italy which the Adornes visited. The book ends with a short *conclusio*, which returns to the moralistic tone of the opening, urging the reader (though in this passage James III is not directly addressed) to seek treasures in heaven rather than on earth.

Adornes and his son arrived back in Bruges on 4 April 1471, more than a year after setting out. When he returned, he found Thomas Boyd and the Princess Mary staying in his house in Bruges, and was shortly thereafter (25 July 1471) entrusted by Charles the Bold with a new mission to Scotland: to reconcile Mary with her brother King James, and if possible to obtain pardon for Boyd.[37] They set out from Calais on 4 October, and were in Scotland early in 1472. The mission to reconcile James with his sister was a success, but the king would not accept a reconciliation with Thomas Boyd (who had discreetly remained in England while the negotiations were in progress). A letter of James III to the duke of Burgundy, dated 14 February but without year-date, should be assigned to 1472;[38] it states that Adornes had presented the duke's letter requesting a reconciliation between James and the Boyds some time before, and further suggests that Adornes deserves a reward from Charles for his diplomatic skill; on 18 April 1472 James himself rewarded Anselm with grants of forfeited land formerly possessed by the Boyds.[39] The reward was due, not only for his diplomatic skill, but also because he presented to the king the recently completed account of his travels in the Mediterranean and the Holy Land, with a flattering dedication to James.

Why did Adornes choose to dedicate the *Itinerarium* to James III? If he had been intending to promote a new crusade (which is hardly mentioned in the book), a better choice of dedicatee would have been Charles the Bold himself; as we have seen, the Burgundian ducal house had a strong interest in all late fourteenth- and fifteenth-century crusading ventures. But the *Itinerarium* is not a crusading document, unlike those commissioned by Philip the Good periodically during his reign,[40] and it does not appear that Adornes' visit to the East was primarily inspired by Burgundian interests. Charles the Bold is seldom mentioned in the book, and the editors of the *Itinerarium* rightly remark that 'il semble hasardeux de rattacher ce voyage des Adorni, père et fils, au désir de préparer une croisade éventuelle'. Another writer on the subject points out that the introduction nowhere appeals to the crusading spirit, and is dedicated to James III rather than to Charles of Burgundy.[41]

What seems more likely is that the journey was undertaken out of a mixture of family piety, a genuine desire for travel to foreign parts, and the encouragement of the young James III. Possibly the grant of knighthood, and the safe conducts which must have accompanied Adornes, constituted him in some sense an ambassador to these foreign courts from the king of Scots; the preface states that at foreign courts Adornes had propounded

James's qualities, and caused him to become the most respected western prince in Moslem eyes. A safe conduct given to Adornes by the king of Tunis styled him 'Anselm Adornes of Flanders, knight of the king of Scots'; as far as the Tunisian authorities were concerned, Adornes was acting on behalf of James, and we have no other documents from nations which he visited which can show otherwise. In a charter under the great seal, issued on 10 June 1472, in which James creates Anselm Adornes conservator of the privileges of Scottish merchants in the lands of the duke of Burgundy, he is described as a familiar knighted by the king and raised to honour,

> who was the honour of us and our kingdom before the pope and in Christian lands, and even among the distant and barbaric nations of Saracens and Turks. [42]

Here again the strong implication is that Anselm was acting on James's behalf, in some official or semi-official capacity.

The question must then be asked, what was James III's interest in encouraging Adornes? It has been mentioned that in 1467 he commissioned a copy of the 'Travels of Sir John of Mandeville' to be made for his own use; so it would seem that in his teens James took an interest in books of travel and guides to foreign lands. James also seems to have had ambitions to travel abroad himself, which were discouraged by his parliaments of 1471 and 1472; they urged the king not to seek to increase his glory by travelling abroad, but to set about the administration of law and justice in Scotland, whereby his fame would be carried abroad. [43] But James does not seem to have envisaged his own overseas travels as a crusade. Only in the parliament of May 1471 is a single resolution passed, urging the king to mediate between France and Burgundy, both at war and both Scotland's allies, to prevent war between Christians and help Europe to face the common enemy, the Ottoman Turks. [44] This is a far cry from the sort of enthusiasm which had gripped Burgundy in the 1450s, and which was to be found in Scotland itself a generation later. Probably Adornes' book was designed to suit the temperament of its reader, and to satisfy his curiosity; it is not crusading propaganda, but a careful and detailed account of wide travels addressed to a young man with a genuine interest in that subject.

The closest thing to crusading propaganda in mid-fifteenth-century Scotland was the *Scotichronicon* of Walter Bower, abbot of Inchcolm. Written in the 1430s, this great and diffuse Scottish chronicle has many more digressions on the Crusades than the works of Fordoun and Wyntoun written a generation earlier. Bower was concerned less with telling a continuous history than with cramming in as much information on as wide a range of subjects as possible. Much of Bower's non-Scottish information is drawn from the encyclopaedic *Specula* of Vincent of Beauvais written in the mid-thirteenth century, so that when Vincent's work comes to an end

Bower's continental information becomes much sparser. Bower was a moralist; he regarded Robert Curthose as having been justly punished for refusing the crown of Jerusalem, and allowed himself a pious outburst over the capture of Jerusalem by the princes of the first Crusade:

> O how far removed are present-day princes and knights from those there were at that time, who, inspired by the Holy Spirit, seemingly from every province in their hundreds and thousands took the cross to travel upon this expedition.[45]

Digressions like these, he explains, are inserted

> So that the readers will be more keenly inspired to take up such a worthy expedition; which is much impeded by the English.[46]

Bower's accounts of subsequent crusades are notably Francophile, justifying Philip II's conduct on the third Crusade while minimising the achievements of Richard I and Lord Edward.[47]

This attitude is taken a stage further in the *Liber Pluscardensis*, which is, like Bower, a continuation of Fordun's chronicle, and even more fiercely anti-English. In this, nearly every disaster which ever befell the Crusaders can be directly attributed to the treachery of the English. Richard I becomes a faithless and arrogant vassal of Philip II who plots against his lord and enters into treasonable negotiations with Saladin.[48] Such interpretations of crusading history abound throughout the book, and show how easily history can be distorted to serve the purpose of the propagandist.

While national interests hindered fresh crusades and distorted thinking on the subject, the Knights Hospitallers continued their existence as an international force maintaining a crusading outpost on the eastern fringes of Christendom. In Scotland their vigour seems to have declined in the second half of the fourteenth century, when there were few or no brothers of the order active in Scotland, and to have revived during the schism period.[49] There were Scottish brothers in the order and Scottish laymen taking service at Rhodes around the middle of the fifteenth century.[50] Most Scottish Hospitallers, before they could aspire to the preceptory of Torphichen, were required to spend a number of years at Rhodes in military activities. An exception to this general rule occurred in the 1460s. The preceptor, brother Henry de Livingston, seems to have been grooming a successor in the person of Patrick Scougal, who was an esquire in his household at Torphichen in 1458, and had become a conventual brother serving at Rhodes by 1462, the year of Livingston's death.[51] On learning of Livingston's death, Scougal hurried back to Scotland, gained possession of Torphichen, and administered it through the mid-1460s.[52] But he had not secured regular promotion to the vacant preceptory at Rhodes, and in 1466 this was conferred by the grand master on another Scot, William Knollis.[53] Knollis had not fulfilled the minimum qualification of five years' membership of the order and three years' residence at Rhodes, but he was able to procure dispensations from the grand master and the pope.[54] Scougal returned to Rhodes to dispute the case, lost, and seems to have ended his days as a conventual knight residing at Rhodes.[55]

His adversary William Knollis went on to have a long and distinguished career as a public servant, acting as treasurer to kings James III and James IV, sitting in the baronial estate in parliament, and even appearing as a merchant with ships trading with England.[56] He emerges as a figure of greater secular importance than any of his predecessors, and the secularising tendency at Torphichen is also suggested by hints that the buildings were becoming dilapidated,[57] and by the new and secular-sounding title 'lord of Saint Johns' by which Knollis became known. However, he paid his regular *responsiones* to the convent at Rhodes;[58] two protégés of his, Patrick Knollis and George Dundas, later served as conventual brothers dwelling at Rhodes, while a brother chaplain of the order, Adam Spens, was vicar of the Hospitallers' parish church of Kilbethoc in the 1480s.[59] The Hospitallers' highly developed chancery and organisation prevented even the remote preceptory of Torphichen from becoming totally secularised in the late fifteenth century, before the death of Knollis in 1510. As we shall see, later events were to draw Torphichen closer again to the Hospitallers' central institutions and their crusading origins.[60] But for the time being, it must have appeared that the house of St John of Jerusalem was sharing in the long, slow decline which affected the crusading movement, in Scotland as elsewhere.

NOTES

1. *Clement VII Letters*, 178 and n.

2. A. T. Luttrell, *The Hospitallers in Cyprus, Rhodes, Greece and the West* (Variorum, 1978); J. Delaville le Roulx, *Les Hospitaliers à Rhodes* (Paris, 1913).

3. Nicholson, *Later Middle Ages*, 249ff. passim.

4. *Chron. Extracta*, 235.

5. Nicholson, *Later Middle Ages*, 289.

6. *ER*, v, 156, 179; L. Gilliodts-Van Severen, *Mémoriaux de la ville de Bruges* (Bruges, 1913), no. 7; cf. A. I. Dunlop, *The Life and Times of James Kennedy, Bishop of St Andrews* (Edinburgh 1950), 31, 390, where the reference is incorrectly given.

7. *ER*, v, 156, 179; Dunlop, *James Kennedy*, 31, 390.

8. *Rot. Scot.*, ii, 313.

9. Ibid., ii, 244-6.

10. William Fraser, *The Book of Caerlaverock* (Edinburgh, 1873), 128-9.

11. Ibid., 129.

12. *The Black Book of Taymouth*, ed. C. Innes (Bannatyne Club, 1855), pp. ii, 15.

13. Ibid.

14. *Scots Peerage*, ii, 174-5.

15. SRO GD 45/13/123, f.22r. edited in *Edinburgh St Giles Liber*, 66-7; the name is there printed as 'Dignerus', but 'Diguerus', misreading an original 'Diguetus', seems to be the MS reading. Cf. Cowan, Mackay and Macquarrie, *Knights of St John of Jerusalem in Scotland*, 62-4.

16. Ibid, 168.

17. G. F. Black, *The Surnames of Scotland* (New York 1946), s.n. Duguid; F. H. Groome, *Ordnance Gazetter of Scotland* (1881-1885), s.n. Auchenhove.

18. Safe conducts issued to Meldrum appear in *CDS*, iv, nos. 1058, 1066, 1075, 1104, 1137; one of his few surviving *acta* appears in *Brechin Registrum*, 89-90.

19. Fyvie Castle Muniments, no. 2; Cowan, Mackay and Macquarrie, *Knights of St John of Jerusalem in Scotland*, 49-51.

20. Ibid, 168; Malta Cod. 365, f. 120r.

21. *Taymouth Book*, facing p.10; A. D. Macquarrie, 'Sir Colin Campbell of Glenorchy and the Knights Hospitallers', *Notes and Queries of SWHIHR*, xv (1981), 8-12.

22. *CPL*, xi, 158-9.

23. Ibid., 519.

24. Ibid., 590.

25. Steven Runciman, *The Fall of Constantinople* (Cambridge, 1965), 84; George Phrantzes, *Chronicon*, ed. I Bekker (Bonn, Corpus Scriptorum Historiae Byzantinae, 1838), 244.

26. *CPL*, xi, 36-7, 40, 401-2; Ibid., xii, 417-8, 493-4, 685; cf. Dunlop, *James Kennedy*, 190-3, 206, 252, 335, 368.

27. Quoted in part in Dickinson and Donaldson, *A Source-Book of Scottish History*, ii, 2.

28. Richard Vaughan, *Philip the Good* (1970), 370-2.

29. Ibid., 143-5, 216-8, 268-72, 359-72; Daniel Waley, *Later Medieval Europe: from St Louis to Luther* (1964), 181.

30. Vaughan, *Philip the Good*, 143-5, 359-60.

31. *APS*, ii, 87.

32. Le Comte de Limburg Stirum, 'Anselme Adornes, ou un Voyageur Brugeois au XVe siècle', *Messager des Sciences historiques*, xlix (1881), 1-43, at 9-10; A. D. Macquarrie, 'Anselm Adornes of Bruges: Traveller in the East and Friend of James III', *IR*, xxxiii (1982), 15-22.

33. Bruges, Stadsarchief, fonds de Limburg Stirum, 15 January 1469; Macquarrie, 'Anselm Adornes', 15-16.

34. *ER* vii, 500; cf. *Mandeville's Travels*, ed. M. C. Seymour (Oxford, 1967).

35. *Itinéraire d'Anselme Adorno en Terre Sainte* (1470-1471), ed. Jacques Heers and G. de Groer (Paris, CNRS, 1978); the portion of the text dealing with North Africa had been previously published in R. Brunschvig, *Deux Récits de Voyage inédits en Afrique du Nord au XVe siècle; Abdalbasit B. Halil et Adorne* (Paris, Institut d'Etudes orientales de la Faculté des Lettres d'Alger, 1936). These have been checked against the original MS, Lille, Bibliothèque Municipale, MS 330, for what follows.

36. N. Geirnaert and A. Vandewalle, *Adornes en Jeruzalem* (Bruges, 1983).

37. Comte de Limburg Stirum, op. cit., 22-4.

38. C. A. J. Armstrong, 'Letter of James III to the Duke of Burgundy', *SHS Misc.*, viii, 19-32; Macquarrie, 'Anselm Adornes', 19-20.

39. *RMS* ii, 1060, 1123.

40. Vaughan, *Philip the Good*, 268-9, 271-2; *Itinéraire*, 2-3.

41. *Itinéraire*, 3, 12-17; Brunschvig, *Deux Récits de Voyage*, 144.

42. Bruges, Stadsarchief, Cartulaire Rodenboek, f. 270r-v; Macquarrie, 'Anselm Adornes', 19.

43. *APS*, ii, 104; cf. Nicholson, *Later Middle Ages*, 474-5.

44. *APS,* ii, 104.

45. *Chron. Bower,* i, 279-81.

46. Ibid., i, 282.

47. Ibid., i, 431-8, 440, 492-506; ii, 111-13.

48. *Liber Pluscardensis,* ed. F. J. H. Skene (Edinburgh, 1877), 36-7.

49. A. D. Macquarrie, 'A Problem of conflicting Loyalties? The Knights Hospitallers in Scotland in the Later Middle Ages', *RSCHS,* xxi (1983), 223-32, at 223-9; Cowan, Mackay and Macquarrie, *Knights of St John,* xxxiv-xxxvii.

50. Above pp. 93-5.

51. Macquarrie, 'Problems of Conflicting Loyalties', 230; Cowan, Mackay and Macquarrie, *Knights of St John,* 168.

52. Ibid., 168-9.

53. Ibid., 168-9.

54. Ibid., 169-70, xlv.

55. He was still living in Rhodes in 1477; Ibid., 171.

56. *CDS,* iv, nos. 1567 and 1579.

57. *CPL,* xiii, 212-13; for 'St John of the Hermits' read 'St John of Jerusalem'.

58. *ER,* x, 134, 237, 363.

59. Cowan, Mackay and Macquarrie, *Knights of St John,* 171-3; *CPL,* xv, no. 107; Vatican Archives, Reg. Supp., 853, f. 227 r-v.

60. See below, pp. 114-9.

6

Castles in the Air, 1472-c. 1560

The crusading movement cannot be said to have come to an end in Scotland until after the Scottish church severed its links with the papacy in 1560. Even then the Hospitallers retained a link with Scotland for some three or four years, and after the siege of Malta (1565) some catholic Scots continued to be attracted to join the Knights.[1] Like all great and pervasive movements, the spirit of the Crusades died hard. As we shall see, the movement had one remarkable final burst of activity during Scotland's last century as a catholic (and therefore a crusading) country.

Very few Scots seem to have set out on crusades against the heathen in the late fifteenth century. A rare example is provided by Patrick Menzies, a layman of the diocese of Moray, who in 1479 vowed and decided to fight against the heathen and to visit the shrines of the apostles in Rome; however, when he arrived in Rome he fell ill, and had to be dispensed for not completeing his vow.[2]

Numbers of Scots continued to make the peaceful voyage to Jerusalem during the later years of the fifteenth century and the first half of the sixteenth. The German pilgrim Felix Fabri noted Scottish clergy among the men of many nations who were with him on a Venetian galley bound for Jaffa in the summer of 1483;[3] Sir Cuthbert Hume of Fastcastle returned to Scotland from an extended stay in Egypt and the Holy Land in 1509; Patrick Gillies, bailie of Peebles, had a respite to go to Jerusalem in 1509.[4] Aberdeen Cathedral Library included a book entitled *De Passagio ad Terram Sanctam* in 1464. When Bishop Elphinstone compiled an inventory of the cathedral's relics in March 1497/8, these were found to include relics of St Catherine, St Helen, St Margaret, and the patriarch Isaac (presumably St Catherine of Alexandria, Helen mother of Constantine, and possibly St Margaret of Antioch).[5] One of the best-documented pilgrimages to the Holy Land (cut short by death) was that of Archbishop Blackadder of Glasgow in 1508.

The details of Blackadder's pilgrimage are well known.[6] The archbishop left Scotland in February 1508, shortly after founding an altar to Our Lady of Consolation in Glasgow Cathedral; travelling *via* Rome, he arrived at Venice, where he was formally presented to the Signory on 16 May. Marino Sanudo noted that he had an income of 2,000 ducats (later he referred to him as 'that rich Scottish bishop'), and admired the eloquence of his Latin oration in praise of Venice and expressing James IV's friendship towards the Signory. On 1 June, Blackadder was among the foreign ambassadors who accompanied the doge on his ship for the symbolic espousal and blessing of the sea.[7] Less than a fortnight later, on 13 June, Blackadder drew up his will, which he lodged with the Florentine firm of Nerli.[8] This, as it turned out, was a wise precaution; Blackadder set out in a ship chartered from the Marconi of Venice early in July, with thirty-five other pilgrims (presumably all his own suite), and of these twenty-seven were killed by disease, including, on 18 July, the archbishop himself.[9] News of the disaster at sea was brought back to Scotland quickly, as it was known to the chapter of Glasgow Cathedral by 9 November 1508.[10] The ship that had carried him towards Jaffa did not return to Venice until about 14 November 1508, bearing news of the death of the pilgrims, including 'that rich bishop of Scotland, the king's relation, who was treated with distinction by the Signory'.[11]

Foreign travel was clearly as common for Scots at the close of the middle ages as it always had been; an increase of documentary evidence makes it appear that there was an increase in overseas voyages, but this may well be a distortion. Whatever the case, there must have been many Scots like Master John, whose travels are described in 'The Thre Prestis of Peblis', a poem written probably towards the end of James III's reign:

> For he has bene in mony uncouth land:
> In Portingale and in Civile the grand;
> In fyve kynrikis of Spane all has he bene,
> In four Cristin and ane hethin I wene;
> In Rome, Flandaris and in Wenys towne,
> And uther landis syndry up and doun.[12]

These travels must have been made before the final conquest of Granada by Castile was completed in 1492; but there was one Scottish knight among the foreigners who aided the Spanish conquest. Many English knights had been made redundant by the general pacification in England following Henry Tudor's dramatic victory at Bosworth in 1485, and their names, along with those of French, German, Swiss, Swedish and others, have been preserved in the Archives of the crown of Aragon (as the campaign was directed by Ferdinand of Aragon, husband of Isabella of Castille). Among these names appears that of 'Joannes Villesetun ciuitatis de Neuburch regni Escocie' under the date 4 March 1492.[13] It is doubtful if he can be identified with any certainty. It is possible that his name may simply have been Seton, rendered into Spanish as Ville Setun. Neuburch is probably Newburgh in Fife, or less likely Newburgh in Aberdeenshire. What is of interest is that, even as opportunities for crusading activity grew more limited, and perhaps tended to be replaced by peaceful pilgrimages, there were still a few Scots, like John of Newburgh, who sought out the last remaining outlets for sacred belligerence.

There can be no doubt, however, that by 1500 such belligerence had become exceptional. More common was a peaceful and scholarly interest in foreign travel, of a sort fostered by the *Itinerarium* of Adornes and the books held in Aberdeen Cathedral Library, the *De Passagio ad Terram Sanctam* already mentioned, and *De Mirabilibus Mundi;* such an interest is reflected in the heraldic ceiling of the nave of St Machar's Cathedral c. 1540,[14] and more widely ranging in the curious list of the rulers of the kingdoms of the world copied into a blank folio at the back of the cartulary of St Nicholas' Church, Aberdeen, in a hand of the late fifteenth century.[15] Some of the names on the list are familiar from the writings of Marco Polo and from Sir John of Mandeville, but many are not. At the end of the list (which contains some 147 names) is a note attributing it to 'Monsieur Robert de Pufflit chevalier natif de Lauduthie de garles', who spent twenty-eight years visiting all these kingdoms.[16] This person cannot be identified as Scottish; he may well be Welsh, as 'Lauduthie' looks suspiciously like a Welsh place name beginning in Llan- (e.g. Llandaff), and 'de garles' might be a misreading or misspelling of 'de Galles' i.e. Wales. As the list, like this note, is in French, the whole may have been copied from a French travel book which had been acquired by one of the canons of St Nicholas. There are a few marginal notes in a later (early sixteenth-century?) hand: 'le Roy de Lettoria – Crestyne with fyr' (which indicates only that the list dates from later than the conversion of Jogailo in 1386);[17] 'le Grant Cane de Castenne [i.e., the Khan of Cathay] – hethynne'; and one which suggests an interest in natural history: 'le Roy de Harzem – her ar ye olifants'.

Most of the interest in the Holy Land so far in this chapter has been peaceful, removed from the aggressive crusading spirit. But in the early years of the sixteenth century the crusading movement underwent a remarkable revival in Scotland, led by the extraordinary personality of James IV. It is uncertain from what source James derived his interest in the crusade. Certainly, there was much talk during the early years of the sixteenth century throughout Europe of a new crusade to push back the Ottoman menace, as it swept on past Constantinople towards Vienna. Charles VIII of France is said to have toyed with the idea of using his successful invasion of Italy in 1494-5 as a springboard from which to liberate the Holy Land; Maximilian the Emperor is also said to have had crusading ambitions on the occasions when he was not preoccupied with the dynastic advancement of the house of Habsburg.[18] There was plenty of propaganda favourable to crusading being produced in the early years of the sixteenth century, of which two examples will suffice: one is the curious *Livre des trois filz de Roys,* which has already been mentioned in an earlier chapter;[19] and the other is the poem *The Ship of Fools* by Alexander Barclay.

'*Le Livre des trois filz de roys, cest assavoir de france, d'Angleterre et d'escosse, lesquelz en leur jeunesse pour la foy crestienne soustenir, au service du Roy de secille eurent de glorieuses victoires contre les turcz*' cannot be taken in any sense as historical evidence for any earlier period, such as Earl David's supposed participation in the third Crusade. But as a product of its time, published in Paris in 1504, it can certainly be viewed as an advocacy of peace and co-operation between the rulers of France, England and Scotland from which victories over the Turks could be the eventual outcome. It is couched in the language of a romance, involving stock situations and characters (such as a prince who suppresses his identity and achieves notable victories in a subordinate capacity, and the traditional figure of romance, Fierebras); but its message is essentially a crusading one. *The Ship of Fools* by Alexander Barclay was written probably in 1509, and contains a flattering address to the new young king of England; Henry VIII is told that he may 'get with his owne hande Jerusalem agayne', as he surpasses Hercules in manhood and Achilles in strength, and that he shall attack the Turks and Saracens and recover Jerusalem and the Holy Cross:

> And ye christen Prynces who so euir ye be,
> If ye be destytute of a noble Captayne,
> Take Iamys of Scotlande for his audacyte
> And proued manhode; if ye will laude attayne
> Let hym haue the forwarde, haue ye no disdayne
> Nor indignacion, for neuir kynge was borne
> That of ought of warre can shew the unycorne.

> For if that he take onys his spere in hande
> Agaynst these Turkes strongly with it to ryde,
> None shall be able his stroke for to withstande
> Nor before his face so hardy to abyde;
> Yet this his manhode increasyth not his pryde,
> But euir sheweth he mekenes and humylyte
> In word and dede to hye and lowe degre.

The appeal concludes:

> If the Englisshe Lyon his wysdome and ryches
> Conioyne with true loue, peas and fydelyte
> With the Scottish vnycornes myght and hardynes,
> Than is no dout but all hole christente
> Shal liue in peas wealth and tranquylyte;
> And the holy londe come into christen hondes,
> And mony a regyon out of the fendes bondes.[20]

It is impossible to say whether or to what extent these, or any other, items of propaganda influenced James IV in the formation of his own crusading ambitions. It is clear, though, that propaganda of this kind was very common, and that Christian princes spent much of their diplomatic time paying lip service to the ideals which lay behind it. What is unusual about James IV is the way in which the crusading ideal seems to have become something of an obsession with him; alone among the princes of Europe he took seriously the Ottoman threat, and was also genuinely concerned for the wellbeing of the Holy Land.

What was to culminate in a fatal attempt to promote peace and a new crusade started with a simple desire to go on pilgrimage to the Holy Land. Rumours of the king's intended pilgrimage were circulating as early as March 1507, when Hugh O'Donnell of Tyrone wrote to James trying to dissuade him from a lengthy pilgrimage overseas, as the country needed his presence.[21] James replied that he would not be dissuaded, but that he would not leave his kingdom until it was safe to do so.[22] Towards the end of 1507 and in the early months of 1508 he dispatched a series of letters to Louis XII and his supporters as a result of a meeting with sieur de la Mothe, who had just been to Jerusalem and Alexandria.[23] It is likely that the pilgrimage of Archbishop Blackadder, who left Scotland early in 1508, had been intended to gather information for the king's own intended pilgrimage. There is no doubt that the king and O'Donnell were not alone in taking the project seriously, because in 1508 James received a gift from George Brown, bishop of Dunkeld, of forty chalders and seven bolls of oats towards the financing of his pilgrimage to Jerusalem and the Holy Sepulchre.[24]

But James had also begun to develop plans for the construction of a fleet, which would make Scotland a power to be reckoned with in north European waters;[25] and it was not long before he started thinking about combining his ambitions of military glory with his projected pilgrimage to Jerusalem. Early in 1508 James wrote to the master of Rhodes thanking him for his letters delivered by hand of James's former familiar, brother George Dundas, a man of fine accomplishments who had committed himself to warfare for Christendom; James had learned of renewed warfare between the knights and the Turks, and wishes them success.[26] Towards the end of 1509 James's ideas became more definite. He wrote to Pope Julius II, saying that Louis XII had informed him of the pope's intention to summon an expedition against the Turks and to lead it himself. James declared that he was prepared to shed his blood for Christendom, and may have embarrassed the pope by asking whether he should be ready to set out the following year. In February 1509/10 Julius replied, telling James that he had come to terms with the Venetians, whose position and maritime strength would be invaluable to the proposed crusade.[27] During the first six months of 1510 James was actually involved in secret negotiations with the Venetians in an attempt to have himself provided to the vacant post of captain-general of the Venetian fleet;[28] but by the end of the year the Venetians were more concerned about winning James away from his alliance with Louis XII and into the fold of the 'Holy Alliance' of Spain, England, Venice and the papacy against France.[29]

While James was dabbling innocently with ambitious schemes of world domination, the realities of his position were becoming more difficult. He had perhaps misinterpreted Henry VII's policy of peace and conciliation as a sign of English weakness, and so was unprepared for Henry VIII's unscrupulous aggressiveness. The Holy Alliance made the prospect of a united expedition more remote, and with England becoming increasingly unfriendly, forced James to rely more and more on the effusive promises of the king of France. From 1510 onwards France was at odds with both Venice and the papacy, and for James's plan to have any prospect of success required the co-operation of France, Venice and the pope.

Although the time was inauspicious, James single-mindedly pursued his scheme. At the end of 1510 he sent an ambassador, Andrew Forman bishop of Moray, to France and then on to Rome to negotiate a general peace.[30] Forman presented Louis XII with a detailed calculation of the number of cannon, ships and men that would be required, reminding him of his promise to set James in overall command since he was prevented from going himself due to ill-health.[31] However, in the course of 1511 relations between Louis and Pope Julius continued to deteriorate, as the former would not abandon his strong position in Italy, and the latter found it unacceptable; by June, Forman had been sent back to France by Julius with uncompromising demands, and the duchess of Savoy was informed that 'in conclusion, there is no longer any great hope for this Scottish project'.[32] Later in the summer, James wrote to the pope, regretting the breakdown in negotiations; the latter wrote back in January 1511/2, holding out the (incredible) prospect that the Holy Alliance might turn against the Infidel after France had been defeated, and encouraging James to join it.[33] In the same month, Louis XII informed Forman that the time was no longer propitious for a crusade against the Turks.[34] Events continued to go badly for James and his project, when a creation of cardinals came and went in March 1511/2 without Julius II fulfilling his promise to make Forman a cardinal at the next creation.[35] All indications are that James was being used by the parties in their own interests, with little regard for his aspirations. James's first serious attempt to launch a crusade had failed in its earliest stages.

James, however, was now bent on his project. The response from the princes of Europe had been polite, even flattering; and he still believed that there was a chance of a united Christian expedition setting out against the Turks under himself as leader. James wrote again to the pope about the project, and Julius replied in July 1512 that the project 'may now become feasible'.[36] But by September Louis XII had persuaded James to renew the Franco-Scottish alliance, while James was complaining of the pope's unfairness and harassment by Henry VIII.[37] Certainly throughout 1512 there was a deterioration in relations between Scotland and England, for which Henry must be held largely responsible. In April 1513 Henry insultingly told Cardinal Bainbridge in Rome that King James was 'more anxious to succour the king of France than for the peace of Christendom or any expedition against the Turks, for which he has no wish, and no ability if he had the wish'.[38] Henry also tried in vain to intercept Forman, who was setting out on a fresh mission to try to head off war between France and the Holy Alliance, but Forman arrived at the French court by 17 April 1513.[39] If he and James had hoped for any greater success with Julius II's successor Leo X, they were to be disappointed; Leo angrily wrote to James urging him to break with the king of France,[40] and sent Henry VIII a secret interdict to be published as soon as the Scots broke the peace.[41] James still believed that the best chance for him to be at the leadership of a new crusade was with the help of the king of France, whom he sincerely believed to have been wronged by the pope and by Henry VIII. He showed the English ambassador in Edinburgh 'a little quayr of four sheets of paper sowed together and signed at the end with the Frenshe Kyngs hand', promising James a levy of a tenth on all his kingdom within a year of peace being established, and a number of men-at-arms, guns and ships for the expedition. When James had read this aloud to the ambassador he added, 'Now ye see wherefore I favour the French king, and wherefore I am loth to lose him; for if I do I shall never be able to perform my journey'.[42] James even stated that he was prepared to appeal to the fabulous oriental king Prester John if he could not get justice from the pope, though this was probably meant as a joke.[43]

In the end Henry VIII's harassment and Louis XII's blandishments combined to throw James's weight on to the side of the French. As Henry prepared to cross into France, James 'sent eleven ships into Britanny to assist France, including one of one thousand tons and two of five hundred, the others of less burden. Part of these ships had been built for an expedition against the Infidels', as the Signory of Venice were informed.[44] When Henry did invade France in August, James marched into the north of England, to meet disaster and death at the hands of an English army at Flodden on 9 September 1513, largely due to James's own military incompetence.[45] He died excommunicate, as Henry published the papal bulls against him immediately war was declared.

The battle of Flodden, and the diplomatic manoeuvrings which led up to it, have received plenty of notice from historians, and a number of different interpretations. James IV has been described as a 'moonstruck romantic, whose eyes were ever at the ends of the earth'.[46] On the other hand, it has been commented that 'this project . . . had overtones that were quixotic, and the problems that it raised were possibly insurmountable';[47] but also that 'never before did western Europe stand in greater need of a grand crusade' because of the Turkish menace to Hungary and Austria and in the Mediterranean.[48] Another scholar has contended that 'An alliance of the princes of Europe against the invaders would have made very good sense . . . [but] they lacked James's breadth of vision, and their only interest was their own aggrandisement'.[49] It has also been pointed out that 'James did not [understand] that the dream [of a re-united Christendom] could never be realised'.[50] James IV and his ambitions can only be understood in the context of a continuing historical process – the crusading movement. Scotland stood squarely within that tradition at the beginning of the sixteenth century, as it had done throughout the middle ages. Insofar as it had any validity at all, the crusading ideal was no less valid in 1513 than in 1095; and it must not be forgotten that only the death of Pius II had prevented the departure of a crusading army in 1464. But James IV did not reckon with the greedy, ambitious princes of his day; Julius II, Louis XII, Henry VIII and Ferdinand of Aragon were 'machiavellian' in their approach to diplomacy. Machiavelli himself was almost certainly referring to Ferdinand of Aragon when he wrote in *Il Principe* of 'A certain contemporary ruler, whom it is better not to name, [who] never preaches anything except peace and good faith; and he is an enemy of both one and the other, and if he had ever honoured either of them he would have lost his standing or his state many times over'.[51] To this extent James's ideals were 'medieval' rather than 'renaissance'; but it is doubtful if either designation has much real value except as a label of convenience. It was just possible, for a brief period in 1511 before Julius's final and irreparable breach with Louis XII, that a united crusade could have been organised; had it been, James IV would probably have occupied a prominent place in it. But the opportunity passed, leaving James stranded on the wrong side (in that no crusade could have been organised without papal support, or the help of the Venetians); in the circumstances of 1512-13, the project was much less realistic, and it was in his attempt to pursue it while keeping faith with his allies (which no-one else was prepared to do at the time) that James prepared his own fate. But subsequent interpretations of the events of the previous five years are bound to be coloured by the magnitude of the disaster of Flodden. This could almost certainly have been prevented by more skilful generalship on James's part, and the use of more up-to-date military equipment. As long before as 1498 the Spaniard Pedro de Ayala had detected the tragic flaw in James's military ability: 'He is not a good captain, because he begins to fight before he has given his orders'.[52] The irony of Flodden is that it resulted from an attempt by James to prove to the world that he was a great military leader – and the result was catastrophic.[53]

As news of the magnitude of the disaster spread through Scotland, it was accompanied by a rumour that the king had survived the battle, badly wounded, and had retired to live as a hermit in the Holy Land.[54] With James's death ended the last revival of interest in Scotland in the crusading movement or in the wellbeing of the Holy Land. James V's interest in the church was largely confined to seeing how much money he could extort from it; in diplomatic terms he was much more 'machiavellian' than his father, in that he seldom honoured his promise and was a match for his slippery contemporaries.[55]

There are a few instances of contacts with the Holy Land and the crusading institutions into the sixteenth century. In 1520 a monk of St Catherine of Mount Sinai was in Edinburgh recruiting members for the confraternity of Mount Sinai, and succeeded in recruiting Richard Maitland of Lethington into the confraternity.[56] On the whole, James V's correspondence is devoid of the frequent references to crusading which fill the letters of his father.[57] But the king was impressed by Thomas Doughty, who had fought against the Turks in the eastern Mediterranean and returned to Musselburgh in 1533 to establish a hermitage of Our Lady of Loretto in the burgh, modelled on the shrine of Loretto in Italy;[58] James gave to his chapel materials for making vestments and altar-cloths in 1534 and 1537,[59] but some contemporaries influenced by reforming ideas from the continent were sceptical of the genuineness of the hermit and his miracles.[60] Another hermit, John Scott of Jedburgh, was also under suspicion from men of reformed opinion for his doubtful relics of the Holy Land.[61]

It has been correctly stated that 'as the unity of the medieval church collapsed in the middle decades of the sixteenth century, the Scottish pilgrims to the Holy Land grew fewer and fewer';[62] they also appear to have been treated with less respect on their return. Pilgrimage, like crusade, was a declining fashion. It is worth noting also that when Erasmus published his criticism of warfare against the Turk (1529) he sent a copy, along with a dedicatory letter, to his former pupil and colleague, Hector Boece, principal of King's College, Aberdeen.[63] Boece had been brought to Aberdeen by Bishop William Elphinstone, who had himself been an opponent of the policies which led James IV to Flodden.[64] Boece's *History*, apart from its extended (and, as we have seen, probably fabulous) account of Earl David's participation in the third Crusade, has surprisingly little to say about crusading Scots. In 1248, the Scots who followed Louis IX to Egypt 'war all slayne in Aphrik throw excessyve heeit and pest'.[65] Sir James Douglas in 1330 is made to carry Robert I's heart to the Holy Sepulchre, then 'went with his folkis to vthir Cristin princes quhilkis had scharp weris for the tyme aganis the Saracenis . . . and be frequent victorijs, wan grete honour to all Cristin pepill'. At last he took service with the king of Aragon (*sic*), with whom he won many battles in Spain, until 'he became negligent, havand his inimyis at contempcioun, throw quhilkis he was slayne with all his folkis'. Boece's final judgement on Douglas, reflecting perhaps his views on crusading in general, is that 'oure grete confidence in fortoun . . . bringis mony nobill men to deth'.[66]

Some more conservative writers did not share Boece's doubts about the Crusades. Adam Abell, observant friar of Jedburgh, seems to reflect fourteenth-century attitudes when he equates the English enemy with the enemies of Christ, in a passage partly based on Bower's account of the first Crusade:

> O quhow gret zeill had the Cristin men of that thyme, in regard of thame at now is in the yle of Britaine, at nowthir for fayth na iustice will fecht, bot geweis thame all to cowiteis and carnaill life! Quhar ar the nobill men at wer wont to defend the borduris? All ar now to seik; bot thair ar our mony fosteraris of thewis and fals coleigis of the Ynglismen.[67]

This attitude is perhaps understandable, having been written in a border town c. 1537, after the trouble of James V's minority. It seems something of a throwback to more traditional attitudes when compared with the humanism of Boece.

The most important 'survival' of the crusading movement in sixteenth-century Scotland was undoubtedly the Hospitaller preceptory based on Torphichen. We have seen that William Knollis, preceptor 1466-1510, has a greater significance as a public servant, diplomat and merchant than as a member of a crusading order.[68] This is a development which one might have expected to continue into the sixteenth century; but the process was halted by a quite unexpected turn of events. Brother George Dundas, knight of the Order, was in Rhodes in 1504, where he procured the right of expectation to succeed to the preceptory of Torphichen when Knollis should die or resign.[69] A grant of right of expectation was a common method of succession to Hospitaller preceptories, ensuring continuity without a vacancy and allowing the successor to act as co-adjutor during the last years of the predecessor's preceptorship. At any rate, Dundas, probably nominated by Knollis, was presented by the corporation of English knights, called the English 'tongue' or *langue* at Rhodes, and granted the expectation by the lieutenant grand master on 1 July 1504.[70] In March 1507/8 he was back in Scotland, and presented letters from the grand master to James IV, informing him of the state of war between the Knights of Rhodes and the Turks. James replied to the master that he was delighted to learn that Dundas had committed himself to warfare for Christendom, having formerly been a member of the king's household, and he thanked the master for the Order's continuing favour to Scots and recognition of their deserts.[71] On 30 November 1508 a mandate was issued under the privy seal to admit Dundas to the temporalities of Torphichen, on the grounds that he had been provided by the master of Rhodes. In July 1510, James IV issued a safe conduct for Dundas, 'Lord of St Johns', to pass with a substantial retinue to Rome and Rhodes.[72]

Despite the wealth of documentation about the quarrel which ensued, it is not immediately obvious why the matter of the Scottish preceptory should have become such a *cause célèbre*. James was perhaps concerned partly because of the very influential position which Knollis had occupied when he was master of Torphichen; perhaps also as his own concept of the virtues of war against the Infidel became something of an obsession he felt that the Hospitallers could be used to assist him in achieving his crusading ambitions; a third consideration is that, as Henry VIII became an increasingly difficult neighbour from 1509 onwards, James became increasingly suspicious of anyone who had secured promotion with English help – as Dundas, approved by the English brothers at Rhodes, had undoubtedly done. But most immediately the trouble was started by the ambition of James's secretary, Patrick Paniter. Dundas cannot have been long out of the country when Paniter secured papal provision to Torphichen, 'vacant by the death of William Knollis'.[73] By the summer of 1511 Dundas, who may still have been at Rome, secured a sentence against Paniter at the *curia* upholding his right to the preceptory. During the autumn of 1511 and the early months of 1512 Paniter and his royal patron bombarded various agents at the *curia* with a series of letters putting forward Paniter's claim to Torphichen.[74] Dundas further alienated James IV by enlisting the help of the cardinal of York at Rome, as well as that of the English *langue* at Rhodes. Litigation dragged on into 1513, while the situation between England and Scotland continued to deteriorate. On 31 March 1513 James IV wrote to Guy de Blanchefort, the grand master, expressing his astonishment on learning that preceptories and their expectations in Scotland were granted out by the Turcopolier, the senior officer, and *langue* of England, even if to Scottish subjects, and that Scottish responsions were paid through the prior and treasurer of the Order in England; he complained that Scottish members of the Order must look upon the Prior of England as lord and protector, and take before him cases touching the preceptory of Scotland. James claimed that he had not been aware of this before the case of Paniter against Dundas had brought it to his notice, otherwise he would never have tolerated such a situation.[75]

In the summer of 1513 James and Paniter wrote again to the grand master reasserting that no Scot should be installed at Torphichen if he held the Prior of England as superior 'on the pretext that Scotland is English-speaking' – presumably a reference to the fact that Scotland belonged to the English 'tongue'. Paniter added that he hoped, 'if he lives long enough', to augment the membership of the order in Scotland, revive its services in Scotland which had been 'extinct for so many years', and repair and rebuild the 'houses and half-buried churches of the Order'.[76]

If this is an accurate description of the state of the Order of St John in Scotland, it is certainly not a reflection on the conduct of Dundas. He had

J

left the country late in 1510, a few months after the death of Knollis, and had been unable to return while the hostility of James IV and Paniter was directed against him. Rather, it probably reflects (if true) on the long and seemingly worldly career of William Knollis. James's attempt to substitute another public servant in his place instead of Dundas could hardly have been expected to lead to the 'revival' of the Hospitallers in Scotland.

The death of James IV and others at Flodden was not the end of Dundas's problems in respect of Torphichen. The temporalities were taken over by Alexander Stewart, half-brother of the Duke of Albany.[77] On 20 January 1516/17 the Regent Albany wrote to Pope Leo X on his brother's behalf, complaining that Dundas had still not proved his case satisfactorily, that he would be unreliable in such an important position as the preceptory of Torphichen, that he had obtained bulls through English intervention at Rhodes, and that he had lately had safe passage through England to Scotland and had sent messengers back by the way he had come.[78] Possibly had the Regent continued to oppose Dundas, the latter would never have been able to make his possession of Torphichen effective; but Albany returned to France in the summer of 1517, and the following years saw an Anglo-French *rapprochement*,[79] which must have made George Dundas's division of loyalty easier to accommodate. In October 1521 he was able to resume the payment of responsions to Rhodes *via* John Babington, English receiver of the Common Treasury.[80] He also repaid money loaned him by Thomas Dockwray, Prior of England, for the defence of his rights to the preceptory at Rome, and for his journey back to Scotland, presumably at the end of 1516. But he consistently refused to pay responsions which the Common Treasury demanded for the five years when he was excluded from possession of his preceptory, until in 1526 Dockwray and the Treasury agreed to remit the outstanding debts.[81] Dundas was clearly firmly installed in his position at Torphichen from 1518 onwards. In 1525 his nephew, Walter Lindsay, and John Chalmers, both of whom had fought at the siege of Rhodes in 1522, were received into the English *langue* at Viterbo as brothers on 19 December 1525.[82] In January 1527/8 Chalmers was present in the English *langue* at Nice submitting proofs of his nobility, and he was still there a year later, requesting the expectation of Torphichen provided this did not prejudice Dundas or Lindsay.[83] In September 1530 the grand master wrote to James V, 'one of the Christian princes whom the Order acknowledges as patron and protector', informing him that after the loss of Rhodes and their eight years of wandering the Hospitallers had finally found a new home on Malta.[84] These facts suggest regular and amicable contact between Scotland and the central organs of the Knights of St John during the active preceptorship of Dundas, during which the disputes of the second decade of the sixteenth century were forgotten.

The last thirty years of the history of the Knights of St John in Scotland do not show any evidence of the decline in the religious order which might be expected. George Dundas, whose possession was undisturbed after the period of his enforced absence from 1510 to 1517, died in 1532, and in March 1532/3 Walter Lindsay was in Malta to procure bulls granting him the preceptory of Scotland in succession to Dundas.[85] Although he may have been the only brother resident in Scotland, Lindsay was not the only Scot in the Order at this time; Chalmers, having had confirmation of the pension owed him by Lindsay, was present in Malta in April 1533 attending deliberations of the English *langue*, and in 1538 Alexander Dundas was received as a brother of the English *langue* and in 1539 attended its deliberations.[86] He may not have lived long enough to receive a grant of the *ancienitas* of Torphichen; that concession was granted in 1540 to James Sandilands of Calder, who had safe conduct from James V to go to Malta for that purpose in April of that year, and arrived in Malta by December, where he made proof of his nobility and was received as a brother of the *langue*.[87] In March 1541 the Grand Master de Homedes conferred the grant of *ancienitas* and appointed Sandilands procurator of the Common Treasury in Scotland. On his way home to Scotland Sandilands paused in Rome to secure papal confirmation of his right of expectation.[88]

Walter Lindsay died in 1546. During his preceptorship he compiled a rental of the baronies of Torphichen, Thankerton (Lanarkshire), Denny (Stirlingshire), Temple of Balantrodoch, and Maryculter, the churches of Maryculter, Aboyne, Tullich, and Inchinnan, and various assorted lands (including Galtway), and also of hundreds of tiny crofts and 'templelands' dotted across Scotland from the Solway to the Pentland Firth.[89] Lindsay also erected in 1538 a fine monument in Torphichen church to his uncle and predecessor George Dundas.[90] He was one of the leaders of the Scottish army on the Borders in 1542, in which capacity he was described as 'ane nobill and potent lord . . . who was weill besene and practissit in weiris baitht in Itallie and had fouchtin oft tymeis against the Turkis witht the lord of the Rodis, and thair he was maid knycht for walleiand actis and thaireftir come in Scotland and seruit our king and had great credit witht him'.[91] A career such as his is a caution against assuming that Scots joined the Hospitallers only in order to control the wealth of the preceptory of Torphichen.

In March 1547 his successor, James Sandilands, procured bulls at Malta from the Grand Master de Homedes presenting him to the vacant preceptory of Torphichen, which were confirmed by the pope in May of the same year.[92] It was not until the summer of 1550 that he actually was given formal possession of the spiritualities and temporalities of Torphichen and its pertinents in a ceremony presided over by brother Peter Ourrier, a knight of the French *langue*.[93] In addition to James Sandilands, there seem to have been two other members of the Sandilands family who were Knights of Malta. In May 1555 'Sir James Sandilands the Younger' had a grant of the expectation of Torphichen from the English *langue*,[94] while later there appears a brother John James Sandilands.[95] The senior James Sandilands, Preceptor of Torphichen, was in Malta in 1557, when he quarrelled with John James, and was requested to recover properties of the Order which had been set in feu by his predecessors.[96] He seems to have had associations with the Lords of the Congregation well before 1560;[97] in about 1563 he married a 'noble lady', Janet Murray, who had earlier been enfeoffed with Hospitaller property in Kirkliston. When the Lords of the Congregation sent him to France on an embassy to Queen Mary in 1560, she had observed that he could hardly be called Grand Prior of Scotland, as he had a wife. Finally in February 1563/4 James Sandilands resigned all the property of the Hospitallers in Scotland into the hands of the Queen, and (in consideration of his payment of 10,000 crowns) had a regrant of them as a hereditary barony of Torphichen.[98]

Although in later times catholic Scots had connections with the Knights of Malta,[99] the old base for recruitment and revenue-raising was gone after 1564. Still, it is worth looking at the contrasting careers of two late Scottish Hospitallers. The first of these is brother John James Sandilands, perhaps the last Scottish Knight of Malta before the Reformation. In May 1557 he was imprisoned for his part in a brawl with James Sandilands. In November of the same year (now released) he was allowed a term of one year in which to produce proofs of his nobility to answer James Sandilands' accusations against it. Throughout 1558 and 1559 he frequently attended meetings of the English *langue* at Malta, where he was residing. In December 1559 he requested to be granted the expectation of Torphichen, which seems to have provoked a dispute with brother James Sandilands, Preceptor of Torphichen, the result of which was that the grand master appointed commissioners in August 1560 to give possession of Torphichen to John James when it should next become vacant. But John James's subsequent career was not to be a happy one. Perhaps it was through necessity that he sold his house in Birgù in 1562. In September 1563 he got into a fight in church as a result of a gambling-game, of which the prize seems to have been a black slave (male); this led a few days later to an altercation with a senior officer of the English *langue*, as a result of which John James was deprived of the habit of the Order. Not having learned from his earlier punishments, John James was in trouble again in July 1564, accused of sacrilege and theft in the Church of St Anthony in Malta; he was found guilty and executed.[100]

John James Sandiland's quarrelsome career contrasts strikingly with the steadfastness of James Irving, who fled Scotland rather than subscribe to Confession of Faith c. 1567. He was received into the Order at Malta in 1569, and persuaded the grand master to allow him to petition for a benefice of the English *langue* outside Scotland.[101] In 1572 he went to Rome and on to France, persuading the pope and cardinals that he could do useful work on their behalf in Scotland.[102] He was probably betrayed by English spies at the French court, and was imprisoned and tortured immediately on his landing in Scotland in 1573. In the following year he was at liberty, but subject to such close scrutiny that he can have done little catholicising.[103]

A career such as his suggests that the Knights, with their prestige increased by their victory in the siege of Malta in 1565, still attracted young catholic nobles who were out of sympathy with the reform movement in their own country. But Irving's attempts to restore Scotland to the Roman catholic fold were doomed from the start. He was building castles in the air no less than was James IV sixty years earlier, in a world that was changing too rapidly to allow men time to think about crusading.

NOTES

1. See below, pp. 118-9.
2. Vatican Archives, Reg. Supp. 786, f. 236.
3. 'The Wanderings of Felix Fabri', in *PPTS*, vii, 208-9.
4. McRoberts, 'Scottish Pilgrims', 91; *RSS*, i, no. 1821.
5. *Aberdeen Registrum*, ii, 167.
6. McRoberts, 'Scottish Pilgrims', 92-5; John Durkan, 'Archbishop Robert Blackadder's Will', *IR*, xxiii (1972), 138-48.
7. *CSP Venice*, i, no. 903, 904.
8. Durkan, 'Blackadder's Will'.
9. *CSP Venice*, i, 909.
10. *Glasgow Rental*, ii, no. 288.
11. *CSP Venice*, i, 909.
12. *The Thre Prestis of Peblis*, ed. T. D. Robb (Edinburgh, STS, 1920), 4.
13. Eloy Benito Ruano, 'La Participacion Extranjera en la Guerra de Granada', *Andalucia Medieval*, ii, (Actas del I Congreso de Historia de Andalucia, 1976) (1978), esp. 317-9.
14. J. S. Coltart, *Scottish Church Architecture* (London, 1936), 222.
15. *Aberdeen St Nicholas Cartulary*, i, 276-8.
16. Ibid., 278.
17. Christiansen, *The Northern Crusades*, 158-9.
18. R. W. Seton-Watson, *Maximilian I, Holy Roman Emperor* (London, 1902), passim.
19. See above, p. 31.
20. Alexander Barclay, *The Ship of Fools*, ed. T. H. Jamieson (Edinburgh, 1874), 208-9.
21. *James IV Letters*, 63.
22. Ibid., 70-1.
23. Ibid., 91.
24. *Dunkeld Rentale*, 247.
25. *James IV Letters*, 30.
26. Ibid., 101.
27. Ibid., 166-70.
28. *CSP Venice*, ii, 63, 66.
29. *James IV Letters*, 220-1.
30. Ibid., 184; cf. Ibid., 188-94 for a series of letters from James to the pope, the marquis of Mantua, the duke of Savoy, the emperor Maximilian, the king of Hungary, and the College of Cardinals, encouraging them to strive for peace so that a crusade could be prepared.

31. *Flodden Papers*, ed. M. Wood (SHS 3rd ser. xx, 1933), no. III; Ibid., no. II, is perhaps Louis's reply to no. III.

32. *James IV Letters*, 206-7.

33. Ibid., 211-12, 220-1.

34. Ibid., 222-3.

35. Ibid., 224; cf. Ibid., 200.

36. Ibid., 251-2.

37. Ibid., 265-6.

38. *Calendar of Letters and Papers, Henry VIII*, i, no. 1769.

39. Ibid., no. 1499; *James IV Letters*, 302-4.

40. *CLP Henry VIII*, i, no. 2036.

41. *James IV Letters*, 302-4.

42. *CLP Henry VIII*, i, no. 1735.

43. Ibid., *James IV Letters*, 302-4.

44. *CSP Venice*, ii, no. 268.

45. For detailed accounts of the battle of Flodden and events leading up to it, cf. R. L. Mackie, *James IV of Scotland* (Edinburgh, 1958), 201ff., passim, and Nicholson, *Scotland: the Later Middle Ages*, 594-606; for more analytical summaries, cf. G. Donaldson, *Scottish Kings* (London, 1967), 141-6, and J. Wormald, *Court, Kirk and Community: Scotland 1470-1625* (London, 1981), 6-7.

46. Mackie, *James IV*, 201.

47. Nicholson, *Later Middle Ages*, 594.

48. Ibid.

49. Donaldson, *Scottish Kings*, 142.

50. Wormald, *Court, Kirk and Community*, 7.

51. Machiavelli, *The Prince*, trans. G. Bull (Harmondsworth, 1961), 101-2 (cap. xviii). Machiavelli comments that 'contemporary experience shows that princes who have achieved great things have been those who have given their word lightly, so have known how to trick men with their cunning, and who, in the end, have overcome those abiding by honest principles'. Ibid., 99.

52. Quoted in W. C. Dickinson and G. Donaldson, *A Source Book of Scottish History* (Edinburgh, 1952-4), ii, 3.

53. Professor Donaldson (*Scottish Kings*, 146) suggests that the number of casualties may have been over-estimated because of the large number of important people who died. It has also been suggested that at one point the Scots came close to victory (Nicholson, *Later Middle Ages*, 605).

54. *DNB*, x, 589.

55. James V has been poorly served by biographers. Accounts of his reign by Professor Donaldson (e.g., *James V-James VII*, 43-62) are rather unsympathetic towards the king.

56. *Edinburgh Sciennes Liber* (Abbotsford Club), 84-7.

57. *James V Letters*, 180-2, 188, 211-2, 223-4, 329, 353.

58. *RMS 1513-1546*, 309-10.

59. *TA*, vi, 200-1, 299.

60. *A Diurnal of Remarkable Occurents* (Edinburgh, Maitland Club, 1833), 17; cf. John Knox, *Works*, ed. D. Laing (Edinburgh, Wodrow Soc., 1895), I, 72-6 and nn.

61. David Calderwood, *History of the Kirk in Scotland* (Wodrow Soc., 1842), 101.

62. McRoberts, 'Scottish Pilgrims', 100.

63. Desiderius Erasmus, *Opus Epistolarum*, ed. P. S. Allen and H. M. Allen (Oxford, 1906-1948), VIII, 372-7; the 'Consultatio de Bello Turcis Inferendo' is printed in Desiderius Erasmus, *Opera Omnia*, ed. Peter Vander Aa (Lugduni Batavorum, 1703), v.

64. John Durkan, 'Early Humanism and King's College', *Aberdeen University Review*, clxiii (1980), 259-279.

65. Hector Boece, *The Chronicles of Scotland*, trans. John Bellenden, (STS, 1940-2), ii, 209-12, 229, 241.

66. Ibid., ii, 297-8.

67. Adam Abell, 'The Roit or Quhele of Tyme', NLS, MS 1746, f.79v. Cf. above, p. 101.

68. See above, pp. 101-2.

69. Cowan, Mackay and Macquarrie, *Knights of St John*, 93-5, 172.

70. Ibid., 93-5.

71. *James IV Letters*, 101.

72. *RSS*, I, 1771-2: he was admitted by the Lords of Council on 30 November, 1508 (ADC xxii, 41); *James IV Letters*, 174, 178.

73. *James IV Letters*, 188.

74. Ibid., 210-11, 219, 229-31.

75. Ibid., 234-6, 265-6, 296-7; cf. Cowan, Mackay and Macquarrie, *Knights of St John*, 172-3.

76. *James IV Letters*, 308-9.

77. *James V Letters*, 3.

78. Ibid., 37-38.

79. G. Donaldson, *Scotland: James V to James VII* (Edinburgh 1965), 19-20.

80. Cowan, Mackay and Macquarrie, *Knights of St John*, 113-5.

81. Ibid., 112-3, 173-7.

82. Ibid., 177; *Book of Deliberations of the Venerable Tongue of England*, ed. H. P. Scicluna (Malta 1949), 71. Lindsay was the son of George Dundas's sister; cf. *Royal Commission Inventory . . . West Lothian*, 236.

83. Cowan, Mackay and Macquarrie, *Knights of St John*, 178-9.

84. *James V Letters*, 180.

85. *Royal Commission Inventory, West Lothian*, 236; Cowan, Mackay and Macquarrie, *Knights of St John*, 179; *Book of Deliberations*, 73.

86. Cowan, Mackay and Macquarrie, *Knights of St John*, 182.

87. Ibid., 182-3.

88. Ibid., li-lii.

89. SRO GD 247/101/1a; Cowan, Mackay and Macquarrie, *Knights of St John*, 1-31.

90. *Royal Commission Inventory, West Lothian*, 236 and facing p. 238.

91. Robert Lindsay of Pitscottie, *The Historie and Cronicles of Scotland*, ed. A. J. G. Mackay (STS), i, 396.

92. SRO GD 119/20; Cowan, Mackay and Macquarrie, *Knights of St John*, liii.

93. Ibid, 136-8; in 1561-2, Peter Ourrier was involved in a dispute over the preceptory of Braux (Malta Cod. 91, ff. 48, 51, 75).

94. Cowan, Mackay and Macquarrie, *Knights of St John*, 184.

95. See below, p. 118.

96. Cowan, Mackay and Macquarrie, *Knights of St John*, 142-4.

97. Donaldson, *James V to James VII*, 80, 103.

98. SRO GD 119/34, 35 and 41; *Hardwicke Papers* I, 37; *RMS, 1546-1580*, no. 1499.

99. McRoberts, 'Scottish Pilgrims', 102.

100. Cowan, Mackay and Macquarrie, *Knights of St John*, liv-lv, 184-90, passim.

101. Ibid., 190-1.

102. *CSP Rome*, i, 42-3, 63.

103. Ibid., 143-5, 389; *Cal. Scot. Papers*, iv, 563, 565 (nos. 650, 652); *TA*, xii, 383; *CSP Rome*, i, 143-5.

7

Conclusions

After such a detailed survey of a narrow theme over a period of five centuries, it must be asked what conclusions are to be drawn from widely scattered material. First, it is clear that we are not dealing simply with 'rumours of wars'; all the major Crusades of eleventh, twelfth and thirteenth centuries did involve some degree of actual Scottish participation, however modest. Second, it is clear that the summoning and financing of crusades had an important impact in Scotland, especially between 1187 and 1291. Third, it can be seen that the crusading movement had an impact in Scotland which can be gauged in other ways: in the generosity of laymen towards crusading foundations such as the military orders and other related foundations, in the crusading ambitions of kings, in the writings of church chroniclers concerned to record events connected with the Crusades, and conversely in the hostile attitudes towards the crusading ideal which emerge towards the end of our period. In drawing together the various threads which have run through this narrative, each of these aspects will be discussed in turn.

Although there was no Scottish presence at the Council of Clermont in November 1095, when Urban II preached the Crusade for the first time, there was a 'great stir' throughout the British Isles around Easter 1096; this was such that, in the words of William of Malmesbury, fields and cities were deserted as whole families marched away to liberate Jerusalem. Even the Scots abandoned their 'familiarity with fleas', and Guibert de Nogent saw them arriving at the seaports of northern France 'with bare legs, shaggy cloaks, a purse hanging from their shoulders', offering the help of their faith and devotion to the Franks. These native Celtic Scots, whose language was so uncouth and barbaric to the Franks that it required gestures to communicate their crusading purpose, joined the army of Robert duke of Normandy (who had been in Scotland in 1085), and were still with the Crusade on the march from Nicaea to Antioch in the summer of 1097. They were not rated as effective fighting men; Guibert calls them 'ferocious among themselves, unwarlike elsewhere', and comments on their ridiculous armaments. The name of only one of these exotic barbarians is known; he was Lagmann, king of Man and the Hebrides, who took the cross in remorse for the cruelty he had shown towards his rebellious brother. He and his followers were probably more typical of the Scots noted by Guibert and Fulcher of Chartres than were Edgar Atheling and Robert son of Godwin, who came to the East in 1102. Edgar Atheling was Malcolm III's brother-in-law, and late in 1097 had placed his nephew Edgar on the Scottish throne with an English army which included Robert son of Godwin; Robert was rewarded with a grant of lands in Lothian, on which he built a castle. He was less fortunate in the Holy Land, for he was captured by the Saracens at the battle of Ramleh in 1102, and martyred for refusing to renounce the name of Christ. Neither he nor the Atheling was typical of the Scottish aristocracy of the time, of whom the king of the Isles was perhaps more representative.

There are indications of Scottish interest in the wellbeing of the crusader states in the first half of the twelfth century. John bishop of Glasgow, tutor and friend of David prince of Cumbria and later king of Scots, visited Jerusalem in 1122, staying in the household of the patriarch Gormond. In 1128 Hugh de Paiens, first master of the Knights Templars, visited Scotland on a recruiting drive which had considerable success, though the army which he assembled failed to capture Damascus in the following year. He introduced the Templars into Scotland, and the Hospitallers soon followed.

David I is said to have desired to end his days fighting in the Holy Land after having laid down the sceptre, but was dissuaded on the advice of councillors and the outcry among his people. This probably means that he wished to join the second Crusade (1147-8); those Scots who had similar desires and fewer responsibilities than their king joined a fleet of Englishmen, Flemings, Normans and Rhinelanders which besieged and captured Lisbon in the summer of 1147. The Scots on this venture still had the same image as those on the first Crusade: the English regarded them as barbaric ('Who would deny that the Scots are barbarians?'), but could not help admiring their constancy and loyalty during the long siege. A northern French Premonstratensian abbot noted a group of Scots on pilgrimage some time around the middle of the twelfth century, who may well have been connected with the second Crusade; he commented on their outlandish mode of dress, and the fact that they wore no underwear. In the early 1150s, in the aftermath of the second Crusade, the earl and bishop of Orkney went to the Holy Land and the court of Constantinople with a large retinue, but the principal influences on their pilgrimage were Norse rather than Scottish; they were true *Jorsalafarir* ('Jerusalem-farers') in the tradition of King Sigurd of Norway, who had visited the Holy Land in 1110, and of the Varangians of the eleventh century. Probably the Scottish pilgrims noted at Lisbon and in Flanders were more characteristic of native Scottish crusaders of the period.

Not until the later years of the twelfth century are there signs of a change in the character and status of Scottish crusaders; Scottish participants in the third Crusade have a much more Anglo-Norman appearance than those in earlier crusades. Robert de Quincy, who had risen rapidly under William I, joined Richard I's army and was entrusted with the captaincy of the English cavalry defending Antioch in 1191-2. We have suggested that possibly Alan the Steward, and probably some of his knightly tenants, also joined the Crusade, although this is not certain. It is less likely that David earl of Huntingdon, King William's brother, was on crusade. Also from Scotland came Osbert Olifard of Arbuthnott, a landowner of lesser rank, who must have taken the cross immediately upon learning of the fall of Jerusalem. This can hardly be described as a 'marked lack of enthusiasm in Scotland for the recovery of Jerusalem after its fall in 1187', as Professor Duncan thought. The reluctance to contribute to the Saladin Tithe in 1188 reflects rather on opposition to English financial demands, a recurring theme which will be discussed below.

The change in the social background of Scottish crusading contingents at this time seems to reflect social change on a wider scale. Going on crusade was a more expensive undertaking than it had been earlier, and required methodical planning rather than spontaneous enthusiasm. In Scotland, by the latter part of William I's reign an Anglo-Norman nobility were firmly established who could contemplate joining their peers from England and France in seeking glory and salvation in the Holy Land. The number of native Celtic crusaders, which seems to have been greatest before the mid-twelfth century, began to decline, and by the end of the thirteenth century had virtually disappeared.

However, during the pontificate of Innocent III (1198-1216) some native Celts continued to take the cross. Ranald son of Somerled, who died c. 1207, is said to have 'received a cross from Jerusalem' before his death, which probably means that he took the cross. A major preaching of the cross in Scotland in 1213 attracted large numbers of volunteers, but few of them were from among the rich and powerful men of the kingdom (i.e., few of the Anglo-Norman nobility?). The Crusade against Damietta (1218-21) was joined by a small group of Hiberno-Scottish Gaels, including the bard Muiredhach Albanach and others, some of whose surviving poems describe their feelings as they crossed the Mediterranean from Acre towards Damietta and back *via* Monte Gargano on the Adriatic coast.

In the same period we find David Rufus of Forfar, a local landowner, taking the cross from the hands of a papal legate at Perth in 1202 and setting out on the Crusade which resulted in the sack of Constantinople (1204). From 'among the rich and powerful of the kingdom' when the fifth Crusade was preached came Saher de Quincy, son of the Robert who had joined the third Crusade, who sailed from Galloway in January 1219 and died before the walls of Damietta three days before it fell to the Christians in the following November. Also present at Damietta was the Clydesdale landowner William de Somerville. Some other English participants were closely connected with Scottish families: Ranulf earl of Chester, leader of the

English forces, was Earl David's brother-in-law, and John de Lacy, constable of Chester, may well have been brother-in-law of Alan of Galloway.

Frederick II seems to have been accompanied to the Holy Land in 1228-9 by one Scot, the philosopher and translator Michael Scot; but this was not a multinational crusade, and it was not until the time of Louis IX of France that there was a return to large-scale international crusading. The fall of Jerusalem in 1244 and the disastrous battle of Gaza in the following year led to renewed fears for the safety of the kingdom of Jerusalem. A number of Scots set out to join King Louis' crusade, led by Patrick earl of Dunbar, who was sufficiently important to have his death noted by the French continuation of William of Tyre's history. In 1248 a crusade-bound ship sailed from Inverness under the command of the count of St-Pol, and it has been suggested that some Scots may have taken ship with him. The master of the Templars in Scotland was present at the crusaders' defeat in Egypt in 1249, and communicated news of the disaster to Matthew Paris at St Albans. When reinforcements prepared to set out in the summer of 1250, they included a group of Scottish knights from East Lothian, who seem to have had connections with Alan Durward and Roger de Quincy. In view of Durward's own extensive travels, the fact that the son of the crusader earl of Dunbar was also a member of his party during the minority of Alexander III, and that the de Quincy family provided three generations of Crusaders from Scotland, it may be possible to detect in the Durward group a more outward-looking or cosmopolitan attitude, with an interest in the Crusades, while the party led by Walter Comyn earl of Menteith was perhaps more insular or introverted.

The last of the great Crusades, that of Louis IX and Lord Edward in 1270-2, was joined by an even more impressive array of Scots. Some of these were Anglo-Scottish lords who had fought in the civil wars and been loyal to Henry III and Lord Edward; in some cases it is known that they sailed with Lord Edward in the late summer of 1270, or with his brother Edmund the following spring. But there was also a substantial Scottish contingent, led by the earls of Atholl and Carrick, which had left Scotland earlier and was with King Louis when he attacked Tunis in the high summer of 1270. The earl of Atholl was among those who perished of heat or disease at Tunis before the attack was abandoned without success in the autumn and the remnant withdrew to Sicily. At the same time, Lord Edward arrived with an English force. They wintered in Sicily and proceeded to Acre next spring with the earl of Carrick and the remnant of the Scottish force, together with the Anglo-Scottish knights who had come with Lord Edward. The earl of Carrick died of disease at Acre in the summer of 1271. The Scots and Anglo-Scots included Balliols, Bruces,

Mowbrays, John de Vescy, Adam de Gordon, possibly David de Lindsay, and Alexander de Seton, whose esquire was captured by Bedouins during Lord Edward's attack on Qaqun in Caesarea.

We know the names of more Scottish participants in the Crusade of 1270-2 than in any earlier or later venture. It must be asked whether the increase in documentation as the thirteenth century progresses presents a distorted picture of an increase in Scottish interest in the Crusades which is more apparent than real. To some extent this may be the case, but it also seems likely that if there had been Scots of the same importance as those who joined the later Crusades, their names would be known. But in the twelfth century most Scots who went on crusade were regarded as barbarians by those around them. In 1213, few of those who took the cross were from among the rich and powerful men of the kingdom. On the other hand, the earl of Dunbar who died on his way to the Holy Land in 1248 was one of the wealthiest and most munificent men of his age, while the Scots who set out for the East in 1270 were mostly men of wealth and influence, with substantial retinues. There is every indication of a transformation having taken place, which may in part reflect the transformation from a native Celtic aristocracy to an Anglo-Norman one, as Scotland became a European kingdom ready to participate in the corporate ventures of western Christendom. In this change in the background of Scottish crusaders, we can perhaps see a reflection in miniature of changes in the nature of Scottish society as a whole over these two centuries. On the other hand, it must be remembered that as far back as the summoning of the first Crusade itself there had been Scots prepared to listen and respond to the appeal of the cross, while in the 1250s Louis IX had spoken in almost comtemptuous terms of 'a Scot coming from Scotland', though capable of good and faithful conduct. It seems that even at this late stage Scots had still not altogether shaken off their image of being barbarous, though steadfast.

The fall of Acre in 1291 does not mark the end of the crusading movement, although it made the recovery of Jerusalem an increasingly unobtainable objective. Fourteenth-century crusades were directed in a number of different directions, often becoming an outlet for the belligerence of professional soldiers, like the man immortalised by Chaucer in his portrait of the knight in the 'Canterbury Tales'. Sir James Douglas, who died fighting against the Moors in Spain in 1330 while carrying King Robert I's heart to the Holy Land, is an early example of this type; by the time of his death he had been fighting continuously for over twenty years, and possibly had little aptitude or taste for any other kind of life. A crusade like his was to some extent a means of keeping such men occupied during periods of peace, such as might have been expected to follow the Treaty of Edinburgh (1328). Similarly, when the Hundred Years' War came to a temporary halt in 1360 and the 'free companies' were left to roam loose over the north of Italy, the pope tried to interest them in the king of Cyprus's projected crusade. When King Peter of Cyprus launched his raid on Alexandria in 1365, his army included a number of Scottish knights, including the brothers Norman and Walter Leslie; they had the previous year been involved in the dealings of Sir John Hawkwood's notorious 'White Company' at Florence, and had some years earlier taken service with the Teutonic Knights in Prussia.

There is a steady flow of Scottish knights to the Prussian crusade from the mid-fourteenth century, until the battle of Tannenberg (1410) put an end to the Teutonic Knights' expansionist designs in the North. In some cases, it seems than they were profiting by a truce in the intermittent war against England; for instance, Sir William Douglas of Nithsdale may have been taking advantage of the truce which followed the battle of Otterburn (1388) to take a belligerent holiday in the Baltic in 1390-1. If he hoped to have a rest from fighting the English in Prussia, he was sadly mistaken, for he was killed in a brawl between English and Scottish knights on the bridge at Königsberg in 1391. After the battle of Tannenberg, which was witnessed by a mysterious personage described as *le bastarde d'Escoce, qui se appelloit comte de Hembe* (a possible addition to the seemingly interminable list of the illegitimate progeny of Robert II), all trace of Scottish knights fighting in the Baltic disappears.

The Mediterranean had not lost all its attraction for Scottish fighters in the late fourteenth and fifteenth centuries. The administrators of Hospitaller property in Scotland in the later middle ages were mostly men who had served at Rhodes, and there are examples of members of the household of a Scottish preceptor making careers for themselves in the service of the knights of Rhodes in the fifteenth century. Two Scottish brothers, David and Alexander Lindsay, joined the Order of the Passion founded by Philip de Mézières in 1395 as the nucleus of a new crusading army. A group of Scottish knights were fighting the Turks around Constantinople in the early 1450s; they 'became so impoverished that they could not return to their own land without the alms of the faithful' and had to be repatriated by a papally sponsored appeal. One Scot was serving under King Ferdinand of Aragon at the final assault on Granada in 1492. Even in the sixteenth century some Scots were found fighting in the eastern Mediterranean: Walter Lindsay and John Chalmers both fought heroically at the siege of Rhodes (1522) and later joined the Hospitaller order, while Thomas Doughty, claiming to have been a captain against the Turks, founded the hermitage chapel of Loretto at Musselburgh and greatly impressed King James V. Sceptics of reforming sympathies were less impressed, however, and described his relics and miracles as fraudulent.

It appears that as belligerent pilgrimages to the Holy Land declined in the later middle ages, an interest in peaceful pilgrimages increased. There are plenty of examples of Scottish pilgrims to the Holy Land in the fifteenth and sixteenth centuries. The most distinguished pilgrim was probably Archbishop Robert Blackadder of Glasgow, who died between Venice and Jaffa in 1508; but perhaps the most interesting was Anselm Adornes of Bruges, a friend of James III, who in the end settled in Scotland and was murdered in 1483 by the king's enemies. He made an extended pilgrimage to North Africa and the Holy Land in 1470, acting as James's representative, and dedicated his itinerary to his friend and benefactor. James had earlier read Mandeville's *Travels,* and perhaps thereby acquired an interest in distant lands. Mandeville's was a book much admired by Columbus, who hoped that his circumnavigation of the globe would aid the recovery of the Holy Land, and whose commission from King Ferdinand followed soon after the Crusade against Granada.

James III's son and successor, James IV, chose not to devote his energies towards expansion in the New World, but towards a much more conservative scheme for uniting Christian princes in a new crusade against the Turks, under his own leadership. His failure to grasp the political realities of his own times led James to defeat and death at Flodden (1513); and it must be stressed that James's interest in the crusading movement, which has sometimes puzzled Scottish historians, can only be understood as part of a wider movement with roots stretching far back into medieval Scotland. James, although conservative for his time, is not an isolated figure in terms of his own historical context.

The question of how Crusaders were recruited from remote lands like Scotland is at times difficult to answer. For the earliest Crusades the papacy had not evolved an elaborate machinery of preaching; in the twelfth century recruiting drives were mostly carried out by individuals independently of the papacy, such as Peter the Hermit, Hugh de Paiens, St Bernard of Clairvaux, or Archbishop Baldwin of Canterbury. We know that the call of the first Crusade spread throughout western Europe in the winter of 1095-6 with remarkable speed and spontaneity. In the thirteenth century the preaching of the cross was more closely controlled by the papacy. The papal legate John de Salerno preached the cross at a council of the Scottish church at Perth in December 1201; in 1213 Innocent III appointed the bishops of St Andrews and Glasgow to preach the cross in Scotland, and thereafter preachers were appointed by the papacy whenever a new crusade was to be organised. From c. 1230 onwards the new orders of friars took an increasingly important part in the preaching of the cross. The legate Ottoboni sent messengers to Scotland to preach the cross in the late 1260s, but they were not well received; in any case, the bishop of St Andrews had previously been appointed by the pope to preach the cross in Scotland, so it is doubtful whether Ottoboni had much to say that was new.

The problem of recruitment for the Crusades is closely related to that of finance. Again, it is a problem in which we see the papacy becoming increasingly involved in the thirteenth century. This may partly be because warfare was becoming more expensive and armies more elaborately equipped as time went on. Certainly the armies of the thirteenth century were very different from the miscellaneous rabble which followed in the wake of the first Crusade, and it may have become difficult for those other than feudal landowners to afford the journey and all that it entailed; this would partly explain the seeming transformation of Scottish crusaders from the 'barbarians' of the twelfth century into men like the earl of Dunbar in the thirteenth. Earl Patrick provides us with a relatively rare example of a crusader raising money for his journey, when in 1248 he sold his stud farm in Lauderdale to the monks of Melrose. It also seems likely that some knightly tenants of the Steward in Innerwick were raising money for the third Crusade when they set their lands in an extended tack to Kelso Abbey in 1190; and it is also likely that when David Rufus of Forfar granted lands to the monks of Coupar Angus and constituted them his heirs in 1201, when about to set out on the fourth Crusade, he was getting financial assistance in return.

Crusading finance was not simply a problem for the individual. From the time of the third Crusade onwards, money for crusades was raised by taxation, and from the early thirteenth century the papacy imposed regular crusading taxes on the church, and appointed collectors. There are clear signs of reluctance in Scotland to contribute to crusading finance, especially when it was feared that the chief beneficiary might be the English crown. This reluctance made William I and his barons refuse to contribute to the 'Saladin Tithe' demanded by Henry II in 1188, but they were happy to accept better terms from Richard I in 1189 when it was clear that Richard did sincerely intend to go to the Holy Land. Fragmentary evidence shows the 'king's aid' raised by William in 1189-90 in operation. In 1213 we find the earliest examples of papally appointed collectors for the Holy Land subsidy, when Innocent III imposed a tax on the whole church and appointed the bishops of St Andrews and Glasgow to collect it in Scotland. By the middle of the thirteenth century there are examples of Scottish collectors being instructed to hand over money to non-Scottish *crucesignati*. The bishop of Dunblane was ordered to give money to two brothers-in-law of Simon de Montfort in 1247, and in the following year King Alexander II reacted angrily, extracting from Innocent IV an assurance that he should suffer no prejudice by the visit of a Franciscan collector to Scotland, and persuading the pope to instruct Scottish collectors to distribute money to those who had taken the cross and were ready to set out. In 1251 the Durward administration ruling in the name of Alexander III reminded the pope that he had originally intended to distribute sums of money collected in Scotland among Scottish crusaders, but had then changed his mind and awarded them to Henry III; the pope was persuaded that the money should in fact be distributed among Scottish *crucesignati*. It is probably significant that Henry III conspired to have Durward removed from power immediately thereafter. During the majority of Alexander III, the king resisted papal financial demands which might benefit the Plantagenets. The king forbade the export of 2,000 marks raised by the legate Ottoboni in 1268, and Ottoboni complained that Alexander had ordered his subjects not to co-operate with the legate or his messengers. Boece's story that Alexander offered to send men instead of money for the Crusade may well be true, for it agrees with Fordun's statement that the king and clergy refused to pay the Holy Land tenth in 1268 and appealed to the pope, while a substantial Scottish contingent set off to join Louis IX in 1270. A wealth of documentation surrounds the visit to Scotland of the collector Baiamund de Vicci (1275-84), who attempted to revise the calculation on which papal taxation was based, but was forbidden to export the money which he had raised by King Alexander, and was accused by the pope of having lent it out at interest because he could not get it out of the country. It is certain that Alexander's reluctance arose from the fact that the beneficiary of this tax on the Scottish church would have been Edward I. In 1284 the pope awarded the tenth from Scotland to Edward, on condition that he first obtained Alexander's consent and undertook to pay the expenses of Scots who took the cross; then in 1286 the pope authorised Edward personally to select Crusaders from the kingdom of Scotland and to pay them out of the Scottish tenth. It is not surprising that Alexander should have been reluctant to allow Edward I to finance his own party in Scotland out of money raised from the Scottish church for the defence of the Holy Land, but it is incredible that the pope should have considered such a preposterous scheme possible. After the death of Alexander III in 1286, with Edward's increasing control over Scotland in the following years, it seems that Scottish money collected for the Holy Land was being diverted for the benefit of the English crown; the last collector, John de Halton bishop of Carlisle, seems to have been largely successful in his collections between 1292 and the outbreak of war in 1296. Thereafter English control in Scotland fluctuated until it was effectively terminated in 1314. The study of papal finance in the later middle ages, when crusading was seldom more than a pretext, is not part of our study.

If we know this much about actual participation in crusades, and the methods by which crusaders were recruited and financed, what can we say about attitudes, aristocratic, clerical or popular, to the crusading movement? Although no Scottish king ever went on crusade, several expressed a desire to do so, most notably David I, Robert I, David II and James IV. Other kings, such as William I, Alexander II and Alexander III, expressed a reluctance to contribute to crusading taxes, but that was primarily out of a fear that the money would be used to benefit the English crown. William subsequently agreed to contribute towards Richard I's crusade, allowed Robert de Quincy and others to take part in it, and later made a substantial *ex gratia* payment towards Richard's ransom; none of these actions suggest an anti-crusade attitude. The two Alexanders were understandably concerned that money raised from the Scottish church should not benefit Henry III and Edward I's schemes of aggrandisement, but they were content that Earl Patrick and others should join the Crusade of 1248, and that the earls of Atholl and Carrick with a substantial force should join Louis IX in 1270.

Royal and baronial interest in the crusading movement is also evidenced by generosity to crusading orders. The chief beneficiaries of this were the Templars and the Hospitallers, the former of whom enjoyed considerable royal favour from the time of their arrival in Scotland in 1128 until their arrest in 1309. By then they had acquired the lands of Temple of Balantrodoch, Kirkliston and Maryculter, and numerous smaller lands, such as a tenement on the North Inch of Perth by gift of Earl David (d. 1219), and another in Falkirk by gift of the thane of Callander; they also held the churches of Inchinnan, Temple, Aboyne, and other churches in Mar. Some of these were royal gifts, others were from nobles such as Walter Bisset, to whom the Templars owed their possessions on Deeside. The Hospitallers' possessions seem to have been modest by comparison, consisting of Torphichen by gift of David I, and Galtway by gift of Fergus of Galloway, as their main estates of size. But Malcolm IV also granted them a toft in all royal burghs, which may have been the beginning of the network of small tofts and tenements, later known as 'templelands', which they held by the late middle ages. Their chapel of Torphichen achieved parochial status; in the 1190s they held the patronage of the church of Glenmuick on Deeside, and in the 1280s they were given the church of Ochiltree, both of which they subsequently lost to other religious orders. Both the military orders were recipients of charters of privileges and immunities from successive Scottish kings.[1]

Other institutions with connections with the Holy Land or with the Crusades were also the recipients of Scottish generosity. The bishop and chapter of the church of Bethlehem had a hospital at St Germains in East Lothian, probably given to them by the crusader Robert de Quincy;[2] the hospital of St Thomas the Martyr of Acre held lands in Kyle, probably a gift from a Stewart; and in the twelfth century the brothers of St Lazarus of

Jerusalem held the church of St Giles, Edinburgh, which they subsequently lost.[3] The Trinitarians, who devoted a portion of their income to the redemption of Christian captives of the Infidel, had a number of houses in Scotland. That at Dunbar was founded by the countess of Dunbar on the eve of her husband Earl Patrick's departure on crusade, and it is possible that that at Houston, East Lothian was founded by the mother of a de Mowbray crusader under similar circumstances. The Trinitarian house at Scotlandwell in Fife was given to them at the time of Louis IX's defeat in Egypt in 1249, as news of the vast number of Christian captives was reaching the West and as reinforcements were preparing to set out. The one crusading order which is curiously absent from this list is the Teutonic Knights, who do not seem to have had any significant landed endowments in Scotland. In view of the steady flow of Scots to the Northern Crusade in the fourteenth century, this omission is not easy to explain.

Churchmen showed their interest in crusading events by entering details about them in their chronicles and histories. For the most part, these are enthusiastic and often remarkably accurate. Both the Melrose and Holyrood Chronicles have extended accounts of events in the Holy Land which are found in no other source, and which would therefore seem to indicate information reaching Scotland independently, especially in the mid- to late-thirteenth century. The Melrose Chronicle in particular abounds with information about the Crusades. Although an anti-English bias is often apparent in this Border chronicle, the writer is full of praise for Richard I and condemnation of Philip II during the third Crusade; and despite an apparently pro-Montfortian bias, another of the compilers is full of praise for Lord Edward and his exploits in the Holy Land. In a rare departure from the usual practice of describing Muslims as idolaters and polytheists, the Melrose writer in 1270 surprises himself with the discovery that Islam involves the worship of one God, but not in the three persons, and is independent of the Jewish law. The Holyrood Chronicle, which by the late thirteenth century shows signs of having become a Coupar Angus document, contains an account of Holy Land affairs from the 1260s which seems to come from a Hospitaller source.

The chronicles of the late middle ages tend to look back on the early Crusades as a golden age of unified Christian endeavour: 'O how far removed are present-day princes from those who were at that time!' wrote Walter Bower of the first Crusade. But his *Scotichronicon* does nothing to promote Christian unity, and always tends to minimise the role of the English in the Crusades and to glorify the French – a natural prejudice for a nationalistic Scot in the second quarter of the fifteenth century. This anti-English prejudice is even more striking in another fifteenth-century continuation of John of Fordun's *Chronica*, the *Liber Pluscardensis;* in this,

Richard I has become a faithless villain, betraying the trust of the noble Philip of France, 'by which unfaithfulness is shown and manifest the natural and innate quality of the English from the earliest time'. If this writer were to be believed, every disaster that ever fell on the Crusaders could somehow be attributed to the wickedness and treachery of the English. Nowhere in the Scottish chronicles is their any hint of disillusion with the crusading ideal, unless it is in the *Scotorum Historia* of Hector Boece, the friend of Erasmus and Bishop Elphinstone. Erasmus sent Boece a copy of his essay criticising the ideal of warfare against the Turks, accompanied by a friendly dedicatory letter. This is worth remembering when one considers that Boece's annals, apart from his curious disgression about Earl David on the third Crusade, mostly record that Scottish crusaders 'were all slain by heat and pest', in a tone which suggests that he had little time for the subject. On the death of Sir James Douglas, who in Boece's opinion should probably have remained at home in defence of his own country, he sourly comments that 'oure grete confidence in fortoun . . . bringis mony nobill men to deth'. Boece's contemporary Adam Abell, however, wrote a chronicle at his Observant friary at Jedburgh which has a view of crusading much closer to that of Walter Bower and earlier writers.

But setting aside Abell and the grand designs of James IV, the sixteenth century is a period when much more doubt was cast than before on the value of crusading. As early as 1494 a group of Ayrshire 'lollards' had been brought before Archbishop Blackadder accused of upholding heretical beliefs, which included the view that 'it is not lawful to fight, or to defend the faith', and that 'indulgences ought not to be given to fight against the Saracens'.[4] Erasmus held similar views, which he communicated to Boece and Elphinstone, but which had no influence on James IV. James V likewise was impressed by the 'captain against the Turks', Thomas Doughty, and endowed his hermitage of Loretto at Musselburgh, ignoring sceptics who asserted that he and his relics of the East were fraudulent. Scots influenced by Luther and other continental reformers brought similar accusations against the hermit John Scott of Jedburgh. As the Reformation approached, there are clear signs that attitudes were beginning to change. Even the preceptor of the Hospitallers in Scotland was an associate of the Lords of the Congregation, who shocked Queen Mary by retaining his title of grand prior of Scotland even though he had a wife.

This analytical summary, it is hoped, provides an answer to the question posed at the outset of our study: 'what was the impact of the Crusading movement in Scotland?' In oral tradition, in factual participation, in propaganda, in diplomacy, in the writing of history, in generosity to institutions, in the survival and influence of these institutions, the Crusading movement can be seen to have had a significant impact in

Scotland, which did not begin to decline until the sixteenth century, Indeed, much of medieval thinking cannot be properly understood except in the context of crusading thought, and this is true no less of Scotland than elsewhere. The Crusades can be said to have had a significant part in bringing remote little Scotland 'beyond which there is no dwelling place at all' into the fold of unified western Christendom, and thereafter the movement had a long history, some remnants of which are still with us today.[5]

NOTES

1. See Cowan, Mackay and Macquarrie, *Knights of St John of Jerusalem in Scotland,* passim.

2. A. D. Macquarrie, 'The Bethlehemite Hospital of St Germains, East Lothian', *TELAFNS,* xvii (1982), 1-10.

3. *RRS,* ii, 116-7; W. J. Dillon, 'The Spittals of Ayrshire', *AANHSC,* 2nd ser., vi (1958-60), 12-42, at 39; W. J. Dillon, 'Three Ayrshire Charters', ibid., 2nd ser., vii (1961-6), 28-38, at 32-4.

4. Quoted in G. Donaldson, *Scottish Historical Documents* (Edinburgh, 1970), 90-2.

5. Cf. above, p. 7.

Bibliography

Note: Except in the case of journals and society publications, place of publication is London unless stated otherwise.

Part 1: Manuscript Sources
Part 2: Printed Primary Sources
Part 3: Secondary Books
Part 4: Articles
Part 5: Unpublished Theses

Part 1: Manuscript Sources
Aberdeen, University of Aberdeen Archives
King's College Charter Chest
Shuttle 22, nos. 1, 3, 4
Shuttle 25, nos. 18, 34
Shuttle 28, nos. 1, 4, 6, 7, 8, 9, 10, 11
Bruges, Stadsarchief van Brugge
Fonds de Limburg Stirum, 15 January 1469; 4 September, 1472
Cartulaire Rodenboek
Dublin, Library of Trinity College, Dublin
MS 498 (formerly E.2.28) (a *Scotichronicon* MS)
Edinburgh, National Library of Scotland
Adv. 15.1.19 no. 11 (Bull of Alexander IV)
Adv. 16.1.10 (*Liber Albus* of Aberdeen Cathedral)
Adv. 32.6.9 (Rule of the Templars)
Adv. 34.1.10 (Augustine Hay's *Dipplomata*)
Adv. 34.5.1 (Kelso Abbey Cartulary)
NLS Accession 5474 box 20 (Lockhart of Lee Writs)
NLS MS 1746 (Adam Abell's 'Roit or Quhele of Tyme')
Edinburgh, Scottish Record Office
B 10/13, 14 (Crail Writs); 14/2, 9, 23
GD 1/413/13 (Wallace-James Notebooks)
GD 45/13/123 (St Giles Cartulary)
GD 119 (Torphichen Writs) passim
GD 124/1/110, 111, 116, 122, 131, 516, 518, 519, 1048, 1054 (Mar and Kelly Papers)
GD 160/112/4 (Drummond Castle Muniments)
GD 241/254 (Charter of Robert de Quincy)
GD 247/101/1A (Hospitallers' Rental)
NP 1/30, 53 (Alexander Lawson Protocol Books)
RH 6/17, 114, 115, 118, 120, 122, 123, 161, 556A, 558, 924, 925, 992, 1149B, 1244, 1292 (Miscellaneous Charters)
Fyvie Castle, Aberdeenshire
No. 2
Haddington, Colstoun House

Broun-Lindsay of Colstoun Writs, nos. 5, 10, 11, 12, 18, 19, 29, 39, 40, 41, 42, 47, 48

Lille, Bibliothèque Municipale

MS 330 (Adornes' *Itinerarium*)

London, British Library

BM MS Lansdowne 415 (Garendon Abbey Cartulary)

BM MS Harleian 4693 (Charters copied by Sir James Balfour of Kinnaird)

London, St John's House, Clerkenwell

K 32/12-19 (Duntreath Muniments)

Paris, Archives Nationales

L 947 (Bull of Innocent IV)

J 475/77 (Receipt of Ingram de Balliol)

Rome, Vatican Archives

Registrum Supplicationum, vols. 272, 287, 288, 296, 298, 302, 306, 405, 411, 651, 662, 731, 740, 742, 755, 757, 768, 791, 873, 886, 907, 1000, 1493

Troyes, Archives départementales de l'Aube

3 H 332 (Fonds de Clairvaux)

Valletta, National Library of Malta

Knights of St John, Codices nos. 46, 48, 54, 55, 75, 84, 86, 89, 90, 91, 92, 280-432 passim, 2237

Part 2: Printed Primary Sources

Accounts of the Collectors of Thirds of Benefices, ed. G. Donaldson (SHS, 1949)

Accounts of the Lord Treasurer of Scotland (Edinburgh, 1877-)

Acta Sanctorum, ed. the Bollandists (Antwerp and elsewhere, 1643-)

Acts of the Parliaments of Scotland, ed. T. Thomson and C. Innes (Edinburgh, 1814-75)

Adomnán, *De Locis Sanctis Libri Tres*, in *Itinera Hierosolymitana Saeculi IV-VIII*, ed. P. Geyer (Corpus Scriptorum Ecclesiasticorum Latinorum, xxxviiii, 1888)

Adornes, Jean, *Itinéraire d'Anselme Adorno en Terre Sainte*, ed. J. Heers and G. de Groer (Paris, Centre Nationale de Recherche Scientifique, 1978)

Anglo-Saxon Chronicle, ed. G. N. Garmonsway (Everyman, 1953)

Anglo-Scottish Relations, 1174-1328: some selected Documents, ed. E. L. G. Stones (2nd ed., Oxford, 1970)

Annales Monastici, ed. H. R. Luard (RS, 1864-9), iii

Annals of the Four Masters, ed. J. O'Donovan (Dublin, 1856)

Annals of Innisfallen, ed. S. Mac Airt (Dublin, 1951)

Annals of Loch Cé, ed. W. M. Hennessy (RS, 1871)

Annals of the Reigns of Malcolm and William, Kings of Scotland, 1153-1214 (Glasgow, 1910)

Annals of Ulster, ed. W. M. Hennessy and B. MacCarthy (Dublin, 1887-1901)

Bagimond's Roll, ed. A. I. Dunlop, *SHS Misc.*, vi (SHS, 1939), 1-77

Barbour, John, *The Bruce*, ed. W. M. Mackenzie (1909)

Barclay, Alexander, *The Ship of Fools*, ed. T. H. Jamieson (Edinburgh, 1874)

Biblioteca de Autores Espanöles (Madrid, 1848-)

Black Book of Taymouth (Bannatyne Club, 1855)

Boece, Hector, *The Chronicles of Scotland*, trans. John Bellenden (STS, 1938-42)

Book of Deliberations of the Venerable Tongue of England, ed. H. P. Scicluna (Malta, 1949)

Bower, Walter, *Scotichronicon Joannis de Fordun cum Supplementis et Continuatione Walteri Boweri,* ed. W. Goodall (Edinburgh, 1759)

Calderwood, David, *History of the Kirk in Scotland* (Wodrow Society, 1842)

Calendar of Close Rolls, 1288-96 (1904)

Calendar of Documents relating to Scotland, ed. J. Bain (Edinburgh, 1881-8)

Calendar of Entries in the Papal Registers relating to Great Britain and Ireland, ed. W. H. Bliss and others (1893-)

Calendar of the Fine Rolls preserved in the Public Record Office (1911-61)

Calendar of Letters and Papers, foreign and domestic, of the Reign of Henry VIII (1862-1910)

Calendar of the Patent Rolls, Edward III (1891-1916)

Calendar of the Patent Rolls, Henry III (1901-13)

Calendar of Scottish Supplications to Rome, ed. A. I. Dunlop and others (SHS, 1934-70, Glasgow, 1983-)

Calendar of State Papers preserved in Rome (1916-26)

Calendar of State Papers preserved in Venice (1864-1947)

Calendar of State Papers relating to Scotland and to Mary, Queen of Scots (1898-1965)

Calendar of the Writs preserved at Yester House, 1166-1625, ed. C. C. H. Harvey and J. Macleod (Scottish Record Society, 1930)

Cartularium Ecclesie S. Nicolai Aberdonensis (Spalding Club, 1888-92)

Catalogue of the Records of the Order of St John of Jerusalem in the Royal Malta Library, ed. A. Z. Gabarretta and J. Mizzi (Malta, 1964-)

Charters, Documents and Extracts from the Royal Burgh of Peebles, ed. W. Chambers (Burgh Records Society, 1872)

Charters of the Abbey of Coupar Angus, ed. D. E. Easson (SHS, 1947)

Charters of the Hospital of Soltre, of Trinity College, Edinburgh, and of other Collegiate Churches in Midlothian (Bannatyne Club, 1861)

Chartulary of Lindores Abbey, ed. J. Dowden (SHS, 1903)

Chartulary of St John of Pontefract, ed. R. Holmes (Leeds, 1899-1902)

Chaucer, Geoffrey, *The Works of Geoffrey Chaucer,* ed. F. N. Robinson (Oxford, 1957)

Chronica de Mailros e Codico Unico, ed. J. Stevenson (Bannatyne Club, 1835)

Chronica Regum Manniae et Insularum, ed. P. A. Munch (Manx Society, 1874)

Chronicle of Melrose, facsimile edn., ed. A. O. and M. O. Anderson and W. C. Dickinson (1936)

Chronicles of the Reign of Richard I, ed. W. Stubbs (RS, 1865)

Chronicles of the Reigns of Edward I and Edward II, ed. W. Stubbs (RS, 1881-3)

Chronicon de Lanercost, ed. J. Stevenson (Bannatyne Club, 1839)

Collection of Gaelic Proverbs, ed. D. Mackintosh (2nd edn., Edinburgh, 1819)

Corpus Scriptorum Historiae Byzantinae (Bonn, 1828-97)

Councils and Ecclesiastical Documents relating to Great Britain and Ireland, ed. A. W. Hadden and W. Stubbs (Oxford, 1873)

Deux Récits de Voyage inédits en Afrique du Nord: Abdalbasit b. Halil et Adorne, ed. R. Brunschvig (Paris, 1936)

Diurnal of Remarkable Occurents (Maitland Club, 1833)

Documenti per Servire alla Storia della Milizia Italiana dal XIII Secolo al XVI, ed. G. Canestrini (Florence, Archivio Storico Italiano, xv, 1851)

Documents illustrative of the History of Scotland, 1286-1306, ed. J. Stevenson (Edinburgh, 1870)

Documents and Records illustrating the History of Scotland, ed. F. Palgrave (1837)

Durham, Symeon of, *Symeon Dunelmensis Opera Omnia*, ed. T. Arnold (RS, 1882-5)

Early Scottish Charters prior to 1153, ed. A. C. Lawrie (Glasgow, 1905)

Early Sources of Scottish History, 500-1286, ed. A. O. Anderson (Edinburgh, 1922)

Erasmus, Desiderius, *Consultatio de Bello Turcis Inferendo*, in *Opera Omnia*, ed. Peter Vander Aa (Lugduni Batavorum, 1703), v

Erasmus, Desiderius, *Opus Epistolarum*, ed. P. S. and H. M. Allen (Oxford, 1906-48)

Exchequer Rolls of Scotland, ed. J. Stuart and others (Edinburgh, 1878-)

Expeditions to Prussia and the Holy Land made by Henry, Earl of Derby, in 1390-1 and 1392-3, ed. L. T. Smith (Camden Society, 1894)

De Expugnatione Lyxbonensi, ed. C. W. David (New York, 1936)

Extracta e Variis Cronicis Scocie (Abbotsford Club, 1842)

Fabri, Felix, *The Wanderings of Felix Fabri* (PPTS, vii, 1896-7)

Fantôme, Jordan, *Chronicle of the War between the English and the Scots*, in *Chronicles of the Reigns of Stephen and Henry II*, ed. R. Howlett (RS, 1884-9)

Fasti Aberdonensis, 1494-1854 (Spalding Club, 1854)

Flodden Papers, ed. M. Wood (SHS, 1933)

Foedera, Conventiones, Literae et Cuiuscunque Generis Acta Publica, ed. T. Rymer (1816-19)

Fordun, John of, *Johannis de Fordun Chronica Gentis Scottorum*, ed. W. F. Skene (Edinburgh, Historians of Scotland, 1871)

Freising, Otto of, *Gesta Frederici Imperatoris*, ed. Simson (MGH Script. in usus scholarum, 1912)

Froissart, Jean, *Les Chroniques de Sire Jean Froissart*, ed. J. A. C. Buchon (Paris, Société du Panthéon littéraire, 1837-8)

Gesta Francorum, ed. R. Hill (1962)

Great Rolls of the Pipe for the third and fourth Years of the Reign of King Richard I, 1191 and 1192, ed. D. M. Stenton (Pipe Roll Society, 1926)

Historical Letters and Papers from Northern Registers, ed. J. Raine (RS, 1873)

Howden, Roger of, *Chronica Magistri Rogeri de Hovedene*, ed. W. Stubbs (RS, 1868-71)

Huntingdon, Henry of, *Historia Anglorum*, ed. T. Arnold (RS, 1879)

Index drawn up in the Year 1629 of many Records of Charters, ed. W. Robertson (Edinburgh, 1798)

Inquisitionum ad Capellam Domini Regis Retornatorum Abbreviatio (1811-16)

Joinville, Jean de, *Histoire de Saint Louis*, ed. N. de Wailly (Paris, Société de l'Histoire de France, 1886)

King Harald's Saga, ed. M. Magnusson and H. Pálsson (Harmondsworth, 1966)

Knights Hospitallers in England: the Report of Prior Philip de Thame (Camden Society, 1857)

Knights of St John of Jerusalem in Scotland, ed. I. B. Cowan, P. H. R. Mackay and A. D. Macquarrie (SHS, 1983)

Knox, John, *The Works of John Knox*, ed. D. Laing (Wodrow Society, 1895)

Le Baker, Geoffrey, *Chronicon Galfridi le Baker de Swynebroke,* ed. E. M. Thomson (Oxford, 1889)

Le Bel, Jean, *Les Vrayes Chroniques de Jehan le Bel,* ed. L. Polain (Brussels, 1863)

'Letters of Cardinal Ottoboni', ed. R. Graham, *EHR,* xv (1900), 87-120

Letters of James V, ed. R. K. Hannay and D. Hay (Edinburgh, 1954)

Letters of King James IV, ed. R. K. Hannay, R. L. Mackie and A. Spilman (SHS, 1953)

Liber Cartarum Prioratus S. Andree in Scotia (Bannatyne Club, 1841)

Liber Cartarum Sancte Crucis de Edwinesburg (Bannatyne Club, 1840)

Liber Censuum de l'Eglise Romaine, ed. P. Fabre (Paris, Ecoles françaises d'Athènes et de Rome, 1889)

Liber Conventus S. Katherine Senensis (Abbotsford Club, 1841)

Liber S. Marie de Balmorinach (Abbotsford Club, 1841)

Liber S. Marie de Calchou (Bannatyne Club, 1846)

Liber S. Marie de Dryburgh (Bannatyne Club, 1847)

Liber S. Marie de Melros (Bannatyne Club, 1837)

Livre des Faicts du bon Messire Jean le Maingre, dit Boucicaut, ed. M. Petitot (Paris, Collection complète des Memoires relatifs à l'Histoire de France, vi-vii, 1819)

Livre des Trois Filz de Roys, etc. (Paris, 1504)

Machaut, Guillaume de, *La Prise d'Aléxandrie,* ed. L. de Mas Latrie (Geneva, Société de l'Orient Latin, Sér. historique, i, 1877).

Machiavelli, Niccolò, *The Prince,* ed. and trans. G. Bull (Harmondsworth, 1961)

Malmesbury, William of, *Gesta Regum Anglorum,* ed. W. Stubbs (RS, 1887-9)

Mandeville's Travels, ed. M. C. Seymour (Oxford, 1967)

Mariana, Juan de, *Historia General de España,* ed. H. M. Guttierez de la Peña (Barcelona, 1839)

Mémoriaux de la Ville de Bruges, ed. L. Gilliodts-Van Severen (Bruges, 1913)

Miscellaneous State Papers, 1501-1726, ed. Philip Yorke, earl of Hardwicke (1778)

Miscellany of the Spalding Club, ed. K. Stuart (Spalding Club, 1841-52)

Monasticon Anglicanum, ed. W. Dugdale and others (1655-73)

Monasticon Anglicanum, ed. W. Dugdale, new edn. ed. J. Caley, H. Ellis and B. Bandinel (1817-18)

Monstrelet, Enguerrand de, *La Chronique d'Enguerrand de Monstrelet,* ed. L. Douët d'Arcq (Paris, Société de l'Histoire de France, 1857-62)

Monumenta Germaniae Historica, ed. G. Pertz and others (Hanover, 1826-)

Orkneyinga Saga, ed. and trans. A. B. Taylor (Edinburgh, 1938)

Papal Letters to Scotland of Benedict XIII of Avignon, ed. F. McGurk (SHS, 1976)

Papal Letters to Scotland of Clement VII of Avigon, ed. C. Burns (SHS, 1976)

Papers relative to the Royal Guard of Scottish Archers in France (Maitland Club, 1835)

Paris, Matthew, *Chronica Maiora,* ed. H. R. Luard (RS, 1872-3)

Paris, Matthew, *Historia Anglorum sive Historia Minor,* ed. F. T. Madden (RS, 1866-9)

Patrologiae Cursus Completus: Series Latina, ed. J.-P. Migne (Paris, 1844-65)

Peterborough, Benedict of (attrib.), *Gesta Regis Henrici Secundi Benedicti Abbatis,* ed. W. Stubbs (RS, 1867)

L

Pitscottie, Robert Lindsay of, *History and Chronicles of Scotland*, ed. A. J. G. Mackay (STS, 1899)

Poema de Alfonso XI, ed. Yo Ten Cate (Madrid, Revista de Filologia Española, Anejo lxv, 1956)

Procès de Templiers d'après des Pièces inédits, ed. J. Michelet (Paris, 1888)

Processus Contra Templarios in Scotia, in *Conciliae Magnae Britanniae et Hiberniae a 446 ad 1717*, ed. D. Wilkins (1737)

Protocol Book of Gavin of Ros (Scottish Record Society, 1908)

Records of the Templars in England, ed. B. A. Lees (British Academy, 1935)

Recueil des Historiens des Croisades: Historiens Occidentaux (Paris, Académie des Inscriptions et Belles-Lettres, 1844-1906)

Recueil des Historiens des Gaules et de la France, ed. M. Bouquet and others (Paris, 1738-)

Regesta Honorii Papae III, ed. P. Pressutti (Rome, 1888-96)

Regesta Regum Scottorum, ed. G. W. S. Barrow and others (Edinburgh, 1960-)

Register of John of Halton, Bishop of Carlisle, 1292-1324, ed. W. N. Thomson (Canterbury and York Society, 1913)

Register of John le Romeyn, Archbishop of York, 1282-96 (Surtees Society, cxxiii, 1893)

Register of Walter Giffard, Lord Archbishop of York, 1266-79, ed. W. Brown (Surtees Society, cix, 1904)

Registres de Clement IV, ed. E. Jordan (Paris, Ecoles françaises d'Athènes et de Rome, 1893-1945)

Registres de Nicholas IV, ed. E. Langlois (Paris, Ecoles françaises d'Athènes et de Rome, 1905)

Registrum Cartarum Ecclesie S. Egidii de Edinburgh (Bannatyne Club, 1859)

Registrum de Dunfermelyn (Bannatyne Club, 1842)

Registrum Episcopatus Aberdonensis (Spalding and Maitland Clubs, 1845)

Registrum Episcopatus Brechinensis (Bannatyne Club, 1856)

Registrum Episcopatus Glasguensis (Bannatyne and Maitland Clubs, 1843)

Registrum Magni Sigilli Regum Scottorum, ed. J. M. Thomson and others (Edinburgh, 1888-1912)

Registrum Monasterii de Passelet (Maitland Club, 1832)

Registrum S. Marie de Neubotle (Bannatyne Club, 1849)

Registrum Secreti Sigilli Regum Scottorum, ed. M. Livingstone and others (Edinburgh, 1908-)

Reliquiae Celticae, ed. A. Cameron, J. Macbain and J. Kennedy (Inverness, 1892-4)

Rental Book of the Diocese of Glasgow (Grampian Club, 1875)

Rentale Dunkeldense, ed. R. K. Hannay (SHS, 1915)

Reports of the Royal Commission on Historial Manuscripts (1870-)

Rishanger, William, *Chronica et Annales regnantibus Henrico Tertio et Edwardo Primo*, ed. H. T. Riley (RS, 1865)

Rotuli Scotiae in Turri Londiniensi et in Domo Capitulari Westmonasterii asservati (1814)

Sacrorum Conciliorum nova et amplissima Collectio, ed. P. Labbée and G. Cossart (Venice, 1778)

Scottish Annals from English Chroniclers, 500-1286, ed. A. O. Anderson (1908)

Scottish Chronicle known as the Chronicle of Holyrood, ed. A. O. and M. O. Anderson (SHS, 1938)

Scottish King's Household, ed. M. Bateson, *SHS Misc.,* ii (SHS, 1904)

Scriptores Rerum Prussicarum, ed. T. Hirsch, M. Töppen and E. Strehlke (Leipzig, 1861-74)

Selectus Diplomatum et Numismatum Scotiae Thesaurus, ed. J. Anderson (Edinburgh, 1739)

Snorre Sturlusson, *Heimskringla*, ed. E. Monsen (Cambridge, 1932)

Source Book of Scottish History, ed. W. C. Dickinson, G. Donaldson, and I. Milne (Edinburgh, 1958

Spottiswoode Miscellany, ed. J. Maidment (Spottiswoode Society, 1844-5)

Suger, *Vie de Louis VII*, ed. A. Molinier (Paris, 1887)

Templaria, ed. J. Maidment (Edinburgh, 1828-9)

Thre Prestis of Peblis, how thai tald thair Talis, ed. T. D. Robb (STS, 1920)

Traités de Paix et de Commerce et Documents divers concernant les Rélations des Chrétiens avec les Arabes de l'Afrique sèptentrionale au Moyen Age, ed. L. de Mas Latrie (Paris, 1866)

Tudela, Benjamin of, *The Itinerary of Benjamin of Tudela*, ed. and trans. M. N. Adler (1907)

Vetera Monumenta Hibernorum et Scottorum Historiam Inlustrantia, 1216-1547, ed. A. Theiner (Rome, 1864)

Villehardouin, Geoffroy de, *La Conquête de Constantinople*, ed. N. de Wailly (Paris, 2nd edn., 1874)

Vitalis, Orderic, *Ecclesiastical History*, ed. M. Chibnal (Oxford, 1969-81)

Wales, Gerald of, *Giraldi Cambrensis Opera*, ed. T. S. Brewer (RS, 1861-91)

Walsingham, Thomas, *Gesta Abbatum Monasterii Sancti Albani*, ed. T. H. Riley (RS, 1867-9)

Wyntoun, Androw of, *Orygynale Cronykil of Scotland*, ed. D. Laing (Edinburgh, Historians of Scotland, 1872-9)

Part 3: Secondary Books

Argyll, an Inventory of the Monuments: vol. iv, *Iona* (Royal Commission on the Ancient and Historical Monuments of Scotland, 1982)

Atiya, A. S., *The Crusade in the Later Middle Ages* (1938)

Barber, M., *The Trial of the Templars* (Cambridge, 1978)

Baro, Bonaventure, *Annales Ordinis SS Trinitatis Redemptionis Captivorum* (Rome, 1684)

Barrow, G. W. S., *The Anglo-Norman Era in Scottish History* (1980)

Barrow, G. W. S., *The Kingdom of the Scots* (1973)

Barrow, G. W. S., *Robert Bruce and the Community of the Realm of Scotland* (2nd edn., Edinburgh, 1976)

Biographie Nationale de Belgique (Brussels, Académie royale de Belgique, 1866-)

Black, G. F., *The Surnames of Scotland* (New York, 1946)

Blöndal, S., *The Varangians of Byzantium*, trans. B. S. Benedikz (Cambridge, 1978)

Brown, J. M., *Scottish Society in the Fifteenth Century* (1977)

Brunschvig, R., *La Berbérie orientale sous les Hafsides: des Origines à la Fin du XVe Siècle* (Paris, 1940-7)

Burns, J. H., *Scottish Churchmen and the Council of Basle* (Glasgow, 1962)

Calin, W., *A Poet at the Fountain: Essays on the narrative Verse of Guillaume de Machaut* (Lexington, 1974)

Christiansen, E., *The Northern Crusades* (1980)

Clay, R. M., *Medieval Hospitals of England* (1909)

Coltart, J. S., *Scottish Church Architecture* (1936)

Coste, E. de la, *Anselme Adorne, Sire de Corthuy, Pélérin de Terre Sainte* (Brussels, 1855)

Cowan, I. B., and D. E. Easson, *Medieval Religious Houses: Scotland* (1976)

Davis, I. M., *The Black Douglas* (1974)

Delaville le Roulx, J., *La France en Orient au XIVe Siècle: Expéditions du Maréchal Boucicaut* (Paris, Ecoles françaises d'Athènes et de Rome, 1886)

Delaville le Roulx, J., *Les Hospitaliers à Rhodes jusqu'à la Mort de Philibert de Naillac, 1310-1421* (Paris, 1913)

Deslandres, P., *L'Ordre des Trinitaires pour le Rachat des Captifs* (Paris and Toulouse, 1903)

Dictionaire d'Historie et de Géographie Ecclésiastiques (Paris, 1912-)

Dictionary of National Biography (1921-)

Dolley, M., *Anglo-Norman Ireland* (Dublin, 1972)

Donaldson, G., *Scotland: James V to James VII* (Edinburgh, 1965)

Donaldson, G., *Scottish Kings* (1967)

Donaldson, G., *Who's Who in Scottish History* (Oxford, 1973)

Dowden, J., *The Bishops of Scotland* (Glasgow, 1912)

Dufourcq, C. E. *L'Espagne Catalane et le Maghrib au XIIIe et XIVe Siècles* (Paris, 1966)

Duncan, A. A. M., *Scotland: the Making of the Kingdom* (Edinburgh, 1975)

Dunlop, A. I., *The Apostolic Camera and Scottish Benefices* (Edinburgh, 1934)

Dunlop, A. I., *The Life and Times of James Kennedy, Bishop of St Andrews* (Edinburgh, 1950)

Fraser, W., *The Book of Caerlaverock* (Edinburgh, 1873)

Gallia Christiana (Paris, 1715-1865)

Groome, F. H., *Ordnance Gazetteer of Scotland* (Edinburgh, 1881-5)

Hedley, W. P., *Northumberland Families* (Newcastle, 1968-70)

Herkless, J., and R. K. Hannay, *The Archbishops of St Andrews* (Edinburgh, 1907)

Hillgarth, J. N., *The Spanish Kingdoms* (Oxford, 1976)

Hume Brown, P., *History of Scotland* (Cambridge, 1911-29)

Illustrations of the Topography and Antiquities of the Shires of Aberdeen and Banff (Spalding Club, 1843-69)

Jones, J. A. P., *King John and Magna Carta* (1971)

Jones, T., *Chaucer's Knight* (1980)

Jorga, N., *Philippe de Mézières* (Paris, 1896)

Lomax, D. W., *The Reconquest of Spain* (1978)

Lopez, Domingo, *Noticias Historicas de las tres florentissimas Provincias del celeste Orden de la Santissima Trinidad, Redemcion de Cautivos, in Inghilterra, Escocia y Hybernia* (Madrid, 1714)

Luttrell, A. T., *The Hospitallers in Cyprus, Rhodes, Greece and the West* (Variorum, 1978)

McGibbon, D., and Ross, T., *Ecclesiastical Architecture of Scotland* (Edinburgh, 1896)

McKenna, L., *Aithdioghluim Dàna* (Dublin, Irish Text Society, 1939-40)

Mackie, R. L., *King James IV of Scotland* (Edinburgh, 1958)

Macneill, F. M., *The Silver Bough*, i: *Scottish Folklore and Folk-belief* (Glasgow, 1957)

Mayer, H. E., *The Crusades*, trans. J. Gillingham (Oxford, 1972)

Mesnages, J., *Le Christianisme en Afrique: Eglise Mozarabe − Esclaves chrétiens* (Paris and Algiers, 1915)

New Catholic Encyclopaedia (Washington, 1967)

Nicholson, R., *Scotland: the Later Middle Ages* (Edinburgh, 1974)

O'Rahilly, T. F., *Measgra Dánta* (Dublin, 1927)

Parker, T. W., *The Knights Templars in England* (Tucson, 1963)

Powicke, F. M., *King Henry III and the Lord Edward* (Oxford, 1947)

Prior, E. S., and A. Gardiner, *An Account of Medieval Figure Sculpture in England* (Cambridge, 1912)

Purcell, M., *Papal Crusading Policy, 1244-1291* (Leiden, 1975)

Report of the Royal Commission on Ancient and Historical Monuments of Scotland: Midlothian and West Lothian (HMSO, 1929)

Riant, P., *Expéditions et Pélérinages des Scandinaves en Terre Sainte au Temps des Croisades* (Paris, 1865)

Riley-Smith, L., and Riley-Smith, J. S. C., *The Crusades: Idea and Reality* (1981)

Riley-Smith, J. S. C., *What were the Crusades?* (1977)

Ritchie, R. L. G., *The Normans in Scotland* (Edinburgh, 1954)

Runciman, S., *The Fall of Constantinople* (Cambridge, 1965)

Runciman, S., *A History of the Crusades* (Cambridge, 1951-4)

Russell, P. E., *English Intervention in Spain and Portugal in the Time of Edward III and Richard II* (Oxford, 1955)

Scots Peerage, ed. J. B. Paul (Edinburgh, 1904-14)

Scott, Sir Walter, *Guy Mannering* (various editions)

Scott, Sir Walter, *The Talisman* (various editions)

Seton, B. G., *The House of Seton: a Story of lost Causes* (Edinburgh, 1939-41)

Seton-Watson, R. W., *Maximilian I, Holy Roman Emperor* (1902)

Setton, K. M., and others, *A History of the Crusades* (Madison, 1969-)

Skene, W. F., *Celtic Scotland* (Edinburgh, 1880)

Smalley, B., *Historians in the Middle Ages* (London, 1974)

Story of the Stewarts (Stewart Society, 1901)

Temple-Leader, J., and Marcotti G., *Sir John Hawkwood (l'Acuto): the Story of a Condottiere*, trans. Leader Scott (1899)

Thorndike, L., *Michael Scot* (1965)

Vaughan, R., *Philip the Good* (1970)

Waley, D., *Later Medieval Europe: from St Louis to Luther* (1964)

Wormald, J., *Court, Kirk and Community: Scotland, 1470-1625* (1981)

Part 4: Articles

Aitken, R., 'The Knights Templars in Scotland', *Scottish Review*, xxxii (1898), 1-36

Armstrong, C. A. J., 'Letter of James III to the Duke of Burgundy', *SHS Misc.*, viii (1951), 19-32

Bain, J., 'Notes on the Trinitarians or Red Friars in Scotland, and on a recently discovered Charter of Alexander III', *PSAS*, xxii (new ser., x), (1887-8), 26-32

Baker, D., 'Legend and Reality: the case of Waldef of Melrose', *Studies in Church History*, xii (1975), 59-82

Barrow, G. W. S., 'The Aftermath of War', *TRHS*, 5th ser., xxviii (1978), 103-25

Barrow, G. W. S., 'A Bogus Tax-Collector in Lothian, 1306-7', *The Stewarts*, ix (1954), 323-8

Barrow, G. W. S., 'A Twelfth-century Newbattle Document', *SHR*, xxx (1951), 41-9

Beck, E., 'The Hospital of St Germains in East Lothian and the Bethlehemites', *PSAS*, xlv (1910-11), 371-85

Beebe, B., 'The English Baronage and the Crusade of 1270', *BIHR*, xlviii (1975), 127-48

Bergin, O., 'Unpublished Irish Poems, xxviii: A Palmer's Greeting', *Studies*, xiii (1924), 567-74

Brandin, L., 'La Déstruction de Rome et Fierebras: MS Egerton 3028, Musée Britannique, Londres', *Romania*, lxiv (1938), 18-100

Brundage, J. A., 'Cruce Signari: the Rite for Taking the Cross in England', *Traditio*, xxii (1966), 289-310

Bulloch, J. P. B., 'The Crutched Friars in Scotland', *RSCHS*, x (1950), 154-70

Carr, R., 'Observations on some of the Runic Inscriptions at Maeshowe, Orkney', *PSAS*, vi (1864-6), 70-83

Cigaar, K. N., 'L'Emigration anglaise à Byzance après 1066', *Revue des Etudes Byzantines*, xxxii (1974), 301-42

Cook, A. S., 'The Historical Background to Chaucer's Knight', *Transactions of the Connecticut Academy of Arts and Sciences*, xx (1916), 161-240

Dillon, W. J., 'The Spitalls of Ayrshire', *AANHSC*, 2nd. ser., vi (1958-60), 12-42

Dillon, W. J., 'Three Ayrshire Charters', *AANHSC*, 2nd. ser., vii (1961-66), 28-38

Dillon, W. J., 'The Trinitarians of Failford', *AANHSC*, 2nd ser., iv (1955-7), 68-118

Duncan, A. A. M., 'The *Acta* of Robert I', *SHR*, xxxii (1953), 1-39

Duncan, A. A. M., 'The Dress of the Scots', *SHR*, xxix (1950), 210-12

Duncan, A. A. M., 'The Earldom of Atholl in the thirteenth Century', *Scottish Genealogist*, vii (1960), 2-10

Duncan, A. A. M., 'The earliest Scottish Charters', *SHR*, xxxviii (1958), 103-35

Dunlop, D. M., 'Scotland according to al-Idrisi', *SHR*, xxvi (1947), 114-18

Durkan, J., 'Archbishop Robert Blackadder's Will', *IR*, xxiii (1972), 138-48

Durkan, J., 'Early Humanism and King's College', *Aberdeen University Review*, clxiii (1980), 259-79

Easson, D. E., 'Medieval Hospitals of East Lothian', *TELAFNS*, vii (1958), 37-43

Easson, D. E., 'Scottish Abbeys and the War of Independence: a Footnote', *RSCHS*, xi (1951), 63-74

Edwards, J., 'The Knights Templars in Scotland', *Transactions of the Scottish Ecclesiological Society*, iv (1912-15), 37-48

Edwards, J., 'The Templars in Scotland in the thirteenth Century', *SHR*, v (1908), 13-25

Egan, K., 'Medieval Carmelite Houses, Scotland', *Carmelus*, xix (1972), 107-12

Laurent, V., 'Byzance et Angleterre au Lendemain de la Conquête normande', *Numismatic Circular*, lxxi (1963), 93-6

Legge, M. D., 'Quelques Allusions littéraires', *Mélanges de Langue et de Littérature offerts à Pierre le Gentil* (Paris, 1973), 279-83

Limburg Stirum, le Comte de, 'Anselm Adornes, ou un Voyageur Brugeois au XVe Siècle', *Messager des Sciences Historiques*, xliv (1881), 1-43

Macleod, F. T., 'Notes on the Relics preserved in Dunvegan Castle', *PSAS*, xlvii (1913), 99-129

Macquarrie, A. D., 'Anselm Adornes of Bruges: Traveller in the East and Friend of James III', *IR*, xxxiii (1982), 15-22

Macquarrie, A. D., 'The Bethlehemite Hospital of St Germains', *TELAFNS*, xvii (1982), 1-10

Macquarrie, A. D., 'The Crusades and the Scottish *Gaidhealtachd* in Fact and Legend', *The Middle Ages in the Highlands*, ed. L. Maclean (Inverness, 1981), 130-41

Macquarrie, A. D., 'The Ideal of the Holy War in Scotland, 1296-1330', *IR*, xxxii (1981), 83-92

Macquarrie, A. D., 'A Problem of Conflicting Loyalties? The Knights Hospitallers in Scotland in the Later Middle Ages', *RSCHS*, xxi (1983), 223-32

Macquarrie, A. D., 'Sir Colin Campbell of Glenorchy and the Knights Hospitallers', *Notes and Queries of SWHIHR*, xv (1981), 5-10

Macquarrie, A. D., 'Some Charters of the Bruces of Annandale', *TDGNHAS*, lviii (1983), 72-9

McRoberts, D., 'Scottish Pilgrims to the Holy Land', *IR*, xx (1969), 80-106

McRoberts, D., 'Three Bogus Trinitarian Pictures', *IR*, xi (1960), 52-67

Manly, J. M., 'A Knight ther was', *Transactions and Proceedings of the American Philological Association*, xxxviii (1907), 89-107

Matheson, W., 'Traditions of the Mackenzies', *TGSI*, xxxix-xl (1942-50), 193-228

Munro, D. C., 'The Speech of Pope Urban at Clermont', *American Historical Review*, xi (1906), 231-42

Murphy, G., 'Two Irish Poems from the Mediterranean in the thirteenth Century', *Eigse*, vii 1955), 71-7

Murphy, G., 'A Vision concerning Rolf MacMahon', *Eigse*, iv (1944), 79-111

Nicholson, R., 'Magna Carta and the Declaration of Arbroath', *University of Edinburgh Journal*, xxii (1965-6), 140-4

Painter, S. 'The House of Quency', *Medievalia et Humanistica*, xi (1957), 3-9

Prioult, A., 'Un Poète voyageur: Guillaume de Machaut et le *Reyse* de Jean l'Aveugle, Roi de Bohême, 1328-9', *Lettres Romanes*, iv (1950), 3-29

Ruana, E. B., 'La Participacion extranjera en la Guerra de Granada', *Andalucia Medieval*, ii (1978), 303-19

Simpson, J. Y., 'Notes on some Scottish Magical Charm-stones, or Curing-stones', *PSAS*, iv (1860-2), 211-24

Simpson, W. D., 'The Augustinian Priory and Parish Church of Monymusk, Aberdeenshire', *PSAS*, lix (1924-5), 34-71

Somerville, R., 'The Council of Clermont and Latin Christian Society', *Archivum Historiae Pontificiae*, xii (1974), 55-90

Stringer, K. J., 'A New Wife for Alan of Galloway', *TDGNHAS*, xlix (1972), 49-56

Stuart, J., 'Notice of Excavations in the Chambered Mound of Maeshowe', *PSAS*, v (1865), 247-79

Taylor, A. B., 'Studies in the Orkneyinga Saga', *Proceedings of the Orkney Antiquarian Association*, xi (1932-3), 45-9

Thomson, D., 'The MacMhuirich Bardic Family', *TGSI*, xliii (1966), 276-304

Thomson, G., 'De Antiquitate Christianae Religionis apud Scotos', *SHS Misc.*, ii (1904), 115-32

Tipton, C. L., 'The English and Scottish Hospitallers during the Great Schism', *Catholic Historical Review*, lii (1966), 240-5

Waha, M. De, 'La Lettre d'Alexis I Comnene à Robert le Frison', *Byzantion*, xlvii (1977), 113-25

Wallace-James, J. G., 'Order of the Star of Bethlehem', *SHR*, ix (1911-12), 109-11

Watt, D. E. R., 'The Minority of King Alexander III of Scotland', *TRHS*, 5th ser. xxi (1971), 1-24

Wilson, J., 'A Balliol Charter of 1267', *SHR*, v (1908), 252-3

Part 5: Unpublished Theses

G. G. Simpson, An Anglo-Scottish Baron of the thirteenth Century: Roger de Quincy, Earl of Winchester and Constable of Scotland, Edinburgh Ph.D. (1966)

K. J. Stringer, The Career and Estates of David, Earl of Huntingdon, Cambridge Ph.D. (1971)

A book based on Dr Stringer's thesis, due for publication in Edinburgh, 1984, appears too late for inclusion in the present Bibliography. Likewise an Oxford D.Phil. thesis, S. D. Lloyd, English Society and the Crusade, 1216-1307 (1983), has regrettably arrived too late for consultation in the course of this study. This thesis is being revised for forthcoming publication.

Index